The Economics and Political Economy of Energy Subsidies

Jon Strand, editor

CESifo Seminar Series

The MIT Press
Cambridge, Massachusetts
London, England

This book was set in Palatino LT Std by Toppan Best-set Premedia Limited. Printed and bound in the United States of America.

Library of Congress Cataloging-in-Publication Data

Names: Strand, Jon, editor.
Title: The economics and political economy of energy subsidies / Jon Strand, ed.
Description: Cambridge, MA : MIT Press, [2015] | Series: CESifo seminar series | Includes bibliographical references and index.
Identifiers: LCCN 2015041251 | ISBN 9780262034647 (hardcover : alk. paper)
Subjects: LCSH: Energy policy--Economic aspects. | Energy tax credits. | Poor--Energy assistance. | Energy consumption. | Energy development. | Energy industries--Finance.
Classification: LCC HD9502.A2 E225 2015 | DDC 333.79/158—dc23 LC record available at http://lccn.loc.gov/2015041251

10 9 8 7 6 5 4 3 2 1

Contents

Series Foreword

This book is part of the CESifo Seminar Series. The series aims to cover topical policy issues in economics from a largely European perspective. The books in this series are the products of the papers and intensive debates that took place during the seminars hosted by CESifo, an international research network of renowned economists organized jointly by the Center for Economic Studies at Ludwig-Maximilians-Universität, Munich, and the Ifo Institute for Economic Research. All publications in this series have been carefully selected and refereed by members of the CESifo research network.

1 Introduction

Jon Strand

Government subsidies to energy are widespread, and often they are distortionary, and present a heavy burden on public budgets in many countries. While subsidies vary across different countries, the most common subsidies are for motor fuel consumption and for electricity supply and consumption. In general, both the energy producers and the consumers are subsidized. Subsidies that principally favor consumers are particularly harmful as they lead to increases in overall energy consumption (and if fossil fuels are subsidized, increased carbon emissions), and their distortionary effects on consumer behavior in the long run.

Moreover subsidies to the production and consumption of renewable energy are prevalent in some parts of the world. The underlying policy objectives are, however, very different for renewable energy subsidies. In particular, the aim of renewable energy subsidies is usually to reduce carbon emissions, which is opposite to the usual impact of subsidies to fossil fuels.

The chapters in this volume were presented at a conference arranged by CESifo, in Venice in July 2014, and they deal with many energy subsidy concerns: background issues, economic aspects of energy pricing, general political economy issues where explanation of energy pricing behavior is central, substantial energy subsidy levels, and energy poverty, and political corruption. All but chapter 11, which is dedicated to the study of renewables subsides, focus on subsidies to fossils and electricity consumption. Thus, altogether, the contributions nicely reflect the now quite rich and diversified literature and present a significant diverse contribution to this literature.

Energy subsidies come in alternative forms and are tied to alternative energies. The most distortionary types of energy subsidies are those to fossil fuels, and to electricity consumption, given that most of electricity generation is based on fossil fuels. It should, however, be pointed out that not all energy subsidies are necessarily bad or harmful. Two aspects of potentially benign energy subsidies are (1) when they are paid out to renewable energies and (2) when such subsidies lead to improved income distribution or reduced "energy poverty." Subsidies to the development of renewable or other low- or zero-carbon energies used either directly or as inputs into electricity generation, or as directed to the development of energy technologies, are in most cases less distortionary. They are often justified by legitimate policy objectives, particularly in heavy energy-importing countries, but also more generally to spur energy-related technological developments in the right direction and by the right magnitude. Subsidies to renewable (or other "clean") energies can be particularly gainful when they lead to substantial reductions in fossil-fuel consumption (and consequently reduced carbon emissions and pollution) and also when they lead to technology improvements that reduce global renewable energy production costs. Today, by far, the most "harmful" energy subsidies are incurred in developing and emerging economies, and most renewable energy subsidies are provided by high-income (OECD) countries, as discussed in chapter 11 by Fischer and colleagues. The rest of this volume, however, deals with the former and more problematic type of subsidies. By far, most fossil-fuel and direct electricity subsidies are paid out in emerging and developing countries (but not when based on the IMF's "after-tax subsidy" definition, as discussed below); in contrast, by far, the most renewable energy subsidies are paid out in high-income countries.

To be sure, energy subsidies can serve socially gainful purposes as well, notably when "energy poverty" is reduced through energy subsidies to impoverished areas where the income elasticity of demand is less than unity. For "modern" energies such as fossil fuels and electricity, consumption is mostly in high-income countries where the dependence on such energies is virtually universal. In low-income countries, subsidizing kerosene may make sense where otherwise the fuel is wood for heating and cooking. In such countries producer subsidies to facilitate increased access to electricity (for the about 2 billion who do not currently have such access) can be a highly beneficial policy. Removing energy subsidies would have adverse effects, both for income distribution and in a wider welfare sense.

With regard to (harmful) fossil-fuel and electricity consumption subsidies, the global magnitudes of such subsidies have been somewhat contested. The most reliable current estimate of subsidies to energy production and consumption (apart from renewables, which generally will be disregarded in this discussion) is that provided by the International Monetary Fund (see Clements et al. 2013; Parry et al. 2014; Coady et al. 2015). The IMF has developed two measures of energy subsidy: before-tax and after-tax subsidies. These measures are discussed by Ian Parry in chapter 2 of this volume. *Before-tax subsidy* here stands for out-of-pocket expenditures by government for fossil-fuel and consumer electricity subsidies; in other words, the fiscal burden of subsidizing energies (here, disregarding renewables). *After-tax subsidy* is a more radical, and innovative, concept. It is designed to measure the degree to which energies are underpriced relative to an optimal or efficient pricing formula in which, in addition to a standard economywide tax such as a VAT, a Pigovian charge is imposed. The after-tax subsidy is based on the idea that many energies, including fossil fuels and electricity, instead of being subsidized really ought to be taxed at the margin to correct for externality effects caused in their consumption or production.

Clements et al. (2013) estimate that for the year 2011, global before-tax subsidies were approximately $500 billion. About half of the total subsidy amount was provided by Middle East and North African (MENA) country governments, and almost half of the rest in developing and emerging Asian countries. The amount of before-tax subsidies to fossil fuels and electricity in high-income OECD countries (again, disregarding renewables subsidies) was small, only 5 percent of the global total. In terms of categories of spending for before-tax subsidies, the most important were for petroleum products with 44 percent of the total, electricity with 31 percent, and natural gas with 23 percent. Coal received very little direct before-tax subsidy (1 percent), although there is a larger implicit subsidy to coal as an input into the production of electricity.

Global after-tax subsidies were by Clements et al. (2013) assessed to be much larger: in total approximately $2 trillion, or close to 3 percent of global GDP, and 8.5 percent of global government revenues. The percentage share to high-income OECD countries is here dramatically higher, 32 percent, and is also considerably higher in emerging and developing Asia, 29 percent. This is due to most of the overall global externality costs of energy production and consumption being incurred in these two regions. The MENA region's share is still significant, 19 percent. As shares of regional GDP, however, after-tax subsidies were highest in the MENA region (14 percent) and in sub-Saharan Africa (13 percent).

The after-tax subsidy concept captures many of the inefficiencies of energy use that manifest themselves in other ways than their fiscal impacts. Among such inefficiencies, we can identify the following:

1. Excessively rapid depletion of nonrenewable energy.
2. Excessive global carbon emissions, related to factor 1. By some estimates (Clements et al. 2013), global CO_2 emissions would be reduced by around 23 percent if global charges on the various relevant energies, corresponding to the elimination of all after-tax subsidies.
3. A number of other local, regional, and global externality costs associated with the consumption and production of fossil energies and with electricity based on such energies. Prominent examples of such externality costs are those associated with road transport (traffic congestion, local and regional pollution, accidents, noise, and wear of infrastructure) and with coal consumption (local and regional air pollution, outdoors and indoors). [1]
4. Adverse distributional impacts as many or most of the subsidized energies are consumed by high-income rather than by low-income households. This problem is magnified as public energy subsidies reduces governments' scope for using fiscal policy to directly address distributional imbalances, including direct income transfers to poor groups.
5. Potential adverse effects for international trade, including terms-of-trade distortions. In particular, widespread fuel subsidies allow fuel exporting countries to maintain their fuel export prices at higher levels than otherwise, thus further worsening the balance of payments problems of fuel-importing countries.
6. Longer run distortions in countries with widespread energy subsidies, including locking-in of excessively energy-intensive capital, delayed introduction of alternative energy resources and technologies, and insufficient supply of public infrastructure and other public goods that would enhance development over the longer term. This can have adverse impacts on long-run economic growth.
7. Worsened energy security for net energy-importing countries.

Little has been done of try to quantify the magnitude of social losses associated with all these factors. Note, however, that the distortions associated with not correcting for a "Pigou tax," represented roughly by the externalities caused by factors 2 and 3 (e.g., as quantified in

Parry and Small 2005, 2012), are magnified by subsidies that go in the opposite direction from such taxes.

Note that the "gross subsidy" concept developed by the IMF departs from a principle whereby marginal costs of factors 2 and 3 are used to construct the benchmark charge on energy (representing a "Pigou tax"), while the other identified effects are ignored. It is also important to properly distinguish between consumer and producer energy subsidies. By *consumer subsidies*, we generally mean subsidies that (mainly) reduce consumer prices for the relevant energies (fossil fuels and electricity) below the prices that would otherwise prevail. By *producer subsidies*, we mean subsidies that (mainly) reduce producer costs of providing the relevant energies, but with negligible impact on consumer prices. Such subsidies generally increase the profits of domestic energy producers and/or make domestic supply of energy viable. Their objectives could be the reduction of international energy dependence, a general strengthening of the domestic energy sector, or the support to technological progress in the same sectors. Most of the discussion in this volume will center on consumer subsidies, thus defined.

When externalities associated with energy production and consumption are not internalized, the expanded use of energy resulting from subsidies exacerbates the harm done by these externalities, thus increasing the gap between price and social opportunity cost. Subsidies to noncarbon energy sources can also give rise to concerns about various types of externalities, including competition for arable land to grow biofuels and handling of nuclear materials.

Supply-side subsidies that have little or no effect on market prices are less harmful than consumption subsidies. However, they are still likely to imply deadweight losses through production inefficiencies. Moreover they can impinge on government funding of other public goods, increase the debt burden in crowding out other investment, and create deadweight losses from additional taxes. The distributional impacts of fuel subsidies can also be highly adverse. High-income groups are the major consumers of many types of energy and thus also the primary beneficiaries of many energy subsidies. Energy supply subsidies may also be regressive by generating substantial economic rents for suppliers. Finally, the "energy security" implications of energy subsidies often increase energy consumption and vulnerability to energy price shocks, overall worsening the balance of payments.

Another potential problem associated with energy subsidies is that energy policies incorporating subsidies in many countries are an obstacle to the efficient use of resources for sustainable growth. In many ways energy subsidies are more harmful than many other subsidies (e.g., those to foodstuffs), as (1) energy is an important input into production of a number of goods whose production then also is distorted, (2) excessive energy consumption is likely to cause negative externalities including excessive carbon emissions, (3) energy subsidies are often poorly suited as a policy for providing support to meeting basic needs of poor households, and (4) production based on a high level of energy use cannot always absorb much of an initially idle workforce, thus undermining a goal of full employment.

The general "harmful" effects of energy subsidies are by now well documented, starting with the first major discussion by the International Energy Agency back in 1999 (IEA 1999); through subsequent work by Beers and Moor (2001), and IEA (2006, 2008); and more recently, for example, by Kojima (2012a, b), Vagliasindi (2012a, b), and IEA (2013). The fact that (mainly fossil) energy subsidies exist raises a range of important economic and political economy issues that need to be addressed. First, and quite obvious, is that given the general knowledge on how bad and harmful energy subsidies are in so many ways, why does fuel still get subsidized? Second, what are the precise effects of subsidized fuel on energy consumption and distribution, and how much are economies distorted by such subsidies? This includes the magnitude of inefficiency wedges associated with energy subsidies, and in particular, for countries where energy instead ought to be taxed. Third, what are the overall effects of fuel subsidies on economic performance, namely on economic growth and development? This includes systemwide effects of energy subsidies whereby also public sector spending, as affected by public subsidies, should be treated as endogenous.

While information has improved with respect to the direct measurement of energy subsidies in both developed and developing countries, as documented in particular in the recent, above-cited, IMF-based work (Clements et al. 2013), significant data gaps persist. Moreover a relatively limited amount of work has been done to assess their broader economic efficiency, distributional and environmental consequences—particularly for developing countries. Thus part of this informational gap is being closed by currently ongoing work, notably at the IMF by Parry et al. (2014; see also chapter 2 by Ian Parry in this volume). However, the vast majority of detailed studies to assess such costs have been carried out for developed (OECD member) countries.

For the distributional impacts of energy subsidies (and energy pricing more generally), the available work is currently limited. The sweeping conclusion is that lowering energy prices, with subsidies to fossil energies and electricity consumption, is not a useful way of improving income distribution in poor countries such as most of sub-Saharan Africa, South Asia, and Latin America, and neither in the MENA and East Asia regions. In these regions the subsidized energies are mostly consumed by higher income groups; indeed the lowest income groups are often completely barred from the energy markets (as they do not own or use motorized vehicles, nor have homes with access to electricity). In higher income emerging economies, the situation is quite different. In the East Europe and Central Asia (ECA) region, for example, most households have electricity access, but the fraction of income spent on electricity is higher for lower income groups. Thus removing energy subsidies (resulting in higher consumer prices) is likely to lead to a worsened income distribution (e.g., see Laderchi et al. 2013). The same is true in high-income OECD countries for motor fuels and electricity. In these countries the overwhelming fraction of households has private motor vehicles and household power access, but the fraction of household budget spent on motor fuel and electricity is generally higher for lower income than for higher income households broadly defined. For these economies the trade-off is therefore between a positive allocation effect and an adverse distributional effect in phasing out energy subsidies. In principle, the widely prevailing view is that adequately compensating low-income groups for income losses resulting from higher energy prices is not difficult, and not especially expensive, given the possibility of a direct income transfer to low-income groups.

Turning now to the contributions in this volume, chapter 2 by Ian Parry, and chapter 3 by Michelle Harding, Herman Vollebergh, and Supli Sen define the energy pricing problem as a major impediment to economic efficiency and put it in the context of the current worldwide level of energy subsidies. Chapter 2 in fact complements this introductory chapter. Mainly it sums up the results from the two IMF publications cited above, Clements et al. (2013) and Parry et al. (2014).

In chapter 3 the authors discuss and analyze the wider issue of energy pricing, and thus not only energy subsidies in high-income countries. Harding, Vollebergh, and Sen discuss an interesting new database on energy taxation developed by the OECD, and describe how it can be implemented to investigate energy policy related issues.

This dataset relates existing nominal tax rates of a wide category of energy products in OECD countries to their underlying energy tax bases in 2012. Accordingly, the data provide the effective tax rates, namely levels of energy and carbon tax rates that account for exemptions or even zero rates applied on part of the potential energy tax base. These data, and some insights derived from estimations based on these data, are used not only describe effective tax rates and (implicit) energy subsidies but also how energy consumption across countries is sensitive to differences in tax rates in different countries and across products and sector applications.

Chapters 4 through 10 deal with the theoretical and empirical aspects of energy subsidies. The many political economy issues related to energy subsidies and their possible reform have in fact been given scant consideration in the analytical and empirical literature, even though addressing them is central to making headway on the goals of reducing, or better eliminating, energy subsidies. There is compelling evidence that current energy policies are very heavily distorted, in the direction of heavy subsidies to various energies, in many low- and middle-income countries. There are thus, rather generally, evident aggregate efficiency gains to be achieved by changing these policies.[2] The obvious question to ask is: Considering all the harmful effects of energy subsidies, for governments' fiscal position, income distribution, and overall economic performance, why are energy subsidies still so popular and widespread? Clearly, the problems in most cases have their basis in complex political economy issues that impact countries with poor or distorted governance relations. The core themes in recent political economy analysis involve such legal and social issues as well.[3]

While recent policy-oriented work specifically dealing with energy subsidies is relatively sparse, chapter 4 in this volume, by Marco Pani and Carlo Perroni, and chapter 5, by Strand, take the analytical literature forward in different directions. Pani and Perroni study how reelection incentives for incumbent politicians may distort energy policies in the direction of excessive subsidies. In their study, possible subsidy reform is impeded by a classical time-inconsistency problem confronting policy makers, which interacts with the electoral decisions of voters. They show how energy subsidy reform could lead to risk of losing future elections for incumbent politicians, to challengers that focus on populistic policies. The incumbent may then, strategically, choose to postpone subsidy reform in order to maintain an electoral advantage on the subsidy issue. Pani and Perroni suggest, as a main remedy for the time-consistency problems leading to an excessive political reliance on energy subsidies, that automatic mechanisms for energy pricing be established, or that the authority to set such rates be delegated to technical committees, although they recognize that this is in itself often politically very difficult.

My own chapter 5 in this volume represents a follow-up to my previous World Bank paper, Strand (2013). In my previous paper, a political-economy model was developed, focusing on the fact that energy subsides are easier to observe and commit to than more complex goods by politicians. The main new perspective in the current chapter 5 relates to trade-offs between the short and long run, when investment in transport infrastructure is an additional policy option to governments that also subsidize fuels. Overall, taking a long-term view tends to be welfare enhancing, but it does not need to reduce potential corruption. It is shown, for example, that multiple "bribing equilibria" may exist where the target of bribing from part of the populace is fuel subsidies supplied by politicians who can, in this way, be swayed.

The empirical literature focusing on political-economy aspects of energy subsidy policy is also slim, mostly due to the lack of good panel-type data for energy subsidies on the basis of which such analysis could be carried out. Some headway has recently been made through a World Bank project I stewarded to collect the appropriate data, which is available in Beers and Strand (2013) and is based on findings that the behavior of governments with respect to energy subsidies differs systematically between democracies and autocracies, and in predictable ways. In democracies, subsidy levels are generally lower than in autocracies, and they are in addition being reduced as the democracy matures in a given country. In autocracies, by contrast, there seems to be no tendency for energy subsidies to be phased out as the autocratic regime grows older. This is very well in line with the theoretical predictions set out above.

Chapter 6, by Christos Kotsogiannis and Leonzio Rizzo, and chapter 7, by Christina Kolerus and Albert Touna-Mama, present empirical analyses of the political economy of energy pricing. Kotsigiannis and Rizzo discuss federalism aspects. Kolerus and Touna Mama consider political factors behind energy subsidies in sub-Saharan countries.

Kotsigiannis and Rizzo start with the observation that fuel-price subsidies are pervasive and widespread around the globe, but that the amount of empirical work on their determinants and, in particular, on the extent to which their presence (and their magnitude) is associated with countries that suffer significantly from corrupt practices, is very limited. This short chapter aims to contribute toward rectifying this shortcoming in the literature. The authors explore empirically the link between fuel-price subsidies and a measure of the degree to which public power is exercised for private gain and the state is 'captured' by private interests. Using panel data over the period 1991 to 2008 (essentially, the same database as that for Beers and Strand 2013), they show that in countries with relatively low level of corruption, when corruption is reduced (corruption control increases), fuel subsidies decrease; for high level of corruption (low level of control of corruption), increasing corruption control has only a small effect on the fuel subsidy rate. These results hold independently of the level of per capita income of a country. This suggests that from a policy perspective, a prerequisite for a substantial reduction in fuel subsidies is an increase in the control of corruption, when corruption is *already relatively low*.

Kolerus and Touna Mama approach fuel subsidies by studying the price-setting processes for gasoline, diesel, and kerosene and the influence of political institutions on this process. They provide both quantitative and qualitative evidence that political factors on the whole influence domestic fuel price-setting in sub-Saharan Africa. A main conclusion from this study is that implementing successful price adjustments or reforms of fuel subsidies is likely to involve two main elements. The first is that one needs to build a coalition with gasoline and diesel stakeholders, even if this implies reaching beyond the typically targeted low-income stakeholders. The second involves improving key aspects of governance in countries where reform is sought; in particular, to improve government effectiveness to credibly commit to policies—including possible compensation packages.

Chapter 8, by Mohammad Habibpur and Neda Seiban, and chapter 9, by Jim Krane, discuss energy subsidy issues with a specific focus on particular MENA countries; the former focusing on Iran, and the latter on the Gulf monarchies. Habibpur and Seiban suggest that in resource-rich developing countries natural resource windfalls, which often lead to a resource curse by which much of the potential gains from the resources are wasted, can change the core social structure in a way that follows from a reduction in female labor participation and hence the gender inequality. If so, commonly proposed policies to address the resource curse, such as distributing the resource revenues widely among the population, through direct transfers of natural resource rents, could also reduce the degree of gender wage inequality. The authors investigated this hypothesis empirically using a survey including more than 6,000 households in Iran, as the only emerging resource-rich country that recently has reduced its fuel subsidies and at the same time transferred a major part of the released funds directly and equally back to the public. They investigate the effects of this subsidy reform plan in Iran, on the wage rates and on gender wage inequality. They end up with suggestions to other resource-rich countries in similar situations, to carry out similar policies.

Krane in his contribution poses the following questions: Do citizens in autocracies feel entitled to cheap energy? How amenable are they to losing the subsidies behind those "entitlements?" In the six Persian Gulf monarchies, where subsidy-fueled energy demand threatens to displace the region's oil exports, these questions have important implications for overall demand management, and in particular how to manage any redistribution of resource rents to the public. A public survey reveals levels of entitlement to energy subsidies that are more subtle than expectations inferred from standard rentier theory. As this theory would predict, on the one hand, there is a cohort of citizens that claims entitlement to national resource wealth, with the additional view that much of this wealth ought to be redistributed through low energy prices, and this group is relatively unwilling to accept higher prices on residential electricity. On the other hand, a substantial portion of the public neither claims entitlement to energy nor opposes higher electricity prices. Citizens were more supportive of higher prices when given a national-interest explanation, and when offered an alternate benefit. A separate survey of experts produced results more consistent with theory, in which citizens were expected to exhibit more "entitled" views of energy and more opposition to subsidy reform. Overall, the chapter's findings suggest that large segments of the Gulf public may be more amenable to necessary reforms of damaging subsidies than the current caution in policymaking implies.

Chapter 10, by Raffaele Miniaci, Carlo Scarpa, and Paola Valbonesi, considers distributional issues raised by subsidies to energy and their removal in Italy. This is an issue of a somewhat different character than that of most of the other chapters in the volume, focusing on a high-income country. The authors discuss potential welfare losses resulting from removing energy subsidies, and where such losses may depend on how well targeted to the poor the initial subsidies are. The discussion centers on the eligibility criterion used in Italy for compensating vulnerable households in the face of such possible welfare losses. The

Miniaci, Scarpa, and Valbonesi argue that this criterion, as currently applied in Italy, is too wide in encompassing a very large set of households many of which are not poor, and that many households that are actually poor are excluded from the benefits scheme. The authors suggest how to better target the scheme, in terms of reducing the poverty impact of higher energy prices, and thus also of higher energy taxes.

Chapter 11, by Carolyn Fischer, Mads Greaker, and Knut Einar Rosendahl, is somewhat distinct from the rest of the volume as the only chapter that discusses aspects of policies to subsidize the manufacturing and/or deployment of renewable ("green") energy. Fischer, Greaker and Rosendahl thus deal with energy subsidies of "type 2" as defined above. This means that, for this type of subsidies, there is no a priori assumption that they are inefficient or wasteful. Indeed, these authors stress, there are several reasons for such subsidies, from a global perspective. Perhaps most important is the global public good aspect of technical development in renewable energy development and provision, whereby neither the individual producer nor the individual country has full incentives to internalize these. It is pointed out that the most effective and efficient solution will entail a combination of taxation of fossil fuels, together with subsidies to renewables; in such cases the latter subsidy may optimally be quite low (as simply the absence of other energy taxes implies an added virtual subsidy). With no taxes (or with subsidies) to fossil fuels, the "optimal" renewables subsidy is likely to be higher to make renewables competitive; but in such cases the fiscal burden of subsidies may "take over" as the overriding problem for governments. The authors recognize that tensions exist between trade and environmental goals, but that the subsidy to production of renewables can, in similar way as taxation on imported fossil fuels, be viewed as trade-distorting and subject to sanctions. This is clearly an area ripe for policy discussions in years to come.

Overall, this mixed set of studies make up a rather consistent whole. Three chapters (those by Parry, by Harding, Vollebergh, and Sen, and by Fischer, Greaker, and Rosendahl) are mainly definitional and provide data overviews; two chapters (those by Pani and Perroni and by Strand) are principally analytical; a third group provides rather general empirical analysis from a political economy perspective (those by Kotsogiannis and Rizzo and by Kolerus and Touna Mama); while the fourth group (by Habibpour and Seidan, by Krane, and by Miniaci, Scarpa, and Valbonesi) focuses on country-specific cases, also taking empirical approaches. The existence of strong cross-cutting areas of analysis, however, serves to unify the contributions into a natural whole. A political economy approach is central to understanding energy subsidies; this is common for virtually all of the chapters (albeit only implicitly in the last chapter by Fischer et al.). A similar cross-cutting theme is, naturally, the discussion of inefficiency associated with energy subsidies. This is central for all the empirical and also the analytical papers, and also underlies Parry's contribution. Corruption is central to two contributions, Strand, and Kotsogiannis and Rizzo. Another cross-cutting topic is distributional impacts including energy poverty. This is also central in all the country case studies, and also in Kolerus and Touna Mama. Finally, several chapters (those by Pani and Perroni, by Habibpour and Seidan, by Krane, and implicitly by Strand) provide guidance to how energy subsidy policies could be fruitfully reformed.

Notes

The work in this book represents the views of the author and not of the World Bank, its management, staff, or member countries.

1. See also World Bank (2010) for discussion, and assessment, of such externality effects.

2. There do exist cases where energy subsidies may, arguably, be justified, either from a distributional point of view (as being more effective than other practically available policy choices), or in terms of efficiency (in particular when the production or consumption of a particular energy type leads to positive externalities). These cases are, however, insignificant for the types of energy discussed here, and will be ignored in the following.

3. For more fundamental analytical work on this topic, consult Persson and Tabellini (2000). For an analysis more specifically directed at low-income countries, see Grindle (2000). For basic background work on related political processes, see Prado and Treblicock (2009), World Bank (2009), and Strand (2013).

4. For definition of "selectorate," see, for example, Gelbach and Keefer (2011), or Keefer and Vlaicu (2008).

References

Andresen, Nils August. 2008. Public choice theory, semiauthoritarian regimes and energy prices: A preliminary report. Fridtjof Nansen Institute, the Norwegian Institute for International Affairs and Econ Pöyry, RUSSCASP project, Working Paper 2008–010.

Beers, Cees v., and Andre d. Moor. 2001. *Public Subsidies and Policy Failure*. Cheltenham, UK: Elgar.

Beers, Cees v., and Strand, Jon. 2013. Political determinants of fossil fuel pricing. World Bank Policy Research Working Paper 6470.

Busch, Per-Olof, and Helge Jörgens. 2005. International patterns of environmental policy change and convergence. *European Environment* 15: 80–101.

Chang, Eric, and M. A. Golden. 2010. Sources of corruption in authoritarian regimes. *Social Science Quarterly* 91: 1–20.

Cheon, A., J. Urpelainen, and M. Lackner. 2013. Why do governments subsidize gasoline consumption? An Empricial Analysis of Global Gasoline Prices, 2002–2009. *Energy Policy*, 56, 382-390.

Clements, Benedict, David Coady, Stefania Fabrizio, Sanjeev Gupta, Trevor Alleyne, and Carlo Sdralevich. 2013. *Energy Subsidy Reform: Lessons and Implications*. Washington, DC: IMF.

Coady, David, Robert Gillingham, Rolando Ossowski, John Piotrowski, Shamsuddin Tareq, and Justin Tyson. 2010. *Petroleum product subsidies: Costly, inequitable, and rising.* IMF Staff Position Note 10/05.

Coady, David, Ian Parry, Louis Sears, and Baoping Shang. 2015. How large are global energy subsidies? IMF Working Paper, WP/15/105. Washington DC: International Monetary Fund.

Commander, S., C. Amini, and Z. Nikoloski. 2011. The political economy of energy subsidies. Mimeo. World Bank.

Deacon, Robert T. 2009. Public good provision under dictatorship and democracy. *Public Choice* 139: 241–62.

Deacon, Robert T., and S. Saha. 2006. Public good provision by dictatorships: A survey. In A. F. Ott and R. J. Cebula, eds., *The Companion in Public Economics: Empirical Public Economics*. Cheltenham, UK: Elgar.

Fredriksson, P. G., X. Matchke, and J. Minier. 2010. Environmental policy in majoritarian systems. *Journal of Environmental Economics and Management* 59: 177–91.

Fredriksson, P. G., and D. L. Millimet. 2004. Comparative politics and environmental taxation. *Journal of Environmental Economics and Management* 48: 705–22.

Gelbach, S., and P. Keefer. 2011. Investment without democracy: Ruling-party institutionalization and credible commitment in autocracies. *Journal of Comparative Economics* 39: 123–39.

Global Subsidies Initiative. 2010. *Defining Fossil-Fuel Subsidies for the G-20: Which Approach Is Best? Policy Brief.* Winnipeg, Geneva: International Institute of Environment and Development, Global Subsidy Initiative.

Grindle, M. 2000. In Quest of the Political: The Political Economy of Development Policy-Making. In *Frontiers of Development Economics: The Future in Perspective*, ed. G. Meier and J. E. Stiglitz. New York: Oxford University Press.

Hammar, H., Å. Löfgren, and T. Sterner. 2004. Political economy obstacles to fuel taxation. *Energy Journal (Cambridge, MA)* 25: 1–17.

IEA. 1999. *World Energy Outlook 1999. Looking at Energy Subsidies: Getting the Prices Right.* Paris: International Energy Agency.

IEA. 2006. *World Energy Outlook 2006.* Paris: International Energy Agency.

IEA. 2008. *World Energy Outlook 2008.* Paris: International Energy Agency.

IEA. 2013. *World Energy Outlook 2013*. Paris: International Energy Agency.

IMF. 2008. *Fuel and food price subsidies: Issues and reform options. IMF Board Paper prepared by the Fiscal Affairs Department*.

Keefer, Philip, and Rezvan Vlaicu. 2008. Democracy, credibility and clientism. *Journal of Law Economics and Organization* 24: 271–306.

Kojima, Masami. 2012 a. *Petroleum Product Pricing and Complementary Policies: Experience from 65 Developing Countries since 2009*. Washington, DC: World Bank.

Kojima, Masami. 2012 b. Oil price risks and pump price adjustments. Policy Research Working Paper 6227. World Bank.

Lachapelle, Erick. 2009. Interests, institutions and ideas: Explaining cross-national differences in the implicit price of carbon. Working Paper. University of Toronto.

Laderchi, Caterina Ruggeri, Anne Oliver, and Chris Trimble. 2013. *Balancing Act. Cutting Energy Subsidies while Protecting Affordability*. Washington, DC: World Bank.

List, John, and Daniel M. Sturm. 2006. Now elections matter: Theory and evidence from environmental policy. *Quarterly Journal of Economics* 121: 1249–81.

OECD. 2005. *Environmentally Harmful Subsidies: Challenges for Reform*. Paris: OECD, Environment Directorate.

OECD. 2006. *Subsidy Reform and Sustainable Development. Economic, Environmental and Social Aspects. OECD Sustainable Development Studies*. Paris: OECD, Environment Directorate.

OECD. 2009. *G20 Leaders' Request: Work on Phasing-Out of Fossil Fuel Subsidies. Working Party on National Environmental Policies*. Paris: OECD, Environment Directorate.

Nur-Tegin, Kanybek, and Hans J. Czap. 2012. Corruption: Democracy, autocracy, and political stability. *Economic Analysis and Policy* 42: 51–66.

Parry, Ian, Dirk Heine, Shanjun Li, and Eliza Lis. 2014. *Getting Energy Prices Right: From Principle to Practice*. Washington, DC: IMF.

Parry, Ian, and Kenneth Small. 2005. Does Britain or the United States have the right gasoline tax? *American Economic Review* 95: 1276–89.

Parry, Ian, and Jon Strand. 2012. International fuel tax assessment: An application to Chile. *Environment and Development Economics* 17: 127–44.

Persson, Torsten, and Guido Tabellini. 2000. *Political Economics: Explaining Economic Policy*. Cambridge: MIT Press.

Prado, Mariana Mota, and Michael J. Treblicock. 2009. Path dependence, development, and the dynamics of institutional reform. *University of Toronto Law Journal* , 59, April 2009, 1-40.

Rock, Michael T. 2009. Corruption and democracy. *Journal of Development Studies* 45: 55–75.

Shleifer, Andrei, and Robert W. Vishny. 1993. Corruption. *Quarterly Journal of Economics* 108: 599–617.

Strand, Jon. 2013. Political economy aspects of fuel subsidies: A conceptual framework. Policy Research Working Paper 6392. World Bank.

Treisman, Daniel. 2007. What Have we Learned about the causes of corruption from ten years of cross-national empirical research? *Annual Review of Political Science* 10: 211–44.

Vagliasindi, Maria. 2012 a. Implementing energy subsidy reforms. An overview of key issues. Policy Research Working Paper 6122. World Bank.

Vagliasindi, Maria. 2012 b. *Implementing Energy Subsidy Reforms. Evidence from Developing Countries.* Washington, DC: World Bank.

Victor, David. 2009. *Untold Billions: The Politics of Fossil-Fuel Subsidies.* Geneva: International Institute of Environment and Development, Global Subsidy Initiative.

World Bank. 2009. *Problem-Driven Governance and Political Economy Analysis: Good Practice Framework.* Washington, DC: World Bank.

World Bank. 2010. Assessing the environmental co-benefits of climate change action. Concept Note for an Environment Strategy 2010 Background Paper.

2 Reforming Energy Prices

Ian Parry

2.1 Introduction

Growing appreciation of the budgetary costs of energy subsidies (especially in light of the surge in debt to GDP ratios since the 2008 fiscal crisis), their perverse environmental and distributional effects, and calls for their removal by the G20 and other prominent authorities, have heightened interest in the reform of energy prices.

Yet countries need to progress much further than eliminating direct energy subsidies. More important is the need for a comprehensive overhaul of energy pricing, not just in developing countries (where discrepancies between supply costs and prices are most pronounced) but also in developed countries, to ensure that energy taxes adequately reflect the major adverse side effects of energy use—not just the global carbon emissions but important domestic externalities (e.g., air pollution) as well.

In this chapter I consider the practicalities of getting energy prices right through *fiscal policies*, specifically how these policies might be designed and how different countries might gauge appropriate energy tax levels. I begin with a brief picture of current energy subsidies, and show that the undercharging for environmental costs (the main focus of this chapter) is generally far more important and pervasive than undercharging for supply costs. I then take a closer look at energy-related externalities and the efficient design of fiscal policies to address them. Following that I discuss the measurement of environmental damages and, for selected countries, estimates of efficient taxes on different fossil fuel products. I end with a brief discussion of how to move the reform process forward.[1]

2.2 Energy Subsidies: A Quick Comparison of Undercharging for Supply Costs and Environmental Costs

2.2.1 Definitions of Energy Subsidies

It is helpful to distinguish two different notions of energy subsidies (e.g., Coady et al. 2015). First is termed *pre-tax subsidies*, which primarily reflect the differences between the costs of supplying fossil-fuel energy and the prices paid for that energy by fuel users. For a particular fuel product shown in figure 2.1 drawn, for convenience, with constant marginal supply costs, pre-tax subsidies are the darker gray rectangle equal to current fuel consumption X_0, times the difference between unit supply costs and the retail fuel price. Often these subsidies come from state-owned enterprises in petroleum-producing countries setting domestic fuel prices below international prices.

Pre-tax subsidies have been calculated using the "price gap" approach (Coady et al. 2015).[2] For internationally traded products—petroleum and, to some extent, natural gas and coal—the price gap measures the difference between an international reference price (adjusted upward for transportation and distribution costs) and the domestic retail fuel price.[3] For nontraded products (notably electricity) the price gap is measured by the difference between estimated cost recovery prices (mostly based on studies of input requirements and input prices) and retail prices.

Pre-tax subsidies also include subsidies on the producer side, which commonly take the form of various tax reliefs for resource exploration and development. However, these are less important, quantitatively, than consumer subsidies, and may have limited effects on domestic fuel consumption (which matters for environmental impacts), at least in small open economies that are price takers in international fuel markets.

The second notion of energy subsidies is *post-tax subsidies*, which equal pre-tax subsidies plus the implicit subsidy from any undercharging for environmental damages.[4] Post-tax subsidies include the lighter gray rectangle in figure 2.1, equal to fuel consumption times the per unit external cost. In Coady et al. (2015), post-tax subsidies were measured using country-level estimates of environmental costs (discussed further below) defined net of any fuel taxes.[5]

Post-tax subsidies are the preferred measure of energy subsidies, as what matters for economic efficiency is the total gap between current fuel prices and efficient prices—that is, prices needed to cover both

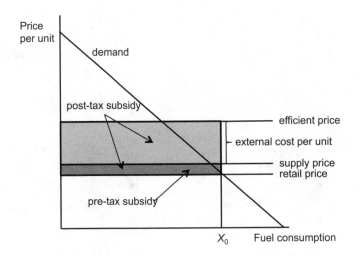

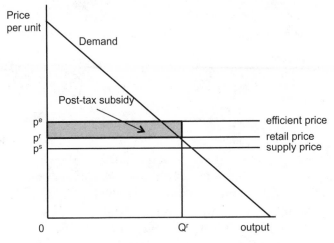

Figure 2.1
Defining pre-tax and post-tax energy subsidies

supply costs and externalities—regardless of the relative contribution of pre-tax subsidies and externalities to this gap.

2.2.2 Size of Subsidies and Their Breakdown by Fuels and Regions

Figure 2.2 summarizes pre-tax energy subsidy estimates for 2013, which totaled $540 billion worldwide (0.7 percent of global GDP). Petroleum accounts for 49 percent of this subsidy, electricity 29 percent,

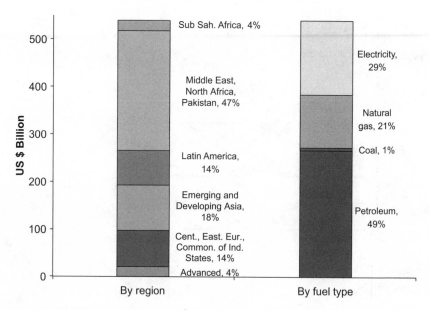

Figure 2.2
Pre-tax energy subsidies by region and fuel type, 2013. Not shown are Pre-tax subsidies in emerging Europe because they are less than 1 percent of the total.
Source: Coady et al. (2015)

and natural gas 21 percent. However, coal, the most carbon-intensive fuel, accounts for just 1 percent, implying only limited carbon benefits from eliminating pre-tax subsidies. Not surprisingly, petroleum-producing countries with administered prices in the Middle East and North Africa account for a large portion of pre-tax subsidies, while advanced countries account for just 4 percent of the subsidy.

However, as shown in figure 2.3, this picture looks completely different for post-tax subsidies. For one thing, the total subsidy is nine times as high at $4.9 trillion, implying that pricing externalities is far more important than removing pre-tax subsidies. For another, coal now accounts for a huge share (52 percent) of the subsidy, reflecting undercharging for its high carbon and local air pollution emissions. Furthermore advanced countries contribute substantially (23 percent) to these subsidies, signaling that energy price reform is a pressing issue not only for developing countries but for developed countries as well.

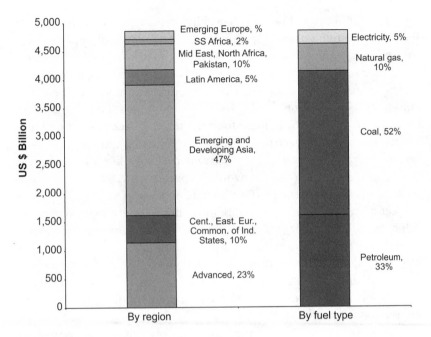

Figure 2.3
Post-tax energy subsidies by region and fuel type, 2013
Source: Coady et al. (2015)

In principle, setting prices to cover supply costs (eliminating pre-tax subsidies) is straightforward, given reasonable information on unit supply costs (or proxies for those costs from international fuel prices). The discussion therefore turns to the more challenging issue of how externalities might be reflected in energy taxes.

2.3   Energy-Related Externalities and Fiscal Instruments to Address Them

This section lays out the case for, and design of, fiscal instruments to address the major environmental externalities from energy use. Subsequent sections get into the empirical size of externalities and efficient energy taxes.

2.3.1   Why Fiscal Instruments?

There are three basic reasons for using fiscal instruments, such as fuel taxes, emissions taxes, or trading systems with allowance auctions, to reflect externalities in energy prices. First is that these instruments are the most effective policies for exploiting the full range of opportunities for externality mitigation—*so long as they are directly targeted at the source of the externality*. For example, as a carbon tax is reflected in higher prices for fossil fuels and electricity, it reduces carbon dioxide (CO_2) emissions by promoting shifting to renewable generation fuels, shifting from coal to gas, and from these fuels to nuclear generation, and reducing the demand for electricity, transportation fuels, and natural gas in homes and industry. Narrowly focused policies—like incentives for renewable generation, which would promote only the first of these responses—are far less effective.[6] To take another example, charges on air pollution emissions from coal plants will promote adoption of emissions control technologies across all plants, shifting to coal with lower pollution content, shifting to other generation fuels, and reductions in electricity demand. In contrast, requirements for control technologies on new plants promote only the first response and only at a subset of plants (and may perversely delay the retirement of older, more polluting plants).

Second is that fiscal instruments achieve a given environmental improvement at the lowest cost overall to the economy—*so long as revenues are used productively*, most obviously to lower the burden of other taxes (e.g., on income, payroll, consumption) that distort economic activity (by reducing incentives for work effort and investments in human and physical capital, promoting informality and shifting to tax-favored goods). A key point from the literature is that pricing policies forgoing efficiency gains from revenue recycling (e.g., trading systems with free allowance allocations, carbon taxes with revenues earmarked for low-value spending) can impose quite large burdens on the economy and are far from cost effective.[7]

The third reason for environmental taxes is that they automatically strike the right balance between environmental benefits and economic costs, promoting only those changes in behavior for which benefits exceed costs—*so long as tax rates are scaled to environmental damages*.[8] Regulatory and other quantity-based approaches are generally not designed to achieve the efficient scale of policy intervention, unless they are converted into tax-like instruments, for example, through supplementary measures that align (implicit or explicit) emissions prices with environmental damages.

As regards the choice between taxes and trading systems, in principle this is less important than implementing one of them and getting the basic design details right—more important is comprehensively targeting the right base, exploiting opportunities for revenue recycling, and establishing stable prices in line with the environmental damages on an ongoing basis. In practice, trading systems are a more convoluted way to achieve these objectives. For example, agencies administering trading systems would need to auction all the allowances and remit the revenues to the finance ministry, and price stability provisions (most obviously tight price collars) are needed (which obviates the need for much allowance trading).[9] Trading systems also add a new layer of administration, rather than modifying (to fully account for externalities) and extending to other fuels administrative systems for road fuel excises, which are long established and widely accepted in most countries.

2.3.2 Major Externalities and Tailoring Taxes to Address Them

The major externalities associated with fossil fuels include carbon dioxide (CO_2) emissions, local air pollution, and further side effects due to vehicle use. Tax design specifics for each externality are discussed in turn below.[10]

CO_2 In the absence of mitigating measures, rising atmospheric concentrations of CO_2 and other greenhouse gases are expected to warm the planet by roughly 3° to 4° centigrade by 2100 (IPCC 2013), but with serious risks of catastrophic outcomes (much higher warming, permanent collapse of ice sheets, reversal of the Gulf stream flow, etc.).

From a tax administration perspective, the most natural CO_2 mitigation policy is simply a charge on the supply of fossil-fuel products equal to the fuel's CO_2 emissions factor (which is well established) times the environmental damage per ton of CO_2. This would be a straightforward extension of motor fuel excises—building a carbon charge into the tax and extending similar charges to the supply of other petroleum products (e.g., at the refinery gate or fuel distribution centers), coal (at the mine mouth or processing plant), and natural gas (e.g., as it enters the pipeline system). These sorts of excises are about the easiest of taxes to administer—in the United States, for example, they would cover only about 1,500 to 2,000 companies (Calder 2015; Metcalf and Weisbach 2009). Alternatively, taxes might be applied directly to emissions at the point of combustion for large stationary sources, though these systems would omit (for administrative reasons) small-scale emitters, involve a new layer of administration (to track emissions rather than fuel use), and require an upstream charging element on fuel supply for transportation and heating fuels.

Local Air Pollution   The main damage from local air pollution is the elevated mortality risk from various heart and lung diseases and strokes whose prevalence is increased by inhaling fine particulates, produced either directly from fuel combustion or indirectly through atmospheric chemical reactions involving sulfur dioxide (SO_2) and nitrogen oxides (NO_x).[11] The World Health Organization (WHO) estimates that outdoor air pollution (from fossil fuels and other sources like biomass) results in over three million premature deaths a year worldwide.

Again taxes can be applied on fuel supply and set equal to the weighted sum of emissions factors for direct particulates, SO_2 and NO_x, where weights are the respective environmental damages per ton. For coal, it is especially important to charge for net emissions out of smokestacks, given the potential for control technologies (e.g., SO_2 scrubbers) to remove most such emissions. Again charges can be levied upfront on coal supply (according to a nationwide benchmark for embodied pollution), with rebates to generators demonstrating valid emissions capture, or on emissions out of the smokestack, though the former is likely the more administratively feasible for many countries.[12]

Motor Vehicle Externalities   Beyond carbon and local pollution, the major externalities associated with motor vehicle use are traffic congestions, traffic accidents, and (to a lesser extent) wear and tear on highway infrastructure. Congestion externalities are mostly due to drivers failing to account for their own impact on adding to traffic volumes and slowing travel speeds for other road users. And while drivers might take into account injury risks to themselves, they may not consider injury risk to pedestrians, elevated injury risks to other vehicle occupants, and risks of third-party property damages and medical costs from their own driving. As for road damage, the externality reflects more frequent need for road maintenance due to wear and tear imposed by vehicles with heavy axle loads.

For given road infrastructure, charging vehicles per kilometer driven on busy roads (monitored, for example, by global positioning systems, electronic debiting from smart cars, or tag plate recognition), with the charges rising and falling with traffic volumes during the course of the rush hour, is the most effective way to promote all behavioral responses for congestion relief (encouraging people to drive sooner or later than the rush hour peak, drive at off-peak hours, take less congested routes, car pool, reduce the number of trips, use public transit). Kilometer-based charges are also the most effective way to internalize accident externalities (given other policies like drunk driver penalties and vehicle and road safety measures), more so if charges could be scaled by driver characteristics (based on insurance ratings for age, prior driving record, and possibly vehicle type), as this penalizes the riskiest driving the most. Road damage is best addressed by kilometer-based charges for trucks, scaled by their axle weight and road surface quality.

Nevertheless, comprehensive kilometer-based charging schemes (applied to all vehicles and set at fully corrective levels) are likely a long way off for most countries.[13] Presently it is wholly appropriate to capture the full range of vehicle externalities in fuel taxes (despite the obvious bluntness of addressing congestion through fuel taxes)—not doing so may forgo substantial welfare gains. One subtlety here in assessing corrective fuel taxes is that externalities varying with kilometers driven should be scaled back by around 50 percent, given a rough rule of thumb that ultimately half of the tax-induced reduction in fuel use will come from reduced vehicle use and the other half from improvements in average vehicle fuel efficiency (the latter does not generate any reductions in distance-related externalities).[14]

2.4   Putting Principle into Practice: Quantifying Corrective Fuel Taxes in Different Countries

This section describes a methodology developed in Parry et al. (2014) for measuring externalities and corrective fuel taxes on a country-by-country basis. A good degree of humility is needed here given that many of the steps in damage assessment (e.g., valuing mortality risks and global warming) are contentious. Nevertheless, it is valuable to lay out a conceptual framework to make transparent the key underlying parameters and accommodate different viewpoints over these parameters,[15] as this helps to discipline the policy debate.

2.4.1   Climate Change

The different views on the appropriate value on CO_2 emissions to charge for global warming damages largely amount to different views on intergenerational discounting and modeling of low-probability, extreme damage outcomes. Parry et al. (2014) use an illustrative value of \$35 per ton of CO_2 for 2010 (based on US IAWG 2013), though the implications of alterative values are transparent from the graphics we discuss below.

2.4.2   Air Pollution Damages from Coal Plants

Parry et al. (2014) use four main steps to quantify the air pollution damage from coal plants. First is that data on the geographical location of coal plants in different countries is mapped to very granular data on the number of people living at different distance classifications from each plant (up to 2,000 km away, given the potential long-range transport of emissions from tall smokestacks). These data are used to extrapolate "intake fractions"—the average portion of a particular pollutant that ends up being inhaled (as fine particulates) by exposed populations (as opposed to the fraction that disperses without harm)—for different pollutants, from a state-of-the-art study for China by Zhou et al. (2006), that are adjusted for population exposure in other countries relative to that in China.

The advantage of this approach is that it circumvents the need to develop complex air quality models relating emissions from different sources in each country to air quality and population exposure in all regions where emissions might be transported to. The drawback is that it cannot account for differences in meteorological conditions (in particular, wind speeds) between other countries and China, affecting regional pollution formation. However, some cross-checks with air quality models in a limited number of cases suggest the bias from omitting these factors is not necessarily large and does not follow a particular pattern.

Second is to obtain elevated mortality risks by country from additional pollution emissions by linking intake fractions to two pieces of information from the WHO's Global Burden of Disease project. One is baseline mortality rates in different regions for fatal illnesses whose prevalence is increased by exposure to pollution.[16] The other is evidence on the relationship between pollution exposure and additional mortality risk (or "dose–response" functions).

Third is to monetize mortality risks. For this purpose, Parry et al. (2014) use estimates of the value per premature mortality for the average OECD country (\$3.7 million, updated to 2010) and of the elasticity of mortality valuation with respect to income (0.8)—both obtained from a meta analysis by OECD (2012) involving several hundred stated preference studies for different countries—in order to extrapolate mortality values for all countries. The mortality value for China, for example, is $1.1 million (though again, the implications of different assumptions are easy to infer from the figures below).[17]

Last is to convert damages per ton of emissions into corrective fuel taxes using an extensive country-level data base of coal plant emissions factors (for SO_2, NO_x, and direct $PM_{2.5}$) compiled by the Institute for International Institute for Applied Systems Analysis (IIASA). The results below are based on current emission factors, reflecting an average over plants with and without control technologies (the appropriate factors are discussed further below). Tax rates are expressed per unit of energy (given significant variation in emissions factors across individual types of coal). The IIASA database also includes emissions factors for CO_2 that are used to express carbon damages per unit of fuels (these factors differ substantially across coal, natural gas, gasoline, and diesel but not across countries).

2.4.3   Air Pollution from Other Sources
The four steps noted above were used to assess corrective taxes for natural gas used in power generation (again expressed per unit of energy).

Local air emissions from ground-level sources—principally vehicles and residential heating—tend to stay locally concentrated (rather than transported over long distances) and this simplifies the assessment of their intake fractions. Parry et al. (2014) obtain ground-level intake fractions for SO_2, NO_x, and $PM_{2.5}$ from over 3,000 cities by pooling estimates from two studies, extrapolate these to the country level, and then follow the last three steps mentioned above (for road fuels, damages are expressed per liter).

2.4.4   Other Motor Vehicle Externalities
In the absence of better data, Parry et al. (2014) regress travel delays from a city-level database on various transportation indicators and then extrapolate delays to the national level using the regression coefficients and countrywide measures of those same indictors. Marginal delay (the delay one extra kilometer driven by one vehicle imposes on other road users) is assumed to be four times the average delay, loosely based on specifications commonly used by transportation engineers. The result is scaled by vehicle occupancy, and monetized based on literature suggesting the value of travel time (on congested roads) is around 60 percent of the market wage.[18]

These estimates understate marginal congestion costs in several ways. For one thing, automobiles impose greater delay to other road users when buses (which have high vehicle occupancies) are a significant share of vehicles on the road. For another, congestion causes broader costs due to creating uncertainty over travel arrival times and may induce people to leave sooner or later than they would otherwise prefer to avoid peak travel.

With regard to accident externalities, Parry et al. (2014) estimate these by country, again in a highly rudimentary way, using data on traffic fatalities and with an assumed breakdown of data between internal and external risks. For example, injury risks to occupants in single-vehicle collisions are assumed to be internal, whereas risks to pedestrians/cyclists and a portion of injuries in multiple-vehicle collisions are assumed to be external. Other components of external costs (e.g., medical and property damages borne by third parties, a portion of nonfatal injuries) are extrapolated from several country case studies.

Road damage costs are obtained from data on road maintenance expenditures (where it is available and extrapolated from other countries where it is not) and assumptions about the amount of wear and tear due to vehicle traffic as opposed to other factors like climate.

2.5 Corrective Fuel Tax Estimates and Impacts of Reform

This section first discusses, for a limited selection of countries, corrective taxes on coal, natural gas, gasoline, and (road) diesel obtained from the above methodology for the year 2010 (Parry et al. 2014 present results, where possible, for over 150 countries). The impacts of policy reform are then considered.

2.5.1 Corrective Tax Estimates

Coal Figure 2.4 shows estimates of corrective taxes on coal for 18 countries, expressed in US$ per gigajoule (GJ). The charge for carbon (the CO_2 emissions factor times the $35 per ton damage) is $3.3 per GJ, which is quite substantial, amounting to about two-thirds of the average world coal price in 2010, and is essentially the same across countries given the minimal differences in CO_2 emissions rates.

More interesting, as figure 2.4 shows, is that the charge for local air pollution (from $PM_{2.5}$, SO_2, and NO_x combined) can also be substantial. For the majority of countries this charge exceeds the carbon charge, but the variation across countries is considerable. For example, the charge

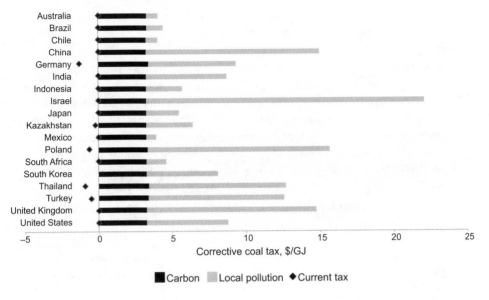

Figure 2.4
Corrective coal tax estimates, selected countries, 2010
Source: Parry et al. (2014)

is relatively modest ($0.8 per GJ) in Australia, where emission rates are relatively low and much of the pollution disperses (across the oceans or to the Outback) without harming exposed populations. In contrast, despite lower assumed mortality values, the local pollution charge for China is much higher ($11.7 per GJ), due to its higher emission rates and especially high population exposure to pollution. As for the United States, the local pollution charge is about half of that for China—even though premature deaths per ton of coal in the United States are only about one-tenth of those for China, this is partially offset by higher mortality values.

In short, coal is pervasively and substantially undercharged, given that coal excises (indicated by the diamonds in figure 2.4) are essentially zero, or slightly negative (most countries do not impose excises on coal analogous to those for road fuels).

One last point about figure 2.4 is that the emission rates underling the air pollution damages are based on average rates across existing plants with and without control technologies—if corrective taxes were introduced (with appropriate crediting for air emissions mitigation) this would create strong incentives for wider deployment of control technologies, thereby lowering the average air pollution damages per unit of coal use.

Natural Gas As indicated in figure 2.5, natural gas (for power generation) is pervasively undercharged as well (in fact in some countries there are significant subsidies for gas), though the degree of undercharging is less pronounced than for coal. One reason is that gas produces 40 percent less CO_2 emissions per unit of energy compared with coal. More important, natural gas produces very minimal amounts of direct $PM_{2.5}$ and SO_2—the two most harmful pollutants for public health—and even NO_x emissions per unit of energy are significantly lower for gas than for coal (for all countries, the charge on natural gas for local pollution is less than the carbon charge).

Gasoline As for gasoline, the corrective tax estimates shown in figure 2.6 are typically substantial, amounting to around 40 to 80 cents per

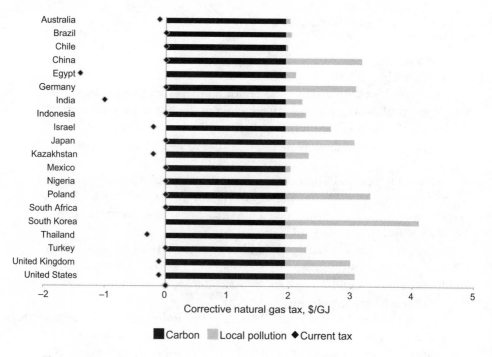

Figure 2.5
Corrective natural gas tax estimates (for power plants), selected countries, 2010
Source: Parry et al. (2014)

liter ($1.60 to $3.20 per gallon) across developed and developing countries alike. Traffic congestion contributes a substantial portion of this corrective charge, particularly in advanced countries where wage rates, and hence the value of travel time, are relatively high. Traffic accidents are another big contributor, particularly in developing countries where road fatality rates are relatively high. Carbon damages (again equal to the CO_2 emission factor times $35 per ton of CO_2) are more modest at 8 cents per liter. Local air pollution damages are smaller still, as gasoline vehicles (e.g., natural gas plants) do not produce the pollutants that are the most harmful to human health.

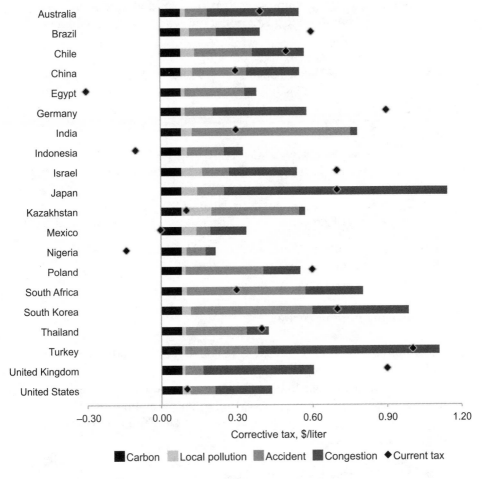

Figure 2.6
Corrective gasoline tax estimates, selected countries, 2010
Source: Parry et al. (2014)

For 15 of the 20 countries shown in figure 2.6, current fuel taxes are below the corrective fuel tax estimates, and even in countries where the opposite applies (e.g., United Kingdom) tax reductions are not necessarily recommended as the corrective taxes are likely understated—far more pressing in these countries (rather than fine-tuning corrective fuel taxes) is to partially transition away from fuel taxes toward distance-based taxes to more effectively manage congestion.

Diesel   Figure 2.7 shows estimates of corrective taxes on diesel fuel, averaged across cars and trucks. The degree of undercharging tends to be more pronounced than for gasoline. This relfects the lower taxation of diesel fuel in many countries, when compared with gasoline, and some of the externalities (e.g., air pollution, road damage) are higher.

2.5.2   Impacts of Reform
Parry et al. (2014) calculate, albeit very crudely, the benefits if all countries move from their existing fuel taxes (which are often zero and sometimes negative in the case of fuel subsidies) to their estimated corrective levels.[19] At a global level, these reforms yield substantial benefits, including

- a 63 percent reduction in premature deaths from fossil fuel air pollution,
- a 23 percent reduction in energy-related CO_2 emissions, and
- new revenues of 2.6 percent of GDP.

Yet, across countries, there is substantial variation in these benefits. For example, revenue gains are over 7 percent of GDP in China, which has a relatively coal-intensive economy.

2.6   Moving Reform Forward

How might these energy price reforms be moved forward in practice? A study of 28 episodes of attempted energy price reforms in a range of countries in Africa, Asia, Latin America, and the Middle East—varying from successful, to partially successful, to unsuccessful—by Clements et al. (2013) concludes that there are several key (and commonsense) ingredients for success.

One ingredient is to communicate to the public and stakeholders the size of energy subsidies and how these groups will benefit from reform, in terms of what other taxes will be reduced with the new revenue,

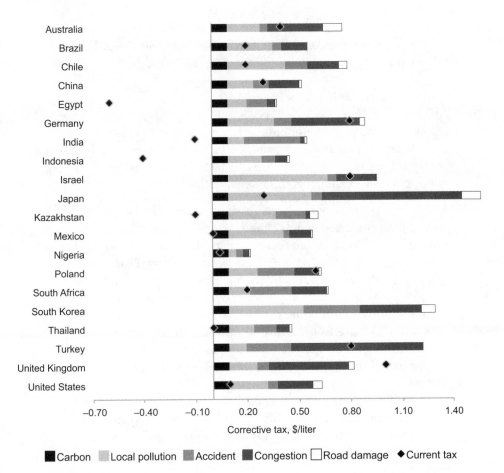

Figure 2.7
Corrective diesel tax estimates, selected countries, 2010
Source: Parry et al. (2014)

how many extra schools and hospitals will be built, the health and environmental benefits, and so on. Another ingredient is to de-politicize the setting of energy prices in countries retaining some price control administration—devolving decision-making processes for linking domestic prices to movements in international prices to an autonomous authority. Sequencing the price reforms may also be useful, for example, leaving till last price reforms for fuels (e.g., kerosene) consumed intensively by the poor and waiting till social safety nets are adequately strengthened before raising prices.

The greatest challenges, however, are overcoming opposition to the potential tax burdens on vulnerable households and firms. These are taken up briefly in turn below.

2.6.1 Burdens on Households

Although all households are potentially affected by higher energy prices, low-income households are a particular concern, not least because access to energy is sometimes viewed as a poverty-alleviation strategy. Here some broad points to bear in mind when designing policy packages to address these sensitivities.[20]

• Energy taxes may not be as regressive as they at first appear. Although in advanced countries the poor tend to spend a greater share of their annual income on electricity, this is less true for transportation and heating fuels, and other consumer products whose prices increase indirectly from higher energy costs (OECD 2014; Parry 2015)—energy taxes could even be progressive in lower income countries with limited vehicle ownership and power grid access. Regressive effects are also less pronounced when incidence is measured against household consumption, which may be a better benchmark against which to measure incidence rather than annual income.

• Holding down energy prices below levels warranted by supply costs and externalities is a highly inefficient way to help low-income households, as most of the benefits leak away to higher income groups[21]—a corollary being that only a minor portion of revenues from energy tax reforms are potentially needed to help low income groups (e.g., Dinan 2015). Indeed there are numerous targeted adjustments to the broader tax/benefit system that might be made to reach these groups at the same time energy prices are increased—the focus should be the distributional impact of the whole policy package, not just the component that raises energy prices.

• But diverting carbon tax revenues from the general budget for compensation involves significant costs, by reducing opportunities for cutting other taxes that distort economic activity. Reasonably accurate estimates of burdens on vulnerable groups are therefore important for gauging appropriate compensation levels. And, insofar as possible, compensation instruments that enhance economic efficiency should be used—higher personal income tax thresholds, payroll tax reductions, earned income tax credits, worker assistance programs, education subsidies, and the like, promote these efficiency gains, whereas lump-sum transfers do not, and means-tested benefits can perversely affect work incentives and economic efficiency.

2.6.2 Burdens on Firms

Higher energy costs for energy-intensive, trade-exposed industries (e.g., steel, aluminum, cement producers) unable to pass through higher energy costs in product prices are a particular concern because of competitiveness impacts and emissions leakage (i.e., offsetting increases in emissions in other countries). But leakage effects may not be that substantial,[22] often trade-exposed firms have to cope with larger changes in energy prices from economic factors, and efficient resource allocation implies that such firms should eventually go out of business if they cannot compete when domestic energy is efficiently priced. Fischer et al. (2015) discuss various options for compensating vulnerable firms (e.g., corporate tax cuts, production subsidies, border tax adjustments, exemptions through rebates for energy costs), though none of them is entirely satisfactory, and these measures should be transitory anyway to ease the needed adjustment (there is, however, an important role for worker re-training and re-location programs).

2.7 Conclusion

The findings discussed in this chapter suggest that there is pervasive and substantial underpricing of energy, across both developed and developing countries, with potentially substantial benefits from energy price reform. And reforms do not need to await an international agreement over carbon pricing, as many of the benefits are in countries' own interests. Using the environmental damage estimates discussed above, Parry, Veung, and Heine (2015) have estimated that, on average across the twenty largest CO_2 emitting countries, a price of $57.5 per ton of CO_2 in 2010 would be warranted by domestic environmental benefits alone (air pollution, reductions in vehicle externalities net of fuel taxes), before even counting the global carbon benefits.

A key theme of the discussion is that energy tax reforms can be a straightforward extension of what most governments are already doing, and have been doing successfully for many years, namely taxing road fuels. These taxes need to be better aligned with external costs in many cases and similar excises applied to other fossil fuels. There are some subtleties (e.g., the need to credit control technologies at power plants and to introduce congestion pricing), but the practicalities should be manageable. Finance ministries have a critical role to play in all of this, not only in administering tax reforms and ensuring that revenues are put to good use but also (given they are often the most powerful voice in government) in championing these reforms—the sooner the better given the stakes.

Notes

1. This chapter largely draws on discussions in Coady et al. (2015) and Parry et al. (2014).

2. This approach (see Koplow 2009 for more discussion) is used widely by international organizations to measure energy subsidies, an advantage being that it captures subsidies that might be off-budget (e.g., reflected in losses at state-owned enterprises) and from any failure to fully apply general consumption taxes to energy products consumed at the household level.

3. Coady et al. (2015) compile retail prices from various sources including publicly available data on the prices of all energy products for advanced countries, survey data for motor fuel prices across a larger group of countries, and responses from ministry representatives.

4. Also included in post-tax subsidies are the value-added or sales taxes applying to consumer products in general that should be applied to household fuel consumption, though this component is typically modest relative to external costs.

5. Where taxes exceed external costs, subsidies are taken to be zero (rather than negative).

6. Studies for the United States (e.g., Krupnick et al. 2010) find that a carbon tax is about five times as effective at reducing CO_2 compared with renewable generation policies. Broader regulatory packages (e.g., an emission per kilowatt hour standard for power generation combined with various energy efficiency standards across different sectors) promote more mitigation responses. Even so, some emission reduction opportunities cannot be regulated (e.g., encouraging people to conserve on vehicle and air conditioner use); extensive credit trading (across firms, sectors, programs, and time periods) is required to contain the costs of regulatory approaches; and importantly, these policies do not raise revenue.

7. For a representative, large emitting country, Parry (2015) puts the annualized cost of a revenue-neutral carbon tax that cuts CO_2 emissions in the order of 0.06 percent of GDP, while the cost of the same policy with no efficiency gains from recycling is more than ten times as high.

8. Early studies (e.g., Bovenberg and Goulder 1996) suggested that despite revenue recycling, optimal environmental taxes are below Pigouvian levels. However, these studies do not capture the full range of distortions created by the broader fiscal system and therefore substantially understate the efficiency gains from revenue recycling and optimal tax levels (e.g., Bento et al. 2012; Parry and Bento 2000). My own view is that for practical purposes, environmental taxes should be set at their Pigouvian levels, with broader fiscal objectives met by some combination of broader taxes (on income, payrolls, etc.) and specific taxes on products (vehicles sales, electricity consumption, etc.) with relatively immobile tax bases.

9. Controlling quantities, rather than prices, is potentially important when the environmental damage function is sharply convex, rather than linear, but this seems to have little relevance for the externalities considered below (e.g., the relation between mortality rates and pollution concentrations appears to be roughly linear in the vicinity of corrective fuel taxes, and the damages from one year's CO_2 emissions by one country are approximately linear given their small contribution to the accumulated concentration of CO_2 in the atmosphere).

10. There are many other externalities associated with energy use, but they are beyond the scope here, because the nature of the externality is difficult to define (e.g., energy security, or indoor air pollution where the people causing pollution are the ones who bear the most cost), or the empirical magnitude of the externality is on a smaller scale than those discussed above (e.g., the annualized costs of oil spills, leakage from fuel storage tanks, de-spoiling of the natural environment at mining sites). See, for example, NRC (2009: ch. 2) for further discussion.

11. Mortality impacts typically account for 85 percent or more of the total estimated damages from local air pollution (other impacts include morbidity, ecosystem damage, building corrosion, reduced crop yields, etc.). See, for example, NRC (2009).

12. Either charging scheme is administratively challenging for vehicle emissions, not least given the dramatically larger number of emissions sources. Here a fuel charge reflecting average pollution damage can be combined with standards or tax-subsidy schemes for vehicle suppliers to promote lower emission rates.

13. Serious nationwide kilometer-based taxes for passenger vehicles (with rates varying with the degree of congestion) have been considered, but not enacted, in the United Kingdom and the Netherlands.

14. See, for example, Glaister and Graham (2002) and Goodwin et al. (2004).

15. A spreadsheet for this purpose is available at www.imf.org/environment.

16. These mortality rates vary substantially across regions. For example, they are relatively high in Eastern Europe where there is high consumption of alcohol and tobacco, and relatively low in African countries where people are more prone to dying first from other diseases.

17. One complication here is the valuation of deaths in other countries caused by pollution transported from a neighboring country. However, Parry et al. (2014) suggest that applying different mortality values depending on where the deaths occur, which can become quite complicated (rather than attributing to all of them the source country's mortality value), would not make a great deal of difference for the corrective tax results.

18. Congestion costs are scaled back to make some adjustment for the weaker sensitivity of driving on congested roads (which is dominated by commuting) to fuel prices, compared with driving on uncongested roads.

19. These calculations are simply based on applying a fuel price elasticity of –0.5 (for all fuels and all countries) to the proportionate increase in fuel prices resulting from the tax reform, to infer the changes in fuel use (relative to 2010 consumption levels). For air pollution from coal plants the reform is assumed to promote adoption of control technologies at all plants, so industrywide emission rates equal rates representative of plants currently using these technologies.

20. For further discussion see, for example, Arze del Granado et al. (2012), Dinan (2015), Metcalf (1999), Morris and Mathur (2015), and Sterner (2010).

21. For example, according to Arze del Granado et al. (2012), the bottom income quintile on average receives only 7 percent of the benefits from petroleum product subsidies.

22. For example, Böhringer et al. (2012) estimate that leakage offsets around 5 to 20 percent of the emissions reductions from carbon pricing, depending on the size of the coalition of countries taking action. This leakage reflects not only the international migration of economic activity but also increases in fossil fuel use in other countries as world fuel prices fall in response to reduced demand in countries with carbon pricing. The latter type of leakage is not easily addressed through policy.

References

Arze del Granado, Javier, David Coady, and Robert Gillingham, 2012. The unequal benefits of fuel subsidies: A review of evidence for developing countries. *World Development* 40: 2234–48.

Bento, Antonio, Mark Jacobsen, and Antung A. Liu. 2012. *Environmental policy in the presence of an informal sector. Discussion paper.* Cornell University.

Böhringer, C., J. C. Carbone, and T. F. Rutherford. 2012. Unilateral climate policy design: Efficiency and equity implications of alternative instruments to reduce carbon leakage. *Energy Economics* 34 (suppl. 2): S208–17.

Bovenberg, A. Lans, and Lawrence H. Goulder. 1996. Optimal 2001 environmental taxes in the presence of other taxes. *American Economic Review* 84: 1085–89.

Calder, Jack. 2015. Administration of a US carbon tax. In I. Parry, A. Morris, and R. Williams, eds., *Implementing a US Carbon Tax: Challenges and Debates*, 38–61. London: Routledge.

Clements, Benedict, David Coady, Stefania Fabrizio, Sanjeev Gupta, Trevor Alleyene, and Carlo Sdralevich, eds. 2013. *Energy Subsidy Reform: Lessons and Implications.* Washington, DC: IMF.

Coady, David, Ian Parry, Louis Sears, and Baoping Shang. 2015. How large are global energy subsidies? Working Paper 15–105. IMF.

Dinan, Terry. 2015. Offsetting a carbon tax's burden on low-income households. In I. Parry, A. Morris, and R. Williams, eds., *Implementing a US Carbon Tax: Challenges and Debates* 120–40. London: Routledge.

Fischer, Carolyn, Richard Morgenstern, and Nathan Richardson. 2015. Carbon taxes and energy intensive trade exposed industries: Impacts and options. In *Implementing a US Carbon Tax: Challenges and Debates*, I. Parry, A. Morris, and R. Williams, eds., 159–177. London: Routledge.

Glaister, Stephen, and Dan Graham. 2002. The demand for automobile fuel: A survey of elasticities. *Journal of Transport Economics and Policy* 36: 1–25.

Goodwin, Phil B., Joyce Dargay, and Mark Hanly. 2004. Elasticities of road traffic and fuel consumption with respect to price and income: A review. *Transport Reviews* 24: 275–92.

IPCC. 2013. *Climate Change 2013: The Physical Science Basis. Contribution of Working Group I to the Fifth Assessment Report of the Intergovernmental Panel on Climate Change.* Cambridge, UK: Cambridge University Press.

Koplow, Doug. 2009. Measuring energy subsidies using the price-cap approach: What does it leave out?" IISD Trade, Investment and Climate Change Series. International Institute for Sustainable Development, Winnipeg.

Krupnick, Alan J., Ian W. H. Parry, Margaret Walls, Tony Knowles, and Kristin Hayes. 2010. *Toward a New National Energy Policy: Assessing the Options.* Washington, DC: Resources for the Future and National Energy Policy Institute.

Metcalf, Gilbert E. 1999. A distributional analysis of green tax reforms. *National Tax Journal* 52: 665–81.

Metcalf, Gilbert, and David Weisbach. 2009. The design of a carbon tax. *Harvard Environmental Law Review* 33: 499–556.

Morris, Adele, and Aparna Mathur. 2015. The distributional burden of a carbon tax: Evidence and implications for policy. In I. Parry, A. Morris, and R. Williams, eds., *Implementing a US Carbon Tax: Challenges and Debates* 97-119. London: Routledge.

NRC. 2009. *The Hidden Costs of Energy.* Washington, DC: National Research Council.

OECD. 2012. *Mortality Risk Valuation in Environment, Health and Transport Policies.* Paris: Organization for Economic Cooperation and Development.

OECD. 2014. *The Distributional Effects of Energy Taxes: Preliminary Report.* Paris: Organization for Economic Cooperation and Development.

Parry, Ian W. H. 2015. Carbon tax burdens on low-income households: A reason for delaying climate policy? In B. Clements, ed., *Fiscal Policy and Income Inequality* 233–254. Washington, DC: IMF.

Parry, Ian W. H., Chandara Veung, and Dirk Heine. 2015. How much carbon pricing is in countries own interests? The critical role of co-benefits. *Climate Change Economics* 6: 1550019-1-26.

Parry, Ian W. H., and Antonio M. Bento. 2000. Tax deductions, environmental policy, and the "double dividend" hypothesis. *Journal of Environmental Economics and Management* 39: 67–96.

Parry, Ian W. H., Dirk Heine, Shanjun Li, and Eliza Lis. 2014. *Getting Energy Prices Right: From Principle to Practice.* Washington, DC: IMF.

Sterner, Thomas. 2010. Distributional effects of taxing transport fuels. *Energy Policy* 41: 75–83.

US IAWG. 2013. *Technical Update of the Social Cost of Carbon for Regulatory Impact Analysis Under Executive Order 12866.* Washington, DC: US Inter-Agency Working Group.

Zhou, Ying, Jonathan I. Levy, John S. Evans, and James K. Hammitt. 2006. The influence of geographic location on population exposure to emissions from power plants throughout China. *Environment International* 32: 365–73.

3 Energy Taxation in OECD Countries: Effective Tax Rates across Countries, Users, and Fuels

Michelle Harding, Herman Vollebergh, and Suphi Sen

3.1 Introduction

Energy use, while critical for modern economies and lifestyles, can have significant environmental consequences through emissions of CO_2 and local air pollutants. Taxes on energy are a key tool available to governments by which they can influence energy use, and consequently emissions of CO_2 and local air pollutants from energy use. Energy taxes, in particular, if levied on fossil fuel tax bases, implicitly tax these pollutants. Since energy taxes can send important price signals that influence energy consumption patterns, energy taxation is often used by governments to reduce emissions (Vollebergh 2012; Parry et al. 2012, 2014; OECD 2013b). Taxes on energy are in fact an important source of government revenue. In some countries these revenues are even earmarked for specific purposes like road infrastructure or non–fossil-fuel support measures. Understanding the structure and level of energy taxes in a country is therefore central to policy discussions regarding energy use. Given the centrality of energy to the economy and the environment, such an understanding is a key reference point for consideration of how policy can best support green growth (OECD 2009).

In this context, the OECD created a new analysis to improve our understanding of the relationship between energy use and taxation by providing a systematic comparative analysis of the structure and level of taxes on energy use in all OECD countries. Building on a highly disaggregated database of energy use and tax information, Taxing Energy Use (TEU) (OECD 2013b) presents effective tax rates on energy use in terms of both energy content and carbon emissions, together with detailed graphical profiles of the structure of energy use and taxes on energy in each country. These effective tax rates do explicitly account for a specific potential tax base in a country and how this tax base is taxed in practice, namely which part of the tax base is subject to a nominal tax rate and which part is not.

A common belief is also that energy consumption is not very sensitive to price or tax changes as energy use would be a typical necessary good with low elasticity, meaning consumption does grow with less than in proportion to income. For example, tax inclusive prices would have relatively little effect on behavior of households to turn down the room thermostat or on firms to shift to other energy products. This is precisely why the energy tax base also provides a potential important revenue source to finance government expenditures. However, if higher tax rates would not lead to lower consumption and revenue loss for energy products with low price elasticities, such as electricity and natural gas used for heating, this would also imply relative sad news from a regulatory perspective. With a more or less stable tax base, energy use and so also (carbon) emissions are less likely to be reduced through (higher) taxes (Vollebergh 2014).

Understanding the cross-country differences in energy taxation is important for its implications about (implicit) energy subsidies. In OECD countries the preponderance of support in the energy market usually takes the form of tax expenditures rather than direct price subsidies. This is one of the main reasons why a discrepancy exists between nominal and effective tax rates. As a result there is a strong relation between tax expenditures and effective tax rates. Therefore estimating tax responsiveness of energy demand can also provide important insights about the consequences of removing the tax support to the energy sector.

The collection of the OECD effective tax rate data provides new opportunities for empirical research. Interestingly, the collection of the OECD effective tax rate data allows us not only to describe effective tax rates but also to estimate how energy consumption responds to differences in tax rates in different countries and across products and sector applications. Using these data, we provide estimates that show the correlations between energy consumption and tax rates in different countries and across products and sector applications. There is a large literature analyzing the price elasticity as a proxy for tax responsiveness. Dahl and Sterner (1991) and Espey (1998) present extensive surveys of this literature. Recently Davis and Kilian (2011) and Li et al. (2014) have estimated tax elasticity directly as in the current study. In this chapter we do not focus on identifying tax elasticity. Our estimations illustrate correlations of tax base with energy taxes and cover whole energy consuming segments and resource types.

3.2 The New OECD Database on Effective Tax Rates

The OECD analysis presented in Taxing Energy Use (OECD 2013b) is based on an underlying database (the TEU database) of energy use and taxation in each OECD country. The TEU database includes all final use of energy by businesses and individuals, as well as the net energy used in energy transmission and in the transformation of energy from one form to another (e.g., crude oil to gasoline, to coal, to electricity). Energy use is highly disaggregated by the fuel and user. By fuel, it is disaggregated into major fuel groups (coal, oil products, natural gas, combustibles and waste, and renewables and nuclear) and within each of these into more specific categories, covering in total 65 fuels (e.g., peat, gasoline, diesel, and hydro). The database is also disaggregated by user. Energy use is grouped into three broad categories: transport, heating and process use, and electricity. These three areas are further disaggregated by user, with data provided for 30 specific users in these categories (e.g., electricity generation, mining, manufacturing, residential, and commercial use).

Data on energy use is taken from the 2009 Extended World Energy Balances (EWEB) (IEA 2011). These data were used as the most recently available disaggregated data when this analysis was undertaken, and as a proxy for current consumption. The TEU database includes data from the Total Final Consumption (TFC) balance from the EWEB, showing end-use of energy by domestic users, whether imported or produced domestically. One departure from the TFC figures is in the treatment of electricity, where the database includes the energy used to generate electricity domestically rather than the energy output shown in the TFC. The amount of electricity used by domestic consumers is recalculated as the total amount of energy used to generate the electricity used by each group, based on the unique fuel mix of electricity generation in each country. Energy used to generate electricity that is exported is excluded, as is imported electricity. In addition the TEU database includes an additional flow showing net losses in energy transformation. Nonenergy use of fuels is excluded. For each product-flow combination, the database shows the amount of energy use expressed in terms of energy value (in terajoules—TJ) and in terms of the carbon emissions associated with its use (in thousand tonnes of CO_2).

The TEU database also includes the rate of specific taxes and related tax expenditures that apply to energy use, against the same disaggregation of users and fuels. The taxes covered are those such as excises levied directly on a physical measure of energy product consumed. Where more than one such tax applies to the same product, tax rates have been aggregated and the total is shown. Taxes that apply to a very broad range of goods (e.g., value-added and retail sales taxes) are not included on the basis that since they apply equally to a wide range of goods, they do not change relative prices. Also excluded are taxes that may be related to energy use but that are not imposed directly on the energy product (e.g., vehicle taxes, road user charges, taxes on emissions such as NO_x and SO_x that do not have a fixed relationship to fuel volume). Production taxes, royalties, and other levies on the extraction of energy resources are excluded on the assumption that because they generally apply to internationally traded goods, they have little impact on prices in the domestic market.

Both taxes on the fuels used to generate electricity and taxes on electricity consumption have been included in the database. Given that the database contains information on the amount of energy used to generate electricity, rather than the energy in the electricity itself, taxes on the consumption of electricity have been translated into implicit tax rates on the underlying fuels used in electricity generation, based on the efficiency and carbon content of each fuel. This was done in order to maintain consistency with the treatment of taxes on other energy sources. Effective carbon tax rates on electricity need to be interpreted carefully when there is a general tax on electricity consumption that applies regardless of the generation source.

Data on tax rates was collected by the OECD as of April 1, 2012, from national sources, including legislation, government websites, and consultation with national officials, as well as from the OECD/EEA database on instruments used for environmental policy (www.oecd.org/env/policies/database) and the European Commission (EC 2012). The TEU database contains information on tax rates in their original units, which are typically set per physical quantity of fuel (liters, kilograms, kilowatt-hours, etc.). These have also been re-calculated as effective tax rates per gigajoule of energy and per tonne of CO_2 emissions based on standard conversion factors, taken from the IEA and IPCC, for each fuel. Tax rates, which were collected in national currency, have been converted to euros using average exchange rates over the period from September 2011 to August 2012.

The Taxing Energy Use database also includes any tax rebates, credits, and other tax expenditures that are reported by the country concerned against the fuel and user combinations to which they apply. Information on the benchmark tax rate and the net level of tax that applies as a result of the concession are included. In this respect the maps are a useful complement to material that focuses on the value of tax expenditures, such as the OECD's Inventory of Estimated Budgetary Support and Tax Expenditures for Fossil Fuels (OECD 2013b). By showing tax expenditures in context, the maps can facilitate discussion about appropriate tax benchmarks for different fuels, uses, and users.

The TEU database also includes information on several other aspects of energy taxation. Where a country has an explicit tax on carbon alongside other taxes on energy, the level of the specific tax on carbon is also shown. For federal countries, sub-national tax rates are shown for an illustrative group of states or provinces. The impact of emission trading schemes in increasing effective prices on carbon has not been included in the database but is indicated in the graphical profiles for each country.

The resulting database of energy use and tax rates is comparable across countries. It permits average effective tax rates to be calculated for a range of energy use and source combinations (e.g., for oil used in road transport, for all agricultural fuels, or for tax rates on diesel used for different purposes). Average effective tax rates in energy terms are the average tax rate per unit of GJ for each flow and product combination, weighted by the amount of energy used at each rate. In carbon terms, they are the average tax rate in tonnes of CO_2, weighted by the amount of CO_2 from energy use at each rate. Zero tax rates are included in the calculation.

3.3 Descriptive Findings

In this section we present a descriptive analysis of the dataset. First, we describe a useful tool, namely the energy map as a way to convey the information contained in the dataset. Second, we present a descriptive analysis of energy use and taxation across OECD countries and energy use categories, which reveals the substantial variation in energy use and taxation.

3.3.1 Country Graphs

In Taxing Energy Use (OECD 2013b) the database was used to generate graphical profiles of energy use and taxation in each country, alternately in energy and carbon terms. In these graphical profiles, energy use is shown along the horizontal axis, and divided into three common categories of transport, heating and process, and electricity generation use of energy. These three broad categories are further divided into more specific subcategories of energy use, varying among countries depending on their specific tax settings. Tax rates that apply to each subcategory of energy use are shown on the vertical axis of the graphical profiles: in local currency on the left-hand axis of the graphical profiles, and in euros on the right-hand axis. For countries subject to the EU-ETS, the NZ ETS, or the carbon price in Australia, which has since been repealed, the graphical profiles note the interaction of tax systems with these trading schemes. For example, an energy category is denoted as [ETS-A] on the carbon map if it is fully or largely covered by the EU-ETS and [ETS-P] if it is only partially covered. The carbon maps also show the average market price for ETS credits for 2010 to 2011 on the vertical axis.

For example, figure 3.1 (OECD 2013b) illustrates the structure of the dataset for Germany. The horizontal axis is the tax base in terms of a common unit that is the CO_2 content of energy consumption by the three different segments of energy use: transport, heating and process, and electricity. As mentioned before, the tax base for the electricity category reflects the carbon emissions in its generation from different energy resources. The vertical axis shows the effective tax rates and benchmark tax rates. The graphs further provide information on tax expenditures. These expenditures can be measured as the area between the benchmark and effective tax rates and indicated by the light gray shading. Dark gray areas are the tax revenues generated by applying the effective tax rates to the corresponding tax bases.

3.3.2 Overview of Energy Use and Taxation in OECD Countries

We now turn to provide an overview of energy use and energy taxation in the OECD countries. Figure 3.2 present the map of energy use and taxation in all OECD countries. The structure of the map is described in the previous subsection. This figure shows that the energy consumption and taxation patterns show considerable variation across energy use and fuel type categories. Following this, by focusing on general patterns and some irregular observations, we present some descriptive

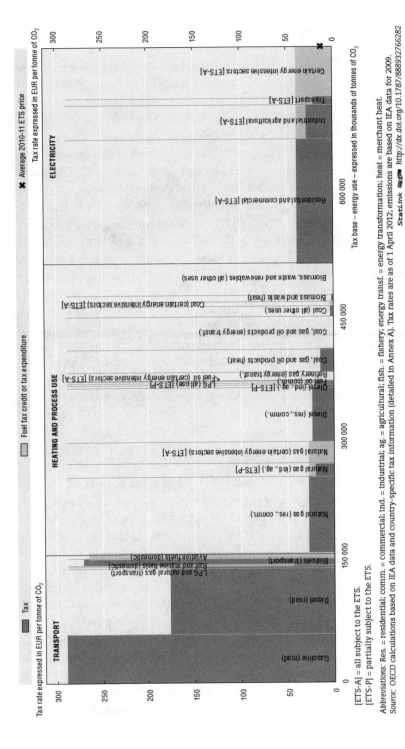

Figure 3.1
Taxation of energy in Germany by carbon content

[ETS-A] = all subject to the ETS.
[ETS-P] = partially subject to the ETS.

Abbreviations: Res. = residential; comm. = commercial; ind. = industrial; ag. = agricultural; fish. = fishery; energy transf. = energy transformation; heat = merchant heat.
Source: OECD calculations based on IEA data and country-specific tax information (detailed in Annex A). Tax rates are as of 1 April 2012; emissions are based on IEA data for 2009.
StatLink ⬚ http://dx.doi.org/10.1787/888932765282

statistics across countries that show how the picture varies substantially across countries.

In total, OECD countries used over 201 million TJs of energy in 2009, although the level of energy use and emissions from each country varies significantly. Within countries, there is also a considerable degree of heterogeneity in the share of different uses of energy as a proportion of total energy use. The transport category varies in size from 6 to 65 percent of total energy use (and 14 to 67 percent of carbon emissions from energy use) in Iceland and Luxembourg, respectively. However, both of these countries can be regarded as outliers: Iceland, because of the high share of energy used in electricity generation, for electricity-intensive industries (particularly aluminum smelting), and Luxembourg, due to its high volume of motor fuels to nonresidents. Excluding these two countries, all other countries are much closer to the simple average of 23 percent of energy use in transport and 27 percent of carbon emissions from energy use from transport energy. Heating and process use of fuels accounts from 20 to 54 percent of energy use and 14 to 71 percent of all carbon emissions, with a simple average of 39 percent of energy use and 46 percent of emissions. The electricity sector varies from 3 percent of energy use in Luxembourg to 71 percent of energy use (yet 0 percent of carbon from energy use due to high use of renewable energy) in Iceland. On a simple average basis across the OECD, electricity makes up 38 percent of energy use and 27 percent of carbon emissions from energy use. Due to the different mix of fuels used to generate electricity it has the most varied carbon intensity of energy use.

If considered by fuel, the proportion of fuel used across OECD countries also varies. On a simple average basis, oil products are the most common fuel source, at 36 percent of total energy on a simple average basis. It is by far the dominant fuel in the transport sector, and is used in smaller proportions in the heating and process sector, and more limitedly, in electricity generation. The proportion of oil ranges from 11 percent in Iceland to 72 percent in Luxembourg, again reflecting the unusual characteristics of energy usage in these two countries. Excluding these two countries, make up from 19 to 57 percent of total energy use. Natural gas, coal and peat, and renewable energy account for similar proportions of total energy use, at between 16 and 22 percent on a simple average basis. Natural gas is used most commonly in the heating and process sector, although also is a significant source of electricity generation energy. Coal is used in the heating and process

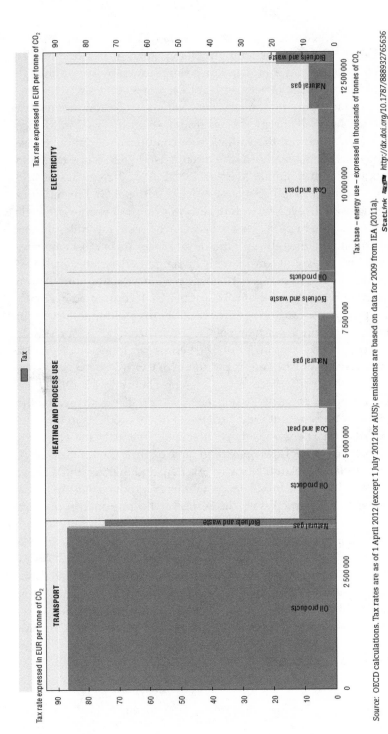

Source: OECD calculations. Tax rates are as of 1 April 2012 (except 1 July 2012 for AUS); emissions are based on data for 2009 from IEA (2011a).

StatLink ⟨⟩ http://dx.doi.org/10.1787/888932765636

Figure 3.2
Taxation of energy in OECD by carbon content

category and in electricity generation. Renewables are almost exclusively used in electricity generation. Biomass and other combustibles account for 8 percent of energy use on a simple average basis, although cross-country variation is very wide for each fuel.

Tax rates on energy use are similarly varied. In 2012 economywide effective tax rates on energy ranged from 0.18 euro per GJ in Mexico (not taking into account the variable rate component of its fuel excise tax, which has been negative in the recent past) to 6.58 euros per GJ in Luxembourg, with a simple average for all OECD countries of 3.28 euros per GJ and a weighted average of 1.77 euro per GJ. Luxembourg has the highest rate even though its tax rates on most energy products are not among the highest. This is because, as seen, Luxembourg has an exceptionally high volume of motor fuel sales. As in most countries motor fuel use is taxed at considerably higher rates than other fuel uses. After Luxembourg, the highest economywide effective tax rate on energy is found in Denmark, at 6.3 euros per GJ. If considered in carbon terms, effective tax rates range from 2.80 euros per tonne of CO_2 in Mexico to 107.28 euros per tonne of CO_2 in Switzerland, with a simple average for all OECD countries of 52.04 euros per tonne of CO_2 and a weighted average of 27.12 euros per tonne of CO_2.

The highest overall effective tax rates on energy in the OECD are found in European countries, where energy-tax policy is shaped by the minimum tax rates set out for a variety of energy products in the 2003 European Union Energy Taxation Directive. Several of the countries with high effective tax rates on carbon have explicit carbon taxes (e.g., Denmark, Iceland, Ireland, Norway, Sweden, and Switzerland). These countries tend to tax a broad range of energy products and to do so more consistently, particularly with respect to heating and process use energy.

Central European and Asian OECD member countries (e.g., the Czech Republic, Estonia, Hungary, Japan, Korea, Poland, the Slovak Republic, and Turkey) typically have lower effective tax rates on carbon. The lowest effective tax rates on energy are found in Australia, New Zealand, and the Americas (Chile, Canada, Mexico, and United States, although subnational rates are not taken into account in Canada), where only fuels used in transport are taxed and generally at lower rates than OECD countries.

3.3.3 Energy Taxation for Transport, Heating, and Process and Electricity Generation Use

Considering the broad categories of energy use used in the graphical profiles, Taxing Energy Use (OECD 2013b) estimates tax rates on each of these different uses of fuels. Transport energy is taxed more commonly and more heavily than other uses of energy, at 11.5 euros per GJ and 181 euros per tonne of CO_2, respectively. Heating and process use of electricity are taxed at lower rates, at 0.9 euros per GJ each in energy terms, and at 12 euros and 13 euros per tonne of CO_2, respectively.

This pattern holds across each individual country, with energy products used in transport (and particularly for road transport) being taxed more commonly and more heavily than energy products used for heating or process use, or to generate electricity. These higher tax rates may be explained by the broader range of policy goals that governments may be attempting to address in the transport category compared to other areas of energy use (e.g., congestion, traffic accidents and noise) although the use of fuel taxes to correct for these externalities is imprecise (see also Parry et al. 2014). Alternately, the higher tax rates on these fuels may simply reflect their historical role in raising revenue, sometimes explicitly or implicitly earmarked for infrastructure purposes.

In the transport sector, oil products account for 94 percent of energy use and 95 percent of carbon emissions. Gasoline and diesel are the most predominant fuels in all OECD countries, accounting for 87 percent of energy used in transport and 88 percent of transport emissions. Diesel for road use is taxed at lower rates in both energy and carbon terms than gasoline used for the same purpose in 33 out of 34 OECD countries. The effective tax rate on diesel is 32 percent lower than that on gasoline in energy terms and 37 percent in carbon terms, on a simple average basis.

Within the heating and process use category, in 18 countries energy products used for industrial or energy transformation purposes are taxed at lower than energy products used for residential or commercial purposes. In ten other countries, however, the reverse holds, and in six countries there is minimal difference in tax rates between the different uses. These differences may reflect deliberate policy choices relating to industrial competitiveness, or alternately, an attempt to protect households from high energy costs. Where differences in tax rates are minimal, this may be a product of the different energy mixes used by these groups. Diesel faces the highest effective tax rates among heating and process fuels, followed by fuel oil and natural gas, with lower rates applying to coal, peat, and other oil products. Nevertheless, patterns of taxation in this category vary considerably, and natural gas and coal, in particular, are often entirely untaxed.

OECD countries vary in the approach they take to taxation of electricity, with the most common approach being to tax only the consumption of electricity (17 countries). A further nine countries tax both consumption and at least some of the input fuels used. Three countries tax only the fuels used to generate electricity. The remaining five do not tax either consumption or generation of electricity. Among electricity fuels, those with the highest rates in energy terms are those that are more efficient, due to the look-through approach described above, including natural gas, renewables and hydro. Coal and peat face lower effective rates on a simple average basis and are frequently untaxed.

3.4   Tax Rate Responsiveness Measured

In this section we investigate the responsiveness of energy consumption to energy taxation. Our main goal is to illustrate some useful aspects of the dataset. We start with illustrating the relation between the tax base and energy tax rates by means of scatter plots. Next we present a more formal analysis.

3.4.1   Descriptive Analysis

It is possible to use TEU also to measure tax rate responsiveness of the energy or carbon tax base. Here we provide a first-pass to such an analysis.[1] In the estimations we use the effective tax rates as computed according to the explanation in section 3.2. We combine the energy use categories into five categories (on-road, off-road, residential, and commercial, industry, electricity production) for five energy resource types (oil, coal and peat, natural gas, waste and combustibles, renewables). The effective tax rate for each category is the average of the effective tax rates (weighted by energy consumption) faced by different segments of society in that category. Importantly, since the effective tax rates are expressed in the same unit, euro per unit of CO_2 emitted, the taxes are comparable across usage and resource categories.

Our detailed dataset has some important advantages. The database allows us to control for country-, user-, and fuel-specific effects. Thus the data also capture, at least implicitly, cross fuel-price effects. Another advantage is that this analysis is one of the first to proxy tax-policy differences across countries, instead of approaching tax impacts through energy price effects that only implicitly include energy taxes. Thus we are able to present energy demand responsiveness that at least implicitly allow for cross-sectional flexibility.

Table 3.1 presents some descriptive statistics for the tax base, tax rates, and some key variables. For both the tax base and the tax rates, mean values are higher than the median values, and the standard deviations are very high compared with the means, indicating a highly dispersed, right-skewed distribution. Our total number of observations is 540. Excluding some outliers reduces this number to 528, which does not change the stated results we present in the chapter. In the following analysis, however, zero tax bases are excluded. Also renewable energy sources are excluded because they have zero tax bases in terms of CO_2 emitted. In total we use 343 observations. While zero tax rates might include valuable information, their inclusion introduces several econometric problems that are beyond the scope the study.

Before proceeding with the regressions, we provide a descriptive analysis in order to reveal some potential concerns that can be addressed by using the current dataset. Figure 3.3 illustrates the relationship between the tax base and tax rates in the full sample. The dots in the figures represent the observations in logarithms, and the line represents the mean relationship derived from a simple ordinary least squares regression. As discussed previously both variables include very small values that can be observed from the scatterplots as negative values in logarithms. The overall relationship between the effective energy tax rates and energy tax base turns out to be negative, as one would expect. However, the slope of the fitted linear line is small, implying a low responsiveness of energy consumption to the tax rates. One explanation may be that the estimate is too small because of the heterogeneity within the user and fuel categories.

Table 3.1
Descriptive statistics

	Units	# Obs.	Mean	Median	Std. dev.	Min.	Max.
Tax base	Ths. ton. CO_2	528	24537.778	3637.883	106606.392	0.225	1746318.779
Tax rate	Euros per ths. ton. CO_2	528	48.818	3.584	225.756	0.000	3656.817
GDP ppp.	USD (bln.)	528	9280.275	2510.310	21390.025	80.754	115479.000
Population	Million	528	373.937	108.956	589.572	3.180	3093.497

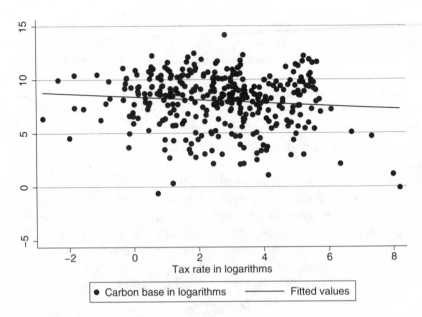

Figure 3.3
Full sample of tax responsiveness

Figure 3.4 and 3.5 illustrate the same simple analysis for different fuel and user categories. Both figures illustrate that there is substantial heterogeneity across and within different categories. For instance, coal and peat do not seem to be very sensitive to the level of the effective tax rate, whereas natural gas clearly does. Also electricity use is lower with higher effective tax rates. Another noteworthy point is that for some categories the slope of line appears insignificant, and even positive for the transport sector. This counterintuitive finding might indicate further problems of within category heterogeneity. Interestingly, our dataset allows us to take such concerns into account.

The "oil-transport" category generally has a larger tax base than both other fuels used in transportation and other energy use categories consuming oil products. The tax rates are also higher for this specific category across the same dimensions. Such effects lead to the spurious positive correlation between tax rates and tax base. To control for the impact of such effects, first we remove fuel-use specific effects by regressing carbon base on fuel-use fixed effects. Then we proceed by using the residuals from this regression and obtain figure 3.6 as a result. The figure again presents the effective tax rates and fuel tax base for only the transport category after we have first removed the fuel-use

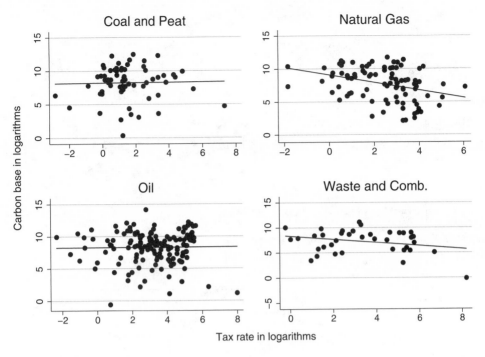

Figure 3.4
Heterogeneity of tax responsiveness by resource category

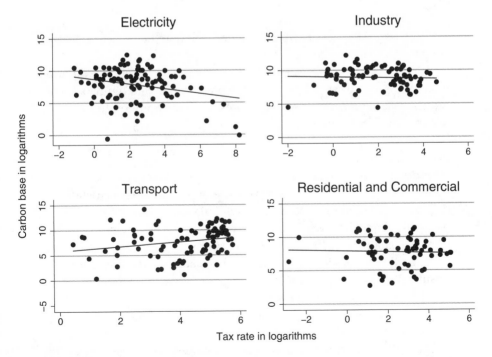

Figure 3.5
Heterogeneity of tax responsiveness by use category

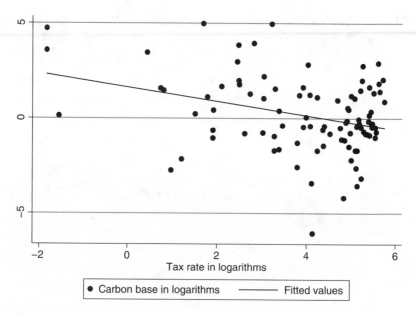

Figure 3.6
Tax responsiveness in the transportation sector when controlled for within-group heterogeneity

specific pair fixed effects. The estimated line now has a clear negative slope after this correction.

When we repeat the same exercise for the whole sample, the estimated slope is clearly higher than the one estimated in figure 3.3. This indicates a higher responsiveness of energy consumption to tax rates, as presented in figure 3.7.

3.4.2 Estimations

The descriptive analysis in the previous section suggests the importance of controlling for unobserved use and resource specific effects. We now present a more formal analysis via OLS estimation. Our goal is to illustrate the correlation between taxes and tax base, and the importance of controlling for resource and user effects.[2]

The OLS estimations are presented in table 3.2. In the regression results of column 1, we controlled for resource and user effects separately, using resource dummies control for systematic energy price differences based on the prices of the underlying fuels. In this result the estimated coefficient of the tax rate is positive, though this is at odds with basic intuition that higher tax rates would go along with lower demand. So, again, we have illustrated that OLS estimates are

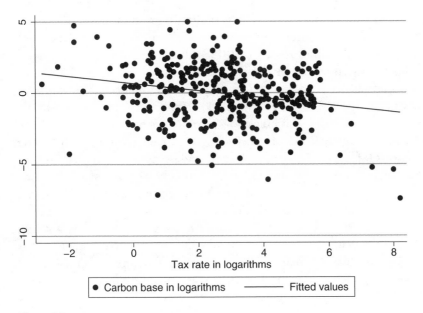

Figure 3.7
Tax responsiveness when controlled for heterogeneity

Table 3.2
Estimation results

	(1)	(2)	(3)
Tax	0.087	0.266*	−0.115*
	(0.100)	(0.133)	(0.066)
Country effects	No	Yes	Yes
Resource effects	Yes	Yes	Yes
User effects	Yes	Yes	Yes
Use-Res. effects	No	No	Yes
Adjusted R^2	0.166	0.178	0.617
AIC	1377.0	1349.1	1072.7
BIC	1415.4	1410.5	1126.4
Observations	343	343	343

Note: Standard errors are in parentheses. In all regressions, standard errors are clustered at the resource-use category level. *$p < 0.10$, **$p < 0.05$, ***$p < 0.01$.

likely to be upward biased due to omitted variables. In the following two columns, we introduce our additional control sets, which reduce the possibility of omitted variable bias substantially.

Including country dummies in column 2 increases the estimated size and significance of the coefficient. Importantly, the increase in adjusted R^2 due to the inclusion of country fixed effects is very limited. Therefore the source of omitted variables is less likely to be the sector and resource invariant country fixed effects. The regression in column 3 additionally controls for use- and resource-specific fixed effects, which increases the explanatory power of the model substantially. The adjusted R^2 is now 0.61, and it is below 0.2 in the previous columns. This reduces the concerns about omitted variable bias. Accordingly, the estimated elasticity in the regression is −0.12 is closer to the expected range. It seems that some country-invariant characteristics, specific to each tax base as defined by the resource and sector combinations, plays a substantial role in explaining the variation in energy consumption.

3.5   Conclusion

This chapter has provided some new descriptive insights into energy taxation across OECD countries and across fuels and user categories. We exploit a new database provided by OECD (2013b) that is based on the TEU database of energy use and taxation in each OECD country. The highly disaggregated form of the database enabled us to analyze energy policy related issues, and thus we describe some aspects of this database that can be applied in empirical research. We also offer some descriptive insights. Our simple analysis of responsiveness of energy demand to energy prices is mostly descriptive, but it reveals some particularly useful applications of the dataset. A more technical treatment is in progress, in a separate work in which we plan to provide firmer insights on energy taxation.

Our regressions using this new dataset illustrate that the different energy use categories matter a lot. Our results illustrate the importance of controlling for unobserved heterogeneity, due to fuel and/or use specific effects, in estimating the effects of energy taxation on energy consumption. Our findings indicate that the energy tax base may be more responsive to effective tax rates than a quick look at the data indicates. A relative inelastic tax base may imply that energy taxes are not effective in reaching environmental goals. This becomes an issue, in particular, where the relation between the energy tax base and emissions is weak. With a weak relation, a so-called green tax reform that aims to raise green revenue may primarily benefit the treasury without much green impact at all (Vollebergh 2014).

Notes

1. We are examining this issue more extensively in our ongoing work.

2. Note that our results are not informative about the elasticity of energy demand with respect to tax rates, as this requires a functional specification that takes tax exclusive energy prices explicitly into consideration.

References

Dahl, C., and T. Sterner. 1991. Analysing gasoline demand elasticities: A survey. *Energy Economics* 13 (3): 203–10.

Davis, L. W., and L. Kilian. 2011. Estimating the effect of a gasoline tax on carbon emissions. *Journal of Applied Econometrics* 26 (7): 1187–1214.

EC. 2012. Excise duty tables. Part 2: Energy products and electricity. Tech. rep. European Comission.

Espey, M. 1998. Gasoline demand revisited: An international meta-analysis of elasticities. *Energy Economics* 20 (3): 273–95.

IEA. 2011. *Energy Balances of OECD Countries*. Paris: OECD.

Li, S., J. Linn, and E. Muehlegger. 2014. Gasoline taxes and consumer behavior. *American Economic Journal. Economic Policy* 6 (4): 302–42.

OECD. 2009. *Declaration on Green Growth Adopted at the Meeting of the Council at Ministerial Level*. Paris: OECD.

OECD. 2013 b. *Taxing Energy Use: A Graphical Analysis*. Paris: OECD.

Parry, I. W., M. D. Heine, E. Lis, and S. Li. 2014. *Getting Energy Prices Right: From Principle to Practice*. Washington, DC: IMF.

Parry, I. W., J. Norregaard, and D. Heine. 2012. Environmental tax reform: Principles from theory and practice. *Annual Review of Resource Economics* 4 (1): 101–25.

Vollebergh, H. 2012. Environmental taxes and green growth. PBL Background Studies 500229001. PBL Netherlands Environmental Assessment Agency, Bilthoven.

Vollebergh, H. 2015. Green tax reform: Energy tax challenges for the Netherlands. Policy Brief 1501. PBL Netherlands Environmental Assessment Agency, Bilthoven.

4   Energy Subsidy Reform and Policy Makers' Reelection Incentives

Marco Pani and Carlo Perroni

4.1 Introduction

Energy subsidies are widespread and substantial. The International Energy Agency (IEA 2011) estimated the total world amount of energy subsidies in 2010 at about $410 billion (about 0.6 percent of world GDP[1]); similarly Coady et al. (2013) estimated that global "pre-tax" subsidies (that do not take account of the cost of consumption externalities) amounted in 2011 to $492 billion, equivalent to 0.7 percent of global GDP. Estimates reported in Shang et al. (2013) suggest that in 2011 the sum of petroleum, natural gas, coal, and electricity subsidies may have exceeded 5 percent of GDP in at least 20 countries and 10 percent in at least seven countries, and, according to Bauer et al. (2013), in at least ten countries total public expenditure on energy subsidies exceeds that on health and education.

Despite their popularity, fuel subsidies are highly inefficient. They encourage waste, excessive consumption, the maintenance of energy-intensive processes and habits, and discourage the development and adoption of technologies that could reduce energy consumption. They also entail large (and not fully transparent) fiscal costs, encourage smuggling and fraud, and promote excessive pollution and CO_2 emissions.

So why are energy subsidies so widespread? To some extent, this could reflect an irrational outcome stemming from imperfect information: while their costs are not easily observable, are hard to quantify, and are not well understood by the majority of citizens, their benefits are highly visible and are generally shared (albeit to different degrees) by various income groups.

But energy subsidies are also rationalized as a way to help the poor, who spend a large share of their low income on energy and energy-related items. To this purpose, however, energy prices appear to be a very inefficient instrument. As a growing body of evidence has documented, energy subsidies disproportionately benefit the rich and middle classes, who consume a lot more energy than the poor (although they spend on it a lower portion of their income).[2] Alternative schemes to help the poor—such as targeted means-tested cash transfers or an enhanced provision of the public goods and services most needed by low-income households—would provide a stronger enhancement to the welfare of the poor at a lower cost for the rest of the citizens.

Yet, energy subsidies are popular, and reforming them is politically difficult. In this chapter we explore this issue further by analyzing the policy dilemma confronting a public official elected to decide the level of subsidies who wants to promote energy-saving investment but is also concerned about the welfare of the poor.[3] A classical problem of intertemporal commitment failure arises as this official, regardless of his personal preferences, would always have an incentive to increase the subsidies ex post (after the citizens have made their energy-saving investment) in order to benefit the poor; as a result, the rate of subsidy that he would announce ex ante would not be credible, given that the official would have a strong incentive to raise it later. In other words, a policy maker may announce subsidy reforms in order to induce the citizens to purchase new, energy-saving, equipment, though, once this investment has been made, he may give in to pressures to postpone the reform or significantly reduce its scope. Knowing this, the citizens will not believe any announcement about subsidy reform.

In principle, this problem could be solved if the policy maker could credibly commit to announced subsidy rates—for instance, by delegating decisions to an independent technical committee or by proposing legislation that sets up an automatic formula to determine the retail price of energy. In practice, however, if citizens had different policy preferences (and energy consumption needs), not all elected policy makers would be willing to make this commitment, since retaining discretion on the level of subsidies could enable them to be reelected or to facilitate the election of a candidate they favor. In particular, when the same elected official is responsible for making decisions in several areas of policy (as is normally the case), a commitment to a specific action on one policy issue removes that issue from the agenda and thereby alters the political equilibrium reached on the other remaining issues; in these conditions an elected official may refrain from making an irreversible commitment to a specific level of subsidies in order to keep that issue on the agenda.

Hence the availability of energy-saving technologies and of institutional arrangements to commit to subsidy reforms does not, in itself, guarantee that these devices will be used; unless the political economy is also favorable, high subsidies and wasteful consumption could persist even if they result in a highly inefficient outcome.[4]

4.2 Energy Subsidies and the Commitment to Reform

In this section we describe how an official appointed to choose the appropriate level of energy subsidies may have an incentive to deviate from any announcement he may make once the other citizens have taken irreversible decisions that affect their energy consumption. More specifically, if citizens can reduce their energy needs by investing in costly technology, the official in charge may prefer to announce a large reduction in subsidies in order to induce the citizens to make this investment; once the investment has been made, however, the same official may prefer to maintain a high level of subsidies (or implement much milder cuts) out of redistributive or "horizontal equity" considerations. Anticipating this behavior, the citizens will not believe his announcements.

This problem arises because, in the area of energy subsidies, distributional objectives are sometimes traded off against efficiency objectives. Energy subsidies are essentially a (generally inefficient) instrument of redistribution that softens the impact of energy costs for the largest consumers at the expense of the smallest consumers and of the taxpayers in general.[5] However justifiable from a social and ethical perspective, this redistribution is inefficient because it weakens private incentives to save energy and invest in energy-saving technologies, and because the collection of taxes to finance the associated public expenditure is, itself, a source of distortions and inefficiencies. Any public decision about subsidies balances the benefits of redistributions with the costs of the associated inefficiencies. Before consumers make their investment decisions, investment-related inefficiencies are present and there is thus a strong incentive to keep subsidies low (or reduce them significantly, if a high level of subsidies has been inherited from the past); after the investment has been made, however, one source of inefficiency is removed, or in any way cannot be changed, and the incentive to keep subsidies low (or reduce them) becomes thus much weaker.

Consider a country where different citizens have different income levels and different energy consumption needs, which depend on circumstances they take as exogenous; for instance, citizens have different skills and other factor endowments, and they live in different locations entailing different commuting costs to their work places, with those individuals living in remote locations not served by public transportation facing comparatively high costs. Energy consumption needs can vary also as a result of other factors: some citizens may live in warm, temperate areas that require low heating or air-conditioning costs while others live in cold areas or torrid zones. For simplicity, we will assume here that energy consumption needs are uncorrelated with (gross) income; that is, rich and poor citizens are equally likely to be high or low energy consumers.[6]

All citizens need to consume some energy, but energy consumption alone does not provide any benefits to the citizens: it is a costly necessity, in that it is an intermediate input for the production of their income or consumption—unlike the purchase of other consumption goods and services such as food, clothes, or vacation tours, that provide a direct utility to the user. Also assume that the country is a net energy importer; its domestic "wholesale" price of energy depends on the price of imported energy inputs that is set in international markets. The retail price of energy (the price of fuel "at the pump") can, however, be reduced by the public authorities through subsidies. These subsidies can take many forms (e.g., the government may set the retail price administratively and reimburse retailers for their losses; or it may fix the selling prices of a state-owned refinery and charge the losses of this enterprise to the public budget; or, again, it may set administrative constraints on the retail price of energy and grant special tax advantages to energy producers and traders), but the ultimate objective is the same: to reduce the retail price of energy below the producer price by charging the difference to the public budget.

All citizens would, of course, prefer to pay a low price for energy, but the costs of reducing this price through subsidies are ultimately borne by the citizens themselves both directly, through taxes, and indirectly, through tax-induced inefficiencies and distortions. As a result only the citizens with strong consumption needs prefer to keep the price of energy low through public subsidies; citizens that do not need to consume much energy prefer to pay a higher price for energy in order to have lower taxes and fewer distortions.

This picture changes, somewhat, if each citizen cares not only about his own welfare but also about the welfare of the other citizens—in particular, about the welfare of those that are least well off. In the setting we are describing, the least well off citizen will simply be the citizen with the lowest income and with the highest energy consumption needs. All citizens with comparatively high energy consumption needs (rich or poor) would, ceteris paribus, favor a high rate of energy subsidies, since this would reduce the cost of their energy expenditures, leaving a higher disposable income that can be spent on utility-enhancing consumer goods. Citizens with a comparatively lower consumption need would, if concerned only about their own welfare, favor a low rate of energy subsidy; but to the extent that they care about the "energy poor" (those among the poorest individuals who also have high energy needs), they will be willing to support a rate of subsidy above that which would be optimal from their purely private point of view, balancing their own preferences for a (comparatively) low level of subsidy with the least well-off citizen's preference for a much higher subsidy rate.

Since the citizens have different preferences over the appropriate subsidy rate, the choice of the subsidy rate entails a collective choice problem that must be resolved by political means, which in most high-income countries involves the election of a representative. Like all other citizens, the elected official will have individual views and preferences that will influence his decisions; indeed, consistently with a large political-economy literature that characterizes representatives as "citizen-candidates," we take here the extreme assumption that the elected official will base his decision *only* on his own personal preferences (that include his concerns about the welfare of the poor), and will not be influenced either by the preferences of the majority or by any pre-electoral promise that he may have made (hence any such promises would not be believed).[7]

This assumption highlights an essential feature of representative (as opposed to direct) democracy, where collective decisions are taken by elected officials who enjoy a significant margin of discretion and are unable to make binding pre-electoral commitments to specific policy decisions (e.g., see Alesina 1988); even explicit pre-electoral promises to implement a well-defined policy can be reneged once elected owing to unexpected constraints or to the acquisition of new information that was not available before the vote.[8] This ex post discretion plays a critical role in this model: if candidates were able to make binding commitments to specific policy decisions before the election, the inconsistency problem examined in this study would be resolved; the experience of several countries where subsidy reforms have been introduced and later partly reversed suggests, however, that such inconsistencies are more than a mere theoretical hypothesis.

In this model, collective decisions are also taken on a "purely political" basis, in the sense that they are only based on the individual preferences of the citizens composing the community and that each citizen is given the same weight in the aggregation of these preferences. This contrasts, for instance, with models that include lobbying, campaign contributions, or corruption, where public decisions are influenced by the preferences of entities ("industries," or "special interest groups") other than the citizens, or where citizens who are more willing or capable of devoting money and other resources to lobbying efforts have a larger influence than the others on policy decisions (e.g., Becker 1983; Katz et al. 1990; Baron 1994; Grossman and Helpman 1996; 2001; Glazer and Gradstein 2005). By abstracting from this possibility, we show that the reform of inefficient energy subsidies can be delayed even in a country where the lobbying influence of powerful interest groups related to the energy sector is absent or effectively neutralized.

When they elect the official that will decide the level of subsidies, citizens base their voting decisions on the energy subsidy preferences of the different candidates. We will assume that these preferences are known publicly (e.g., citizens know whether a candidate lives in the city center or in an outer suburb). Candidates with particularly high consumption needs will not receive many votes because they can be expected to set subsidies too high (resulting in high taxes and inefficiencies), and candidates with particularly low consumption needs will not be popular either because they will set energy subsidies too low. The most "electable" candidates will therefore have "average" energy consumption needs.

The citizens' vote, however, depends critically on when the subsidy rate is irrevocably fixed:

• If the subsidies are fixed *before* the citizens make their energy-saving investments and cannot be changed (e.g., the official establishes once and for all a rule that determines the retail price of energy on the basis of an automatic formula), the citizens know that whichever candidate they elect will set a comparatively low level of subsidy that will encourage all citizens to invest in energy saving. Of course, this "low" level of subsidies will be higher, the higher the energy consumption needs of the candidate.

- If instead the subsidies are decided *after* any energy-savings investments have been made (e.g., retail prices are adjusted periodically by a committee that maintains a large degree of discretion), the citizens know that each candidate, ceteris paribus, will set a comparatively high level of subsidies, since the subsidy rate in this case has no effect on energy-saving investments.

As an illustration, consider an economy composed of N citizens. Each citizen must consume a number of energy units equal to j; we scale the units on the maximum amount that any citizen would need to consume in the absence of energy-saving investment, so that the largest value of j among the citizens is 1. Assume that j is uniformly distributed among the population over the interval $[0, 1]$.

Each individual earns an income of Y dollars ($Y > 1$). Income is spent to purchase fuel, pay taxes, and buy other goods or services (including personal financial investment). The *producer* price of energy is one dollar per unit, while the *retail* price of energy, p, is equal to the producer price if no subsidies are granted, and is below the producer price if energy is subsidized; if s is the rate of subsidy (the amount of subsidy paid per unit of energy consumption), then the consumer price of energy is $1 - s$.[9]

If the government subsidizes energy consumption, the financial cost, F, of this measure is financed through a uniform lump-sum tax not related to income;[10] collecting this tax entails a variety of administrative costs (directly or indirectly borne by the taxpayer) and creates inefficiencies and distortions (e.g., tax-avoidance efforts and public spending to combat tax evasion). As a result the total cost, $C(F)$, eventually incurred by the taxpayer (comprising the portion of the tax revenue used to pay the subsidies and administrative costs, as well as the losses due to other distortions) is larger than the financial costs that the taxes are supposed to cover. We assume here that the total cost (hereafter called "the tax") is a quadratic function of F, equal to $F/N + (F/N)^2$.[11]

While a citizen cannot change the amount of energy j that he needs to consume, he can reduce the energy input (the amount of fuel he needs to *purchase*) by investing in energy-saving technologies. The scale of this investment can vary, but a larger investment results in stronger energy savings. For instance, a citizen could purchase a more expensive car that consumes less gasoline (or purchase a hybrid car), install double-glazed windows to reduce his house's heating costs, or install solar panels; and firms could replace or upgrade their equipment with newer machines that consume less energy.

Measure the investment, a, as the amount of energy that is saved compared to that citizen's energy requirement: after the investment, the citizen only needs to purchase $(1 - a) j$ amount of energy, instead of j. Energy-saving investments bear benefits in the long term and are decided with a long-term perspective (one does not, usually, buy a new car, or replace all windows, to save only on one year's energy costs). And investment is, of course, costly; we assume, here, that to reduce energy consumption by a fraction a, a citizen has to pay an amount $a^2 j$ in investment costs.[12] Note that we are assuming that the investment costs increase with the total amount of energy saved: for instance, buying a car that consumes 10 percent less gasoline per mile entails a higher initial purchase price but also higher recurrent costs of maintenance that are proportional to the distance traveled (and hence to the amount of gasoline consumed); indeed the more one travels, the more often the car needs to be replaced. Similarly the purchase and maintenance costs of solar panels may depend on their size, which, in turn, depends on the amount of energy needed.[13]

How much will each citizen invest in order to save energy? The answer, of course, depends on the price of energy that each citizen expects he will have to pay in the future. Since the producer price is, by assumption, given,[14] the price paid by the consumer depends only on the rate of subsidies; hence, citizens base their investment decisions on the expected rate of subsidies. If a citizen expects the rate of subsidy to be s, he will make the investment $a = \theta(s)$ that minimizes his total energy-related costs ERC (direct energy costs plus costs of investing in energy-saving technologies). The latter are equal to $ERC = p (1 - a) j + a^2 j = (1 - s)(1 - a) j + a^2 j$, and are minimized by setting $a = \theta(s) = (1 - s)/2$.[15] Unsurprisingly, subsidies discourage energy-saving investment: the lower the expected consumer price of energy, the less each citizen is willing to pay to reduce his energy consumption. Note that the amount of investment, a, is the same for all citizens: all citizens make the same (proportional) energy-saving investment, which depends on the expected rate of subsidy but not on a citizen's consumption needs (this particular result derives from the assumption that investment costs are proportional to the reduction in energy consumption).

Once all citizens have made this investment, the total energy consumed by all citizens (measured in physical units) is

$$E = N\int_{j=0}^{1}(1-a)dj = N(1-a)\int_{j=0}^{1}dj = \frac{N(1-a)}{2}, \tag{4.1}$$

and the financial costs for the government of paying a subsidy rate of s is thus equal to

$$F = sE = \frac{sN(1-a)}{2}. \tag{4.2}$$

The tax paid by each citizen, in turn, is equal to

$$T = \frac{F}{N} + \left(\frac{F}{N}\right)^2 = \left(\frac{1-a}{2}\right)s + \left(\frac{1-a}{2}\right)^2 s^2. \tag{4.3}$$

When s is known in advance, a depends on s because the citizens take the rate of subsidy into account when they decide how much to invest; then, after replacing a with $\theta(s) = (1-s)/2$ into (4.3), the tax can be expressed as a function of the expected subsidy rate:

$$T(s) = \frac{1-\left(\frac{1-s}{2}\right)}{2}s + \left(\frac{1-\left(\frac{1-s}{2}\right)}{2}\right)^2 s^2 = \frac{4s + 5s^2 + 2s^3 + s^4}{16}. \tag{4.4}$$

Notice that a higher subsidy rate increases income taxes in two ways: by raising the amount that has to be paid in subsidies on each unit of energy consumed, and by discouraging investments that would reduce the consumption of energy.

The disposable income of a citizen whose consumption needs are equal to j, net of income taxes, of the cost of energy-saving investment, and of energy costs (net of subsidies), thus equals

$$y(Y, s, j) = Y - T(s) - a^2 j - (1-s)(1-a)j$$
$$= Y - T(s) - (\theta(s))^2 j - (1-s)(1-\theta(s))j$$
$$= Y - \frac{4s + 5s^2 + 2s^3 + s^4}{16} - \left(\frac{1-s}{2}\right)^2 j - (1-s)\left(1-\left(\frac{1-s}{2}\right)\right)j \tag{4.5}$$
$$= Y - \frac{4s + 5s^2 + 2s^3 + s^4}{16} - \left(\frac{3 - 2s - s^2}{4}\right)j.$$

Marco Pani and Carlo Perroni

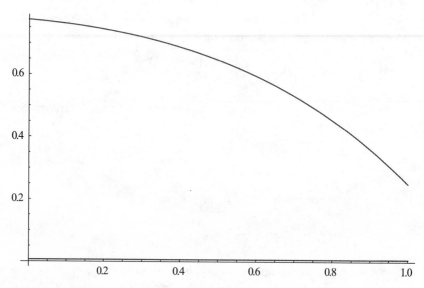

Figure 4.1a
Disposable income as a function of the subsidy rate (s) for a citizen of type $j = 0.3$

This is the amount that a citizen can spend on goods and services
that, unlike taxes or energy-related expenditures, provide him a direct
and tangible benefit. Notice that a citizen's gross income Y appears as
an additive constant in (4.5); hence the value of s that maximizes a citizen's disposable income does not depend on his gross income; citizens
with the same consumption needs will have the same preferences about
s, regardless of their gross income. Figures 4.1a and 4.1b show how the
disposable income changes as a function of s for a citizen with consumption needs equal to $j = 0.3$ and $j = 0.7$, respectively.[16]
    As discussed above, citizens also care about the welfare of the citizen
with the largest energy-consumption needs ($j = 1$). Each individual's
"ex ante utility" (achieved when the rate of subsidy, s, is known in
advance—ex ante—allowing the citizen to optimize his investment) is
thus equal to a weighted average of his own disposable income, $y(Y,
s, j)$, and of the disposable income of the poorest citizen with the largest
energy consumption needs (for whom $j = 1$), that is, $y(Y_L, s, 1)$, where
Y_L is the gross income of the poorest citizen:

$$U^A(Y, s, j; w) = wy(Y, s, j) + (1 - w)y(Y_L, s, 1). \tag{4.6}$$

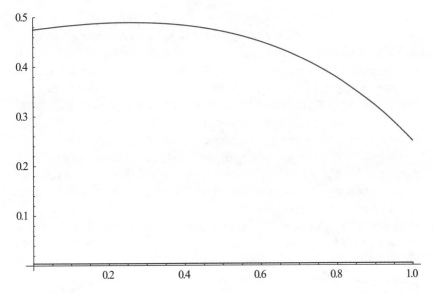

Figure 4.1b
Disposable income as a function of the subsidy rate (s) for a citizen of type $j = 0.7$

From (4.5), and after some simplifications, we obtain

$$U^A(Y, s, j; w) = wY + (1 - w)Y_L - \frac{4s + 5s^2 + 2s^3 + s^4}{16} - \left(\frac{3 - 2s - s^2}{4}\right)x, \quad (4.7)$$

where $x \equiv w j + 1 - w$ is, in the rest of this section, called the citizen's "type."[17] This utility is maximized, for each citizen, by some "ideal" subsidy rate $s^*(x)$ that satisfies

$$\frac{\partial}{\partial s} U^A(Y, s, j; w) = -\frac{2 + 5s + 3s^2 + 2s^3}{8} + \left(\frac{1 + s}{2}\right)x = 0. \quad (4.8)$$

Differentiating this expression with respect to s^* and x yields

$$\left(-\frac{5 + 6s + 6s^2}{8} + \frac{x}{2}\right)ds + \left(\frac{1 + s}{2}\right)dx = 0, \quad (4.9)$$

whence

$$\frac{ds^*}{dx} = \frac{1 + s}{\frac{5 + 6s + 6s^2}{4} - x} > 0, \quad (4.10)$$

which ensures that s^* increases in x: citizens of higher type (with stronger energy consumption needs), predictably, prefer a higher level of subsidy. Notice that when $s = 0$, we have $dU^A/ds = 0$ for $x = 1/2$, which implies that the ideal subsidy of the citizen with $x = 1/2$ is zero; citizens with $x < 1/2$ prefer a negative subsidy (a tax) while citizens with $x > 1/2$ prefer a positive subsidy. When $w \leq 1/2$ (citizens are sufficiently "altruistic"), then $x \geq 1/2$ for all citizens and the ideal level of subsidies is positive (more generally, nonnegative) for all.

Table 4.1 and the lower line in figure 4.2 show the amount of subsidy preferred by citizens of different types, with different consumption needs, when $w = 0.5$. Notice that in this case all citizens prefer a nonnegative subsidy (nobody wants to *tax* energy).

Compare this with the ex post utility that a citizen derives when the amount of subsidy is known only ex post—after he has made his investment. In this case his disposable income is equal to $1 - C(F) - a^2 j - (1 - a)(1 - s) j$, with a fixed and $F = (1 - a) s/2$, and his ex post utility (taking account of his concerns for the poorest citizen) is equal to

$$
\begin{aligned}
U^P(Y, s, x; w) &= wY + (1-w)Y_L - \left(\frac{1-a}{2}s + \frac{(1-a)^2}{4}s^2 \right) \\
&\quad - \left((1-a)(1-s) + a^2 \right)x \\
&= wY + (1-w)Y_L - \frac{1-a}{2}s - \frac{(1-a)^2}{4}s^2 \\
&\quad - (1-a)x + (1-a)sx - a^2x,
\end{aligned}
\tag{4.11}
$$

Table 4.1
Desired subsidy level by citizen type

j	x	s^*
0	0.5	0
0.1	0.55	0.066
0.2	0.6	0.132
0.3	0.65	0.196
0.4	0.7	0.258
0.5	0.75	0.317
0.6	0.8	0.375
0.7	0.85	0.430
0.8	0.9	0.483
0.9	0.95	0.534
1	1	0.583

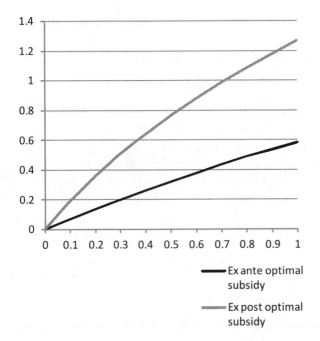

Figure 4.2
Desired subsidy level (s^*) by citizen type (j)

which is maximized at $s^{**}(x; a) = (2x - 1)/(1 - a)$.

As mentioned above, the citizen elected as official in charge of setting the subsidy rate would behave differently depending on whether the subsidy can be irremovably fixed *before* or *after* the citizens make their investment decisions. In the first case, the elected official would set the subsidy at the rate that maximizes his own ex ante utility, since the subsidy rate will affect the citizens' decisions on how much to invest to reduce energy consumption. In the second case, the subsidy will have no effect on these decisions, which will have already been made, and the elected official will set it at the level that maximizes his own ex post utility. Any announcement on his part to set the rate at a different level will not be credible.

Assume, for instance, that the elected official announces a subsidy rate before the citizens decide on their investment, but this rate is not irrevocably fixed and can be changed after the investment is made. If the citizens—naively—believed the announcement, the best option for the elected official would be to set s equal to $s^*(x)$. The citizens would thus make an investment $a = \theta(s^*) = (1 - s^*)/2$; at this point, the official's best choice would be to set

$$s = s^{**}(x, a) = \frac{2x-1}{1-\theta(s^*)} = \frac{4x-2}{1+s^*}.$$

(4.12)

It is easily seen (table 4.2, figure 4.2) that this level is higher than s^*;[18] intuitively, since the citizens can no longer *reduce* their investment in response to a lower energy price, the cost of lowering this price (increasing the subsidy) is now lower, yielding an incentive to reduce the price. Formally, this can be proved by replacing $x = 1/2 + s^{**}(1 + s^*)/4$ in the expression (4.8) above, yielding[19]

$$\frac{\partial}{\partial s}U^A(Y, s, x; w)\Big|_{s=s^{**}<0} = -\frac{2+5s^{**}+3s^{**2}+2s^{**3}}{8}$$
$$+\left(\frac{1+s^{**}}{2}\right)\left(\frac{1}{2}+\frac{s^{**}(1+s^*)}{4}\right)$$
$$=\left(-\frac{2+5s^{**}+3s^{**2}+2s^{**3}}{8}+\left(\frac{1+s^{**}}{2}\right)\frac{1}{2}\right)$$
$$+\left(\frac{1+s^{**}}{2}\right)\frac{s^{**}(1+s^*)}{4}$$
$$=\frac{\partial}{\partial s}U^A\left(Y, s, \frac{1}{2}; w\right)\Big|_{s=s^{**}<0}+\left(\frac{1+s^{**}}{2}\right)\frac{s^{**}(1+s^*)}{4},$$

(4.13)

which is positive since, when $x = 1/2$, U^A is maximized at $s = 0$ and therefore $dU^A/ds > 0$ for all $s < 0$. In any case, unless the elected policy maker is of type $x = 1/2$ (in which case he would set $s = 0$ both ex ante and ex post), the citizens anticipate that ex post he will change the rate of subsidy (or tax) if he is allowed to do so, and therefore do not trust any announcement that is not backed by a credible (legal or institutional) commitment to keep the subsidy rate at the announced level.

The previous discussion has been cast in terms of a very specific distributional goal driving the use of energy subsidies, namely lowering the energy costs faced by the "energy poor," but the commitment problem we have described does not hinge on the specific structure of the distributional problem as we have characterized it, and would equally apply, for example, to a scenario where subsidies to energy production are the result of lobbying pressure by industry stakeholders

Table 4.2
Subsidies announced ex ante and implemented ex post if the announcement is believed, depending on the elected official's type

Elected official's energy consumption needs	Elected official's type	Subsidy announced ex ante	Investment if the announcement is believed	Optimal subsidy ex post if this investment has been made
j	x	s^*	a	s^{**}
0	0.5	0	0.5	0
0.1	0.55	0.066	0.467	0.187
0.2	0.6	0.132	0.434	0.353
0.3	0.65	0.196	0.402	0.502
0.4	0.7	0.258	0.371	0.636
0.5	0.75	0.317	0.341	0.759
0.6	0.8	0.375	0.313	0.873
0.7	0.85	0.430	0.285	0.979
0.8	0.9	0.483	0.258	1.080[a]
0.9	0.95	0.534	0.233	1.173[a]
1	1	0.583	0.209	1.263[a]

a. Hypothetical optimal values returned by the formulas of the model; of course, the subsidy rate must be less than 1.28

(e.g., electricity companies). No matter what the distributional aims of the subsidy are, those aims will be traded off ex ante with the adverse efficiency effects of subsidies on investment choices; ex post, however, those efficiency effects disappear, raising the ex post subsidy choice above the corresponding ex ante choice.

4.3 Subsidy Reform and Reelection Incentives

In this section we examine whether—and under what conditions—an elected official may refrain from undertaking a credible commitment to reform energy subsidies out of electoral concerns. We assume that the citizens are concerned about two policy issues, energy subsidies and another unrelated policy topic ("education"). Decisions on both issues are taken by the same official, who is elected for only one period. The game runs for two periods; energy subsidies are set in each period by the official elected at that time, but the policy maker elected in period 1 can implement a reform of energy subsidies that sets, irreversibly, the rate of subsidy applied in period 2, removing from the official

Marco Pani and Carlo Perroni

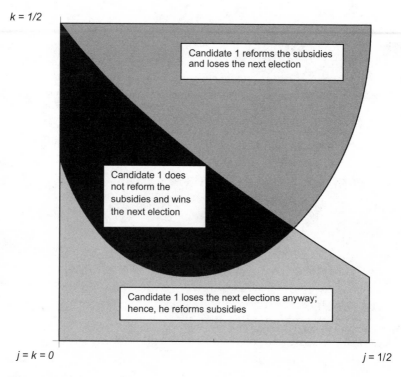

Figure 4.3
Candidate 1's decisions on subsidy reform and electoral outcome by candidate 1's type

that is elected in that period any authority to discretionally alter the rate of subsidy (an action hereafter described as "commitment" or "reform"). On the issue of education, instead, the decisions taken in one period are valid only for that period, and no long-term reforms are possible; the official elected in period 1 cannot constrain the educational policies that are adopted in period 2. On the basis of their expectations about the rate of subsidies that will be implemented in period 2, the citizens decide in period 1 how much to invest in energy-saving technology. Both the costs and the benefits of this investment accrue in period 2 (e.g., the citizens finance their investment with a loan that is repaid in full in period 2).

Suppose that the citizens differ in their energy consumption needs j, as discussed in the previous section, and also in their preferences concerning education, which are represented by a second parameter k. The couple (j, k) that represents the preferences of each citizen along the two policy dimensions is hereafter called the citizen's "type." Types are uniformly distributed over a square support of unit side: the cumulative distribution function is $F(j, k) = j\,k$; note that the distributions of j and k are statistically independent.

Additionally suppose that all voters live for two periods, and that their preferences over policies are additively separable, independent of each other, and separable across periods. Preferences for first-period policies are described by the utility function[21]

$$U(s; j) + V(z; k) = 1 - T(s) - (1 - s)x - 0.2(z - k)^2, \qquad (4.14)$$

where $x = w\,j + 1 - w$, while $T(s) = F(s)/N + F(s)^2/N^2$ and $F(s)/N = s\,(1 - a)/2$, as discussed in section 4.2, while $V(z; k) = -0.2\,(z-k)^2$ is the utility perceived by a citizen of preferences k from an educational policy equal to z.[20] For a citizen of type (j, k), this function is maximized by the policies $s = s^o(x)$ and $z = k$, where $s^o(x) = s^{**}(x, 0)$ because no energy-saving investment has been made yet at this stage.

The candidates who compete to be elected as officials cannot precommit to implement a certain policy action after they have been elected; any pre-electoral promises are not credible. Hence the citizens assume—correctly—that each candidate will implement the policies that he prefers (i.e., that maximize his own utility), regardless of any pre-electoral promises. The officials do not derive any direct utility from holding office per se; the only advantage of being elected is the opportunity to implement one's own favored policies.

Consider the decisions that need to be taken by the official elected in period 1: he has to choose a subsidy rate and an educational policy for period 1 (s and z, respectively), and to decide whether or not to set the subsidy rate for period 2. The first choice is simple: he just sets $s = s^o(x)$ and $z = k$, where (j, k) is his own type; the second decision has, however, implications not only on the energy-saving investment and future energy consumption but also on the outcome of period 2 elections and on the ensuing policy choice on both s and z.

The decisions confronting the candidate elected in period 2 depend on the action taken by the official in period 1: if the latter has fixed the level of subsidies, the official in charge in period 2 can only set policies on education (setting $z = k$); subsidies are now off the policy agenda. If instead the period 1 official has not fixed the level of subsidies, the period 2 official must decide both the educational policies ($z = k$) and the rate of subsidies; since any energy-saving investment has, by this time, already taken place, the decision is taken ex post on the basis of the ex post preferences discussed in section 4.2 ($s = s^{**}(x, a)$). The outcome of the elections is different in these two scenarios: if the subsidy rate is fixed, the citizens elect a period 2 official only on the basis of the educational preferences of the candidates (parameter k); in the other case, they take into account *both* their educational views *and* their energy consumption needs (j and k).

The policy decisions of the official elected in period 1, and the electoral behavior of the citizens, depend on the policy preferences of the electable candidates. In principle, in a democracy, it should be assumed that any citizen can stand as a candidate. In practice, however, the set of "electable" candidates is often constrained by various factors: for instance, to credibly contest an election, a candidate needs to have access to large financial resources, have a strong educational and professional standing, and be well known by the other citizens through personal and network connections and media coverage. These characteristics are not uniformly distributed among the population and are likely to be correlated with a candidate's policy preferences. In the context of our model, one could argue, for instance, that credible candidates are more likely to reside in urban areas where energy consumption needs related to commuting are lower and a higher value is placed on the provision of public education.

For simplicity, we will assume here that, after some process of selection, only two alternative credible candidates are suitable to be elected as officials. One of these candidates ("candidate 1") is of type (0.2, 0.3), while the other ("candidate 2") is of type (0.5, 0.5) (coinciding with the median voter). Notice that candidate 1's views on education are more distant from those of a majority of citizens than those of candidate 2; hence, if only education were (or remained) on the policy agenda (as occurs when period 2 subsidies are fixed by the official incumbent in period 1), candidate 2 would obtain more votes than candidate 1 and would thus be elected.

If candidate 2 is elected in period 1, he may set s for period 2 at his preferred ex ante value—equal to 0.317—in which case he would be reelected in period 2 and get a utility equal to 0.460; if instead he leaves the choice to the official that is elected in period 2, the voters elect candidate 1 who would set $s = 0.306$ (his preferred ex post value); anticipating this choice, the voters would select a level of energy-saving investment $a = 0.347$, and candidate 2 would receive a utility equal to 0.452 (table 4.3). Obviously, in these conditions he would prefer to fix the future level of subsidies and be reelected.

Table 4.3
Median voter's and candidate 2's utility depending on the reform decision and on the outcome of period 2 elections

Candidate 2's reform decision	Candidate elected in period 2	Period 2 subsidy rate s	Energy-saving investment a	Median voter's utility[a]			Candidate 2's utility in period 2[a]
				Period 1	Period 2	In total	
Reform	1	0.317	0.342	0.313	0.452	0.764	0.452
Reform	2	0.317	0.342	0.313	0.460	0.772	0.460
No reform	1	0.306	0.347	0.313	0.452	0.764	0.452
No reform	2	0.618	0.191	0.313	0.428	0.741	0.428

a. Based on a gross income of 1. For gross incomes larger (smaller) than one, the values reported in the table should be increased (reduced) by the difference between the actual gross income and 1.

Table 4.4
Median voter's and candidate 1's utility depending on the reform decision and on the outcome of period 2 elections

Candidate 1's reform decision	Candidate elected in period 2	Period 2 subsidy rate s	Energy-saving investment a	Median voter's utility[a]			Candidate 1's utility in period 2[a]
				Period 1	Period 2	In total	
Reform	1	0.132	0.434	0.282	0.444	0.726	0.553
Reform	2	0.132	0.434	0.282	0.452	0.736	0.545
No reform	1	0.306	0.347	0.282	0.452	0.734	0.546
No reform	2	0.618	0.191	0.282	0.428	0.710	0.472

a. Based on a gross income of 1. For gross incomes larger (smaller) than one, the values reported in the table should be increased (reduced) by the difference between the actual gross income and 1.

The same, however, would not apply to candidate 1, if he is elected in period 1 (table 4.4). If this candidate sets s at his own ex ante preferred level, equal to 0.132 (or, for that, at any other level), he loses the next elections; in period 2, the citizens elect candidate 2 who sets $z = 0.5$ and candidate 1's utility in period 2 is thus equal to 0.545. If, however, candidate 1 left the level of subsidies to be decided by the official elected in period 2, the citizens would reelect him, since he would set lower subsidies than candidate 2. In this case, his period 2 utility would rise to 0.546. Candidate 1 clearly prefers to refrain from fixing the future subsidy rate, even if this leads to some inefficiencies.

More generally, the space of candidates that oppose candidate 2 can be divided as in figure 4.3: the monotonically decreasing curve represents the candidate 1 types (j, k) for which candidate 1 is indifferent between reforming the subsidies (and losing the elections) and being reelected (by not reforming the subsidies). Candidates whose types lie below this curve prefer to refrain from reform in order to be reelected, while candidates whose types lie above the curve prefer to reform the subsidies even at the cost of losing the next elections. The nonmonotonic curve represents instead the candidate types for which, if candidate 1 refrains from reforming the subsidies, he gets as many votes as candidate 2 at the next elections; candidate 1 types above this curve are reelected if they do not reform the subsidies, while candidate types below this curve lose the next elections in any case. The darker shaded area in the figure represents the set of candidate 1 types who not only could win the next elections by refraining from reforming the subsidies but would also be willing to do so. If a candidate of one of these types is elected in period 1, there is no energy subsidies reform.[22]

Going back to the previous example (where candidate 1's type is (0.2, 0.3), which lies in the dark shaded area), it is easy to see that in period 1 candidate 1 would not be elected in the first place: if he were, the median voter's utility would be equal to 0.282 in period 1 and to 0.452 in period 2 (since he would not reform the subsidies and he would be reelected); by electing candidate 2 instead, the median voter would reach a utility of 0.313 in period 1 and of 0.460 in period 2; hence he—and therefore a majority of citizens—would be better off in both periods if candidate 2 were elected in period 1 (and then reelected in period 2).

But assume that candidate 2 were not standing and that all other candidates were further away from the preferences of the median voter than candidate 1. In this case candidate 1 would be elected in period 1 in essentially uncontested elections and would reform the subsidies, fixing their rate at his own preferred ex ante level of 0.132, because the reform would induce the citizens to invest more in energy-saving technology without hampering his reelection prospects. In this situation the appearance on the scene of a credible challenger in the person (and of the type) of candidate 2 would upset this outcome, inducing the incumbent candidate 1 to revise his plans and refrain from reforming the subsidies in order to remain in power.

There are also situations where the citizens would rationally prefer to elect a candidate who would not fix the level of subsidies even when other credible contestants are available. Assume, for instance, that candidate 2 were instead of type (0, 0.5). If this candidate were elected in period 1, he would still reform the subsidies (indeed he would abolish them altogether) and be reelected in period 2. If candidate 1 were elected in period 1, he would not reform the subsidies and would be reelected in period 2, as in the previous example. The median voter's total utility in this case (defined as the sum of his utility in periods 1 and 2, with no intertemporal discounting) would, however, be equal to 0.688 in the first case and to 0.734 in the second; as a result, in period 1, a majority of citizens would prefer to elect candidate 1 even if he would not reform the subsidies, anticipating that, once reelected, he would keep the subsidies at a positive level in line with the preferences of a majority of citizens (table 4.5).[23] A similar situation would occur if candidate 2 were of type (0.9, 0.5) (table 4.6).

Table 4.5
Median voter's and incumbent candidate's utility depending on the reform decision and on the outcome of period 2 elections (candidate 2's type = (0, 0.5))

Candidate elected in period 1, and reform decision	Candidate elected in period 2	Period 2 subsidy rate s	Energy-saving investment a	Median voter's utility[a]			Period 1 official's utility in period 2[a]
				Period 1	Period 2	In total	
1, Reform	1	0.132	0.434	0.282	0.444	0.726	0.553
1, Reform	2	0.132	0.434	0.282	0.452	0.734	0.545
1, No ref.	1	0.306	0.347	0.282	0.452	0.734	0.546
1, No ref.	2	0	0.5	0.282	0.438	0.720	0.542
2, Reform	1	0	0.5	0.25	0.430	0.680	0.617
2, Reform	2	0	0.5	0.25	0.438	0.688	0.625
2, No ref.	1	0.306	0.347	0.25	0.452	0.702	0.595
2, No ref.	2	0	0.5	0.25	0.438	0.688	0.625

a. Based on a gross income of 1. For gross incomes larger (smaller) than one, the values reported in the table should be increased (reduced) by the difference between the actual gross income and 1.

Table 4.6
Median voter's and incumbent candidate's utility depending on the reform decision and on the outcome of period 2 elections (candidate 2's type = (0.9, 0.5))

Candidate elected in period 1, and reform decision	Candi- date elected in period 2	Period 2 subsidy rate	Energy- saving invest-ment	Median voter's utility[a]			Period 1 official's utility in period 2[a]
		s	a	Period 1	Period 2	In total	
1, Reform	1	0.132	0.434	0.282	0.444	0.726	0.553
1, Reform	2	0.132	0.434	0.282	0.452	0.734	0.545
1, No ref.	1	0.306	0.347	0.282	0.452	0.734	0.546
1, No ref.	2	0.932	0.034	0.282	0.297	0.579	0.299
2, Reform	1	0.534	0.5	0.273	0.436	0.709	0.354
2, Reform	2	0.534	0.5	0.273	0.444	0.717	0.362
2, No ref.	1	0.306	0.347	0.273	0.452	0.724	0.337
2, No ref.	2	0.932	0.034	0.273	0.297	0.570	0.284

a. Based on a gross income of 1. For gross incomes larger (smaller) than one, the values reported in the table should be increased (reduced) by the difference between the actual gross income and 1.

Hence an elected official may refrain from committing to a specific subsidy rate for the future (subsidy reform), despite the losses and inefficiencies that this lack of action entails, in order to maintain the issue of energy subsidies on the policy agenda and thereby ensure either his own reelection or, more generally, the election of a candidate that he likes; anticipating this decision, the voters may still prefer to elect him if the other alternative candidate(s) have preferences in terms of subsidies that are too distant from those of the majority.

This may explain why much-needed subsidy reforms may be delayed for a long time. Since reforming the subsidies can alter the subsequent political game, the stronger advocates for subsidy reforms are likely to have more radical views on the issue than a majority of the citizens; candidates with more moderate positions may prefer to delay the reform in order to preserve their comparative political advantage. In these conditions, the citizens may also prefer to maintain the status quo, despite its inefficiencies, rather than to delegate the reform to candidates whose preferences and views on the subject are too different from their own.

4.4 Discussion

A number of policy options have been explored with the purpose of reducing (or phasing out) inefficient energy subsidies: the adoption of automatic pricing formulas, delegation of authority to price-setting committees, subsidization of energy-saving investments, as well as more narrowly targeted transfers.

Our preceding analysis offers a specific, political economy-based interpretation of the obstacles to reform, and a specific lens through which those various policy alternatives can be assessed.

Automatic pricing formulas   These formulas typically provide that the (administered) retail price of selected energy products (e.g., gasoline) is determined by applying a fixed discount to the total cost of the inputs (imported energy products plus any local refining costs, transportation and distribution costs, labor costs, and a "fair" profit margin for the local firms involved) and is automatically adjusted at fixed intervals (e.g., once a month) in response to changes in the costs of these inputs. The difference between the cost of the inputs and the retail price is typically charged to the public budget. In principle, these formulas provide an institutional instrument to credibly commit to a specific subsidy rate: if, for instance, the formula establishes that the retail price of gasoline is determined by applying a 20 percent discount on the price of imported gasoline (abstracting from transportation and distribution costs), then, until the formula is revised, the subsidy on gasoline will remain equal to 20 percent and the retail price will automatically change in response to the import price in order to maintain this proportion. By adopting a formula such as this, the elected official renounces his authority to discretionally adjust the administrative price of energy, and commits instead to a fixed discount rate.

The practical experience suggests, however, that a pricing formula approach is not always effective as a way of achieving commitment: in some cases the presumably automatic periodic adjustment is not carried out (especially when international prices rise), and the retail price is left unchanged for prolonged periods;[24] in other cases, the determination of important elements of the formula (such as excise taxes or retailers' operating costs) contain a large margin of discretion that enables the policy maker to make significant adjustments to the level of subsidies.

The results of our theoretical analysis suggest that the presence of these margins of discretion (including the possibility of skipping periodic adjustments) may not be unintentional: under certain conditions, elected policy makers may deliberately choose to retain discretionary influence on the level of subsidies in order to gain the voter support that they lack in other policy areas.

Price-setting committees Delegating the determination of the retail price (and hence of the level of subsidies) to an independent committee can serve different purposes, depending on the powers, composition, and tenure of the committee. An elected official can credibly commit to a specific subsidy rate by delegating the authority to modify the subsidies to a long-standing committee composed of experts with specific views on the topic, who would— ex post—prefer to enforce the rate that he sets ex ante (a process that is analogous to the delegation of the authority to set monetary policy to a "conservative" central banker; see Rogoff 1985). Alternatively, delegating power to a committee may serve to separate the subsidy issue from other policy issues: a committee may include representatives of various organizations and professional groups (truck drivers, environmental protection organizations, chamber of commerce, etc.), each of whom separately elects its own representatives to the committee, while political competition for broader political representation only revolves around other issues. This would remove strategic incentives for noncommitment on the part of general representatives. [25]

However, to the extent that the delegation decision is left to elected policy makers, the preceding analysis suggests that they may choose not take advantage of this option, and that the reform of energy subsidies might need to be underpinned by institutional reform, rather than being left to the routine policy-making of elected representatives.

Subsidizing energy-saving technologies If the government subsidizes energy-saving technologies, citizens invest more in them and therefore reduce their energy consumption needs, reducing the need for subsidies. This would reduce the subsidy rate preferred by each citizen and the number of citizens that would support a positive subsidy rate, thereby reducing the level of subsidies that is adopted in a political equilibrium. [26] In our highly stylized model, if an investment subsidy reduces the cost of investing in energy-saving technologies by a rate s_a, from a^2 to $(1 - s_a) a^2$, and if the official elected selects a level of abatement subsidy s_a and then announces the energy subsidy s before the consumers make their investment, it can be shown that the levels of subsidy that the official prefers ex ante and ex post coincide. Thus, in principle, the introduction of subsidies on energy-saving investments can make an institutional commitment to reform unnecessary: any official willing to reform the energy subsidies ex ante will also be willing to implement the same reform ex post, after the citizens have already reduced their energy consumption needs.

In practice, however, investment subsidies cannot be targeted as precisely as energy subsidies—energy subsidies directly reduce the price of energy, while abatement subsidies reduce the price of investments that might be only imperfectly correlated with energy use and could thus leak beyond their intended purpose (supporting investments that do not reduce energy consumption), or even encourage the use of energy (e.g., subsidies on electric car sales could discourage people from commuting by bus). More important, when there is political competition and multiple potential decision makers, the choice of subsidies on energy-saving investments and the subsequent choice of energy subsidies might not be made by the same official, further complicating an incumbent's strategic incentives. In other words, an incumbent could face political incentives to use the investment subsidy strategically, departing from his preferred level of investment subsidy in order not to accommodate the energy subsidy choice of a potentially elected challenger and, by so doing, ensuring his own reelection. Subsidizing energy-saving technologies does not therefore eliminate the problem of energy subsidy reform: the strategic noncommitment problem with respect to energy subsidies would translate in such a scenario into a strategic nonoptimal investment subsidy—which in turn would make the ex post choice without commitment by the incumbent nonoptimal.

Targeted transfers   A frequently voiced suggestion in the debate on energy subsidies is to replace inefficient subsidies on energy with more efficient transfers specifically targeted at the poor. In our theoretical setup this would be achieved by imposing a flat income tax on all citizens to finance a graduated transfer that benefits the citizens with the strongest energy needs (the largest value of j). Unlike subsidies on the retail energy price, these transfers (1) would not benefit all citizens, but only those with the strongest needs, and (2) would not depend on actual energy consumption, and hence would not discourage energy-saving investments (if anything, they may encourage them by providing the poorest citizens with increased financial means to undertake them).[27] In principle, this measure should result in a more efficient outcome, with more energy-saving investment, less energy consumption, and a more efficient use of resources. In practice, it may not be easy to implement, as j is to a large extent private information to the individuals (even when its *distribution* among the population is common knowledge).

Such a measure may also have further political economy implications and may raise further questions. How would the threshold for eligibility to the transfer be defined? What would its level be in political equilibrium? For a given degree of altruism, a higher threshold would translate into voters preferring a lower energy subsidy (since their concerns for the poor would be addressed by the targeted transfer), and if the threshold is sufficiently high, the subsidies would be completely abolished. When there are more than one policy dimensions, however, voters may elect an official who sets a comparatively low threshold in order to secure reelection. Thus targeted transfers may themselves be used as a strategic tool of political competition.

Acknowledgments

We gratefully acknowledge CESifo's sponsorship of this study. We would like to thank Caterina Gennaioli, Tom Moerenhout, Carlos Mulas-Granados, Ian Parry, Leonzio Rizzo, Jon Strand, Cees van Beers, and other participants to the 2014 CESIfo Venice Summer Institute Conference on "The Economics and Political Economy of Energy Subsidies" for comments and suggestions. Support from Warwick's CAGE is gratefully acknowledged.

The views expressed in this chapter are those of the authors and do not necessarily represent the views of the IMF, its Executive Board, or IMF management.

Notes

1. Based on IMF estimates of world GDP at about $64 trillion in 2010: IMF, *World Economic Outlook Database*, April 2014.

2. In low- and middle-income countries, on average, 43 percent of fuel subsidies accrue to the richest 20 percent of households, and only 7 percent accrue to the poorest 20 percent (Bauer et al. 2013; see also Clements et al. 2010, and IEA 2011). Despite these leakages to the rich, hydrocarbon subsidies can be important for the poor (e.g., see IEG 2009 for the case of Bolivia).

3. Some countries that heavily subsidize energy are not ruled by governments that are elected in fairly contested elections, but similar considerations apply to a nondemocratic government in which the rulers are selected (or manage to remain in power) by gathering sufficient support from different, heterogeneous constituencies within the ruling elite.

4. The incentives for elected policy makers to make a credible commitment to implement specific policy measures have been widely studied in the literature (Persson and Svensson 1989; Alesina and Tabellini 1990; Aghion and Bolton 1990; Milesi-Ferretti and Spolaore 1994; Milesi-Ferretti 1995). The political economy of reforming energy subsidies remains, however, comparatively unexplored and, to our knowledge, has not yet been analyzed in reference to this time-inconsistency problem.

5. More generally, energy subsidies benefit most those consumers for whom a reduction in the price of energy results in the largest marginal increase in utility; this includes low-income households whose energy consumption may be modest in terms of physical units but accounts for a large proportion of total household expenditure.

6. The empirical evidence from household surveys shows that the volume and value of energy consumption generally increase with household income, but the share of income spent on energy decreases with household income. As stated in note 10 below, qualitatively similar results can be obtained from an extension of the model where energy consumption increases with income.

7. The Downsian model of representative democracy (Downs 1957) predicts that under certain conditions representative democracy can produce outcomes that are consistent with direct democracy. This conclusion requires that commitment be feasible and enforceable (e.g., see Banks 1990). However, there is abundant evidence that elected politicians often renege on their campaign promises (e.g., Krukones 1984). This evidence, and the ensuing debate, has led to the widespread adoption of the "citizen-candidate" model of representative democracy (Osborne and Slivinski 1996; Besley and Coate 1997). In such framework elected policy makers can only make policy decisions that are aligned with their ex post preferences given any constraints they may have inherited from previous policy makers. Thus, even if institutional mechanisms for constraining future policy choices are available, prior to being elected, political candidates cannot rely on such mechanisms to make binding campaign promises—although they may choose to constrain future policies once they are in office. Note that this does not mean that elected policy makers do not care about the interest of the citizens, only that their assessment of what constitutes this interest may be heavily biased by their own personal situation and experience, and that no binding campaign promises can be made not to act on those views once in office.

9. Subsidies can also be *negative*, if the government imposes special taxes on energy products. These taxes, aimed at encouraging energy-savings techniques and habits, are common in advanced economies. Consequently the retail price of energy is higher than the producer price.

10. This assumption simplifies the analysis. It could also be assumed that the subsidies are financed through distortionary income taxes. The preferred level of subsidies would depend on a citizen's income as well as on his energy consumption needs. The analysis

in this study abstracts from the redistribution that can be achieved through progressive income taxes; it can be assumed, for instance, that—given the economic structure, institutional development, and governance capacity of the country—the structure of income taxes is already set to achieve an optimal balance between redistribution and efficiency, so that any additional redistributive goals must be pursued through other instruments such as energy subsidies. An extension of the model that includes proportional income taxes and assumes that energy consumption needs are positively correlated with income yields qualitatively similar results.

11. More generally, it could be assumed that the tax $C(F)$ is a continuous and twice differentiable function of F, increasing in F at an increasing rate.

12. More generally, the cost of reducing energy consumption by a fraction a could be assumed to be a continuous, thrice differentiable function $c(a)$ with $c(0) = 0$, $c'(a) > 0$, $c''(a) > 0$, and $c'''(a) \geq 0$. An additional condition $c'(1) > 1$ ensures that no citizen can afford to reduce energy consumption to zero.

13. The cost of other energy-saving investments may, however, be more weakly linked to the total amount of energy saved. The cost of installing double-glazed windows or adding fiberglass under the roof, for instance, does not directly depend on the households' heating bill.

14. Producer energy prices, of course, vary over time; the international price of oil, for instance, has fluctuated from 2003 to 2012 between \$29 and \$105 dollars per barrel (IMF, *World Economic Outlook Databases*, April 2014; simple average of the Dated Brent, West Texas Intermediate, and Dubai Fateh spot prices). This price is, however, largely beyond the control of national government authorities. One could assume that citizens base their investment decisions on "consensus" projections about future developments in producer prices based, for instance, on demand and supply projections like those published by the IEA in its annual *World Energy Outlook*.

15. The first derivative of ERC with respect to a is $-(1-s)j + 2aj$, which is equal to zero if and only if $a = (1-s)/2$. The second derivative, $2j$, is always positive, ensuring that the second-order condition for a minimum is met.

16. In this example Y is normalized to 1.

17. Notice that income appears once again as an additive constant in the utility function; as a result the value of s that maximizes utility does not depend on income.

18. This is true only for those citizens with $x > 1/2$, who prefer a positive subsidy ex ante; when $w = 1/2$, as assumed in table 4.2 and figure 4.2, this group includes all the citizens, except those with $j = 0$, for whom $x = 1/2$ and $s^* = s^{**} = 0$. More generally, citizens with $x < 1/2$, who ex ante prefer a tax (negative subsidy) on fuel, would prefer an even larger tax ex post: for them, $s^{**} < s^*$ because ex post higher energy taxes can no longer induce citizens to save energy, which increases the revenue yield that can be collected by raising energy taxes (citizens who consume little energy prefer to tax those who consume a lot and redistribute the revenue evenly across citizens).

19. A condition ensuring that $s^* > -1$ for all citizens is required to ensure that $a < 1$; namely citizens will not reduce their energy consumption to zero by investing enough in energy-saving technology, an outcome that is mathematically feasible in the simplified setting of our model but that would not be technically feasible in most real-life situations (although it could apply in some limited cases: e.g., some people may reduce their commuting gasoline consumption needs to zero by relocating within walking distance to

their workplace). Since $a = (1 - s)/2$, if s is equal to or less than -1 (energy is taxed by at least 100 percent), then in our model $a \geq 1$, violating this requirement.

20. We assume here that the possible policy choices concerning "education" can be compared using a cardinal measure. This might apply to some type of decisions (e.g., concerning class size, the length of the school year or weekly hours) but not to others (e.g., content of the curriculum).

21. Citizens also consider the welfare of the "poorest" citizen whose energy consumption needs are highest, as discussed in section 4.2; this is reflected by the use of x in place of j in some formulas.

22. Candidate 1 types in the lighter shaded area at the bottom, could never defeat candidate 2, and would therefore reform the subsidies as they have nothing to lose (and something to gain) by doing so. Candidate 1 types in the lighter shaded area at the top, are willing to reform the subsidies even if this costs them the next elections.

23. This would also hold if the citizens discounted period 2 utility, for instance, at a 10 percent rate.

24. For instance, in Ghana, the executive retains discretion on the application of the formula and prices are infrequently adjusted; in Namibia, retail prices adjustments did not keep pace with the rise in world prices in 2008; in contrast, an automatic pricing mechanism appears to have been effectively implemented in South Africa; see David et al. (2013).

25. Several countries that have reformed energy subsidies (including Armenia, Kenya, the Philippines, South Africa, and Turkey) have delegated responsibility for reforming and regulating the sector to an independent agency (Alleyne et al. 2013).

26. Some governments, for instance, have subsidized the conversion to less costly LPG for cooking (Indonesia) or transportation (Philippines) (Nozaki and Shang 2013).

27. In Ghana, Niger, Nigeria, and Turkey, for instance, a reduction in energy subsidies was accompanied by the extension of subsidies to the public transport sector, which is used more intensely by the poor. In Namibia, the government subsidizes transportation costs to remote rural areas. In Brazil, low-income families are provided with gas vouchers to purchase LPG. Cash transfer schemes have been introduced in a number of countries, including Brazil, Indonesia, and the Philippines (Dizioli et al. 2013; Nozaki and Shang 2013).

28. A rate larger than one could make sense if each citizen's physical energy consumption were fixed; high energy users would benefit if the government paid an energy subsidy larger than the energy costs incurred, financed from income taxes. This arrangement, of course, would be difficult to justify politically and would encourage energy waste.

References

Aghion, P., and P. Bolton. 1990. Government domestic debt and the risk of default: A political-economic model of the strategic role of debt. In R. Dornbusch and M. Draghi, eds., *Public Debt Management: Theory and History*, 315–45. Cambridge, UK: Cambridge University Press.

Alesina, A., and G. Tabellini. 1990. A positive theory of fiscal deficits and government debt. *Review of Economic Studies* 57: 403–14.

Alesina, A. 1988. Credibility and policy convergence in a two-party system with rational voters. *American Economic Review* 78 (4): 796–805.

Alleyne, T., B. Clements, D. Coady, S. Fabrizio, S. Gupta, C. Sdralevich, B. Shang, and M. Villafuerte. 2013. Reforming energy subsidies: Lessons from experience. In B. Clements, D. Coady, S. Fabrizio, S. Gupta, T. Alleyne, and C. Sdralevich, eds., *Energy Subsidy Reform: Lessons and Implications*, 23–41.Washington, DC: IMF.

Baron, D. 1994. Electoral competition with informed and uninformed voters. *American Political Science Review* 88 (1): 33–47.

Banks, K. 1990. A model of electoral competition with incomplete information. *Journal of Economic Theory* 50: 309–25.

Bauer, A., D. Coady, A. Kangur, C. Josz, E. Ruggiero, C. Sdralevich, S. Singh, and M. Villafuerte. 2013. Macroeconomic, environmental, and social implications. In B. Clements, D. Coady, S. Fabrizio, S. Gupta, T. Alleyne, and C. Sdralevich, eds., *Energy Subsidy Reform: Lessons and Implications*, 15–21. Washington, DC: IMF.

Becker, G. 1983. A theory of competition among pressure groups for political influence. *Quarterly Journal of Economics* 98 (3): 371–400.

Besley, T., and S. Coate. 1997. An economic model of representative democracy. *Quarterly Journal of Economics* 112: 185–14.

Clements, B., D. Coady, and J. Piotrowski. 2010. Oil subsidies: Costly and rising. *Finance and Development* 47 (2): 42–23.

Coady, D., S. Fabrizio, M. Hussain, B. Shang, and Y. Zouhar. 2013. Defining and measuring energy subsidies. In B. Clements, D. Coady, S. Fabrizio, S. Gupta, T. Alleyne, and C. Sdralevich, eds., *Energy Subsidy Reform: Lessons and Implications*, 5–13. Washington, DC: IMF.

David, A., F. Gwenhamo, M. Hussain, C. Mira, A. Op de Beke, V. Thakoor, and G. Verdier. 2013. Case studies from the sub-Saharan Africa region. In B. Clements, D. Coady, S. Fabrizio, S. Gupta, T. Alleyne, and C. Sdralevich, eds., *Energy Subsidy Reform: Lessons and Implications*, 43–74. Washington, DC: IMF.

Dizioli, A., J. Kapsoli, M. Nozaki, and M. Soto. 2013. Case studies from the Latin America and Caribbean region. In B. Clements, D. Coady, S. Fabrizio, S. Gupta, T. Alleyne, and C. Sdralevich, eds., *Energy Subsidy Reform: Lessons and Implications*, 103–22. Washington, DC: IMF.

Downs, A. 1957. *An Economic Theory of Democracy*. New York: Harper.

Glazer, A., and M. Gradstein. 2005. Elections with contribution-maximizing candidates. *Public Choice* 122 (3/4): 467–82.

Grossman, G., and E. Helpman. 1996. Electoral competition and special interest politics. *Review of Economic Studies* 63: 265–86.

Grossman, G., and E. Helpman. 2001. *Special Interest Politics*. Cambridge: MIT Press.

IEA. 2011. *World Energy Outlook 2011*. Paris: International Energy Agency.

IEG. 2009. *Climate Change and the World Bank Group: Phase I: Evaluation of World Bank Win-Win Energy Policy Reforms*. Washington, DC: World Bank, Independent Evaluation Group.

Katz, E., S. Nitzan, and J. Rosenberg. 1990. Rent-seeking for pure public goods. *Public Choice* 65 (1): 49–60.

Krukones, M. 1984. *Policies and Performance: Presidential Campaigns as Policy Predictors.* Lanham, MD: University Press of America.

Milesi-Ferretti, G. M. 1995. The disadvantage of tying their hands: On the political economy of policy commitments. *Economic Journal* 105: 1381–1402.

Milesi-Ferretti, G. M., and E. Spolaore. 1994. How cynical can an incumbent be? Strategic policy in a model of government spending. *Journal of Public Economics* 55: 121–40.

Nozaki, M., and B. Shang. 2013. Case studies from emerging and developing Asia. In B. Clements, D. Coady, S. Fabrizio, S. Gupta, T. Alleyne, and C. Sdralevich, eds., *Energy Subsidy Reform: Lessons and Implications*, 75–85. Washington, DC: IMF.

Osborne, M., and A. Slivinski. 1996. A model of political competition with citizen-candidates. *Quarterly Journal of Economics* 111: 65–96.

Persson, T., and L. Svensson. 1989. Why a stubborn conservative would run deficit: Policy with time-inconsistent preferences. *Quarterly Journal of Economics* 104: 325–45.

Rogoff, K. 1985. The optimal degree of commitment to an intermediate target. *Quarterly Journal of Economics* 100: 1169–90.

Shang, B., I. Parry, and L. Sears. 2013. Estimating pretax and posttax global energy subsidies. In B. Clements, D. Coady, S. Fabrizio, S. Gupta, T. Alleyne, and C. Sdralevich, eds., *Energy Subsidy Reform: Lessons and Implications*, 143–64. Washington, DC: IMF.

5 Model of Noncorrupt versus Corrupt Government in Delivery of Transport Services: The Impact of Energy Subsidies

Jon Strand

5.1 Introduction

This chapter represents a follow-up and extension to a World Bank Policy Research Working Paper (Strand 2013). It relates closely to empirical work currently ongoing in the World Bank dealing with energy subsidies and related themes. This general topic area of economic analysis or energy subsidies has recently attracted substantial interest, both in the World Bank, the IMF and elsewhere, with contributions found among others in World Bank (2010), Commander (2011); Kojima (2012a, b), Vaglinasindi (2012a, b), IMF (2013, 2014), Coady et al. (2015), and Kojima and Koplow (2015). Some of the follow-up work, involving this author, has focused on building, estimating, and testing empirical models for fuel (gasoline, diesel, and kerosene) pricing across countries over a more than twenty-year period, much of it based on an extensive dataset for such pricing integrated with various economic and political variables. This work, which includes Strand (2011), Beers and Strand (2013), and Kotsogiannis (2011), deals principally with the political economy of fuel pricing. More recently the data on which much of this work is based have been extended and improved. We have updated the models by adding useful data on car ownership in countries for which we have more current fuel price and consumption data.[1] The new data reflect similar and recent work by the IMF (2013, 2014) on energy subsidy rates as shares of the overall economy.

It is also worth mentioning that the economic analysis of corruption in its relation to economics and politics has a long history, which serves as a backdrop for the current presentation. An earlier strand of literature discussed empirical political economy aspects of fuel pricing, and includes Hammar, Löfgren, and Sterner (2004) and Fredriksson and Millimet (2004). The empirical analysis in these papers is, however, based on more limited datasets than those we now have available. Also most existing work has focused on high-income countries. Our improved data situation opens up for meaningful inclusion of additional political variables such as those representing democratic or autocratic governments, length of regime or regime type tenure, and democratic system (e.g., presidential vs. parliamentarian).

As already noted, the present chapter extends Strand (2013), which attempted to lay the analytical foundations for the political economy analysis of petroleum-based fuel (gasoline and kerosene) subsidies and to show how these policies vary across countries. I there considered both economic and political factors behind differences in subsidy policies across countries, with much of the focus on differences in practices between democratic and autocratic governments. I modeled a political process where the promise of low fuel prices is used as a political tool: in democracies to attract voters and in autocracies to mobilize support among politically powerful support groups. A key approach taken there was that fuel subsidies are easier to observe, commit to, or deliver, or are better targeted at core groups, than other public goods or favors that can be offered or promised by politicians. A main finding was that easier commitment and delivery, for the "commodity" of low fuel prices, as compared to costs of supplying more standard public goods, can explain a high prevalence of fuel policies in autocracies, and in young democracies where the capacity to commit to or deliver complex public goods is incompletely developed.

This chapter extends that framework mainly by including infrastructure investments in politicians' choice sets and a more explicit dynamic formulation. I now focus more on the trade-off between the long run, here simply represented by the infrastructure (road) investments, and the short run, represented by the government's periodic energy pricing policy. I model a democracy with multiple election periods; alternatively, a government under autocratic rule where leaders rely on a necessary, narrower, power base (a "selectorate") to stay in power.[2] Reelection of politicians in democracies (or staying in power for an autocratic ruler) is in the basic model studied in section 5.2 assumed to be affected by three factors: (1) the quality of the infrastructure (provided by the politician in an initial investment period), (2) the rate and amount of fuel subsidies or taxes, and (3) the number of private vehicles, which in turn determines the fraction of the public that has cars and thus gains from motor fuel subsidies. We assume throughout that sitting governments are concerned only with their net utility from governing (in excess of some outside reservation utility), and thus also with their probabilities of remaining in power for future periods.

In sections 5.3 through 5.5 this basic model is extended in different directions. Section 5.3 considers additional public-goods supplies that do not require up-front investments and may have benign effects on growth. Section 5.4 considers the possible growth effects of energy subsidies themselves, which may be negative; this factor may tend to further discourage such subsidies in particular for governments who expect to remain in power for quite some time, and/or have growth concerns high on the agenda. Section 5.5 studies a simple version of corruption in this context. We here assume that politicians may accept bribes in return for providing energy subsidies favorable to particular constituencies. We assume that politicians may be sacked when bribe taking is revealed, but that the probability of this happening is a negative function of average bribe taking. This may easily lead to both very high and very low bribe taking representing equilibria; where the likelihood that the former occurs is higher when politicians place little emphasis on future returns, and/or they, in any case, expect their time in office to be short-lived. Section 5.6 concludes.

5.2   A Basic Model of Noncorrupt Government

In my basic model, transport infrastructure investment, and transport-related energy subsidies or taxes, are the only explicit instruments of government. Consider an infinite-period model where, in period 1, governments can provide an investment T into a transport system, alternatively a collective (train, bus transit, etc.) or road investment benefiting road vehicles (cars and trucks), or a combination of the two. We assume that all voters are affected by this investment, but possibly to differing degrees depending, for example, on whether they have cars. Fuels may be subsidized or taxed. Beneficiaries of net fuel subsidies are only those with cars; the group of households that contains car owners is also called the middle class. The investment T provides public goods only after an initial (perhaps long) construction period, here defined as the unit period of the analysis. We assume that some governments have problems of credibility, in promising T to be actually delivered and transformed into effective and operational infrastructure in the next period.

This section considers noncorrupt, and principally (but not only) democratic governments, and where delivery problems, and/or governments' concern for and interest in the public, may vary. Governments may be not fully democratic, and then rely on a so-called selectorate (smaller constituencies than in standard democracies) for their political support.

We start by defining a variable Z, which represents the politician's periodic utility function while in power, and given by the following terms:

$$Z_t = G_t + U(T_0, s_t) - eV(T_0, N_t, s_t) - qC(N_t, s_t) + H(B_t), \qquad t = 1, \dots \quad (5.1)$$

The individual terms in (5.1) will be explained further below.
The objective function for the sitting government can now be defined as follows:

$$EW_0 = H(B_0) + \delta\Phi(T, s, N)\{[G + U(T, s) - eV(T, N, s) - qC(N, s) + H(B)]\}$$
$$+ [\delta\Phi(T, s, N)]^2 \{.\} + [\delta\Phi(T, s, N)]^3 \{.\} + \dots$$
$$= + H(B_0) + \frac{\delta\Phi(T, s, N)}{1 - \delta\Phi(T, s, N)} Z.$$

$$(5.2)$$

In (5.2) we are considering a steady-state solution only, whereby Z_t (= Z) is assumed to be constant through time. The first two lines in (5.2) look complicated, but we see that they reduce to the simpler expression in the third line, using the expression for Z from (5.1). By assuming an infinite horizon (in principle) for a sitting government, the objective can be expressed as an infinitely discounted sum of periodic utilities, the last term on the right-hand side of the last line, where $\delta\Phi$ represents an "effective degree of discounting" (see immediately below for definitions of individual variables and parameters). Note that Z is counted only from period 1 on, at which time the returns to the investment made in period 0 are starting to be reaped. For period 0 we assume that all terms apart from $H(B_0)$ are exogenous thus playing no role for the government's maximization problem (and thus dropped here and in the following for simplicity). Assume that the sitting government is in power for certain during the initial period 0, and that only T is determined in that period.

We have defined the following symbols:[3]

B_t = budget balance in period t, where we only denote the initial period 0 (and otherwise do not use time subscripts).

$H(B)$ = utility to the sitting government from the current net budget surplus, where $H(B)$ can be positive or negative, and $H' > 0$, $H'' < 0$, so that an improved budget balance is viewed positively by the government, but with a marginal value that drops with budget balance improvements. We may think of $H(B)$ as being positive if and only if B is positive (thus, in particular, $H(B) = 0$ for $B = 0$). Also large budget deficits may be considered as bad at the margin, in the sense here of making H' large.

T = transport infrastructure investment, determined in period 0. As noted, T can be considered as investment in collective transport or road infrastructure.

N = number of private vehicles (defined for simplicity as the fraction of the public that has cars).

s = fuel subsidy rate, considering s as an excise tax (implying $s < 0$), or similar subsidy ($s > 0$).

S = total fuel subsidy amount = $sN(s)$, where $N'(s) > 0$ (assuming that the amount of driving per car is a positive function of the fuel subsidy rate). This expresses the (negative) net fiscal impacts of fuel subsidies.

C = carbon emissions per period.

G = utility to sitting government officials or politicians, due to being in power as such (independent of other sources of utility embedded in equation 5.2).

U = direct utility to government officials or politicians themselves from transport infrastructure and fuel subsidies. U could also reflect (fully or partly) the utility to the general public, depending on the degree of "societal concern" among politicians. We assume that the partial derivatives U_T and U_s are both positive and decreasing in their arguments.

V = marginal externality cost in private transport in the country, assumed to be a negative function of public infrastructure supply; and a positive function of the number of cars and the fuel subsidy. For partial derivatives we assume $V_T < 0$, $V_N > 0$, and $V_s > 0$: externality costs of transport increase in the number of cars and in fuel subsidies, but are reduced when transport infrastructure improves (regardless of whether T represents public transport or road building).

e = the government-internalized costs related to externalities in private transport. A "responsible" government will tend to emphasize efficiency in fiscal and externality policy, put negative weights on high and distortive energy subsidies, and have a high e value. e takes values from 0 (disinterested government) to 1 (fully internalizing fuel externalities).

q = carbon price, such as carbon tax or price under a c-a-t scheme, or a carbon market offset price. For simplicity, we assume that q is constant through time.

Φ = probability that the government remains in power until the following period. We consider both democratic governments (with formal elections), and nondemocratic ones. The process for staying in power is likely to be different under autocracy, often with a "selectorate" determining whether an autocratic government or ruler remains in power. In either case this probability is affected positively by increases in both T and s. Effects of the number of car owners could go in either direction, and may depend on T and s. When T is high (s is low), those without cars are likely to vote for or support the politician; and an increase in N is likely to reduce this voting propensity and thus Φ. When T is low (s high), we it could be opposite: households with cars are likely to care less about public transport, and more about fuel subsidies.

δ = (interest-equivalent) discount factor of government. This factor depends on length of the period (how many years constitute an election period/cycle); on the time lag from investment in transport infrastructure, T, to its effect on infrastructure quality; and on "subjective impatience" of government that may vary by country and government type. It is related to, but not identical to, the standard capital market discount rate, r.

The government's budget balance in period t is found from the following expression:

$$B_t = R_t - rT_0 - S_t - P_t, \qquad t = 0, 1, \ldots, \tag{5.3}$$

where we have defined the following terms:

R_t = total government revenue in period t, considered exogenous.
rT_0 = the government's service payments to pay for infrastructure investment made in period 0.

For simplicity, we assume that the infrastructure investment is fully loan financed and that fixed payments (for interest and principal) must be paid from period 0 and continuously thereafter.[4]

P_t = expenditure on "other public goods" in period t. We assume that these public goods do not require investments, and thus only represent current expenditures. This would among other items include health, education, social services, and other infrastructure. This is here for the moment considered exogenous, but it can in reality be endogenous as perhaps being "squeezed" by the two (endogenous) items S and rT. We will revert to an explicit analysis of such expenditures in the next section below.

For simplicity of exposition and modeling, we can assume that all actions are taken in period 0 with respect to transport infrastructure determined by the government, and determination of the number of private vehicles by the private sector. The government determines its fuel subsidy level in period 1 and subsequent periods, sequentially. We however assume for simplicity that a steady-state level of S is found already in period 1 (but which may differ from the level in period 0). We can assume that S_0 has no impact on following periods' political and economic variables.

We can also assume that the sitting government derives utility from activities and events when being in power, but we do not specify its utility from outcomes occurring when not in power. One way to view this assumption is that the utility level is scaled such that out-of-power utility is set at zero.

The private sector determines the change in the vehicle stock, relative to the previous period, at the start of any given period, on basis of the levels of T and s in the current period (s being, in principle, variable over time):

$$N = N(T, s); N_T' < 0; N_s' > 0; N_{Ts}'' < 0. \tag{5.4}$$

We assume that the private sector acquires more additional motor vehicles when the fuel subsidy rate is higher; and that it acquires fewer vehicles when the quality of public transport is higher.[5] We can further assume that with more public transport, the marginal effect of greater fuel subsidies on the car stock falls. For simplicity, we can assume that cars are rented or leased, period by period, so there are no persistence or stock effects from a given car stock at the start of the period.

The government is assumed to (1) maximize its overall objective function with respect to its period 0 infrastructure decision, T, and (2) maximize its period-by-period utility with respect to the fuel subsidy rate s in periods 1, 2, ..., for as long as the government stays in power.

The latter decision must take account of the relationships (5.3), and $S = sN(s)$ determining the fiscal impact of the fuel subsidy. We assume no persistence effects on future period outcomes from a current fuel subsidy.

The maximization problem for T departs from the last expression in (5.1), which can be maximized directly with respect to T (and where we recognize that all periodic Φ values are affected in the same way by a given change in T in period 0). We first consider the effect on the probability of staying in power, due to improved transport infrastructure, given by

$$\frac{d\Phi}{dT} = \Phi_T + \Phi_N N_T > 0. \tag{5.5}$$

Two components affect the reelection probability in response to improved public transport infrastructure investments: there is a direct, positive political effect, but also an indirect effect on voting as the number of motorists on the road is assumed to be also affected by T. This latter effect may be positive or negative, depending on the nature of the infrastructure investment. First, the derivative Φ_N can be positive or negative, depending on whether the government, overall at the outset, is considered "friendly" or "less friendly" to drivers. This derivative is more likely to be positive than otherwise when T is road investment; although this depends on this government's voter reputations. Second, N_T can be positive or negative: it is much more likely positive when T is road investments, and likely negative when T is public transport investments. Overall, in cases of both road and public transport investments, the last main term in (5.5) is likely positive: in the former case, both factors are positive, and in the latter case, they are negative. We can thus rather safely assume that the overall effect of better transport infrastructure on the probability of reelection is positive.

The condition for optimal infrastructure investment T in period 0 is

$$\frac{dEW_0}{dT} = -\frac{1}{1-\delta\Phi} rH'(B) + \frac{\delta\Phi}{1-\delta\Phi} \{U_T - eV_T - (eV_N + qC_N)N_T\}$$
$$+ \left(\frac{1}{1-\delta\Phi}\right)^2 (\Phi_T + \Phi_N N_T)\delta Z = 0. \tag{5.6}$$

To interpret this condition, it is useful to write it on the following alternative form:

$$H'(B) = \frac{\delta\Phi}{r}\left\{U_T - eV_T - (eV_N + qC_N)N_T + \frac{Z}{1-\delta\Phi}\left(\frac{El_T(\Phi)}{T} + \frac{El_N(\Phi)}{N}N_T\right)\right\}.$$

(5.6a)

The El terms represent elasticities of the Φ function with respect to the specified arguments. The term on the left-hand side expresses the marginal utility cost to the politician of the infrastructure investment in period 0, evaluated at the equilibrium level of the budget surplus, B. This means that the effective marginal cost is inversely related to B. In particular, when B is highly negative, the marginal value to this government of budget improvements is likely to be high.

This term is at the optimum for the government set equal to the marginal benefits of transport infrastructure investments, represented by the two other main terms. Note that a (notional) cost rT is assumed to be incurred by the politician each period for as long as the politician stays in office, but no longer (as the politician then no longer is "responsible for" this cost).

The first of the two major terms on the right-hand side of (5.6a) expresses the "direct marginal utility value" for the government from having a higher level of transport infrastructure for as long at the politician stays in power.[6] Since $V_T < 0$, both the two first utility elements going into this term are positive. The last element is typically positive when T represents public transport investment (as both V_N and C_N are positive, and in this case $N_T < 0$), but negative when T represents investment in roads, as the number of cars is then likely to increase, which leads to greater congestion and carbon emissions. Overall, the main bracket is positive when T is public transport investments but more ambiguous when T is road investments.

The second main term expresses "political" impacts of increased transport infrastructure investment, via changes in future reelection probabilities when infrastructure is improved by the current government. This term tends to be large when $1/(1 - \delta\Phi)$ is large and thus $\delta\Phi$ large (current politicians put a lot of weight on future periods relative to the current investment period, when the discount factor δ is close to unity, and the reelection probability Φ is also high); and when Φ_T is large (a large effect from transport infrastructure on the probability of reelection of the politician, now and in future periods). The latter should be large when T is public transport and voters care a lot about this, which is more likely when few initially have cars (greater T then also discourages car ownership). The last term depends on the sign of

Φ_N that is determined by the propensity of voting for this politician when the number of car owners increases. It is likely positive (negative) when the current government is viewed as positive (negative) to the demands of car owners (including e g currently subsidizing fuels). N_T is likely positive (negative) when T is "mainly" road (public transport) infrastructure. Both the second and third main terms are likely to be negative functions of T. Factors that tend to make each of the terms large for any given T, would also tend to make T large.

We next derive the optimal fuel subsidy rate s. Considering "starting" from period 1 (or assuming that the country is now already in period 1, and the politician is in power, when setting energy subsidies), we define the following discounted expected utility function:

$$EW_1 = G + U(T, s_1) - eV(T, N(s_1), s_1) - qC(N(s_1), s_1) + H(B_1(s_1))$$
$$+ [\delta\Phi(T, s, N)]Z_2 + [\delta\Phi(T, s, N)]^2 Z_3 + \ldots = Z_1 + \frac{\delta\Phi(2)}{1 - \delta\Phi(2)} Z_2, \tag{5.7}$$

where again at a steady state, Z_t (the periodic utility of a sitting government) is for simplicity assumed to be constant through time, and maximized period by period (= Z_2 for all $t = 2, 3, \ldots$) Thus in period 1, Z_1 is maximized taking Z in future periods (with its stationary value denoted by Z_2) as given, thus prompting the last formulation in (5.7). $\Phi(i)$ is shorthand for the probability of political survival, for one more period, being currently in period i. The point here is that setting s_1 in period 1 affects $\Phi(1)$ and Z_1, but no other variables directly as there are no political persistence effects of a given policy beyond the next following period (it is, however, rationally assumed that setting s_i in other periods will then affect Z_i similarly). Let us define

$$\frac{d\Phi}{ds} = \Phi_s' + \Phi_N' N'(s), \qquad \Phi_s' > 0, N'(s) > 0. \tag{5.8}$$

The sign of Φ_N' is here as before indeterminate, but we may reasonably assume that (5.6) is positive. We now find

$$\frac{dEW_1}{ds_1} = \frac{dZ_1}{ds_1} + \frac{1}{\Phi} \frac{1}{1 - \delta\Phi(2)} \frac{d\Phi}{ds} Z_2$$
$$= \{U_s - e(V_s + V_N N_s) - q(C_N N_s + C_s) - H'(B)(sN_s + N)\}$$
$$+ \frac{1}{\Phi} \frac{1}{1 - \delta\Phi} (\Phi_s + \Phi_N N_s) Z_2 = 0, \tag{5.9}$$

where we have dropped subscripts to Φ, as it has a common value in steady state. Also at a steady state, $Z_1 = Z_2$. The first main term on the right-hand side expresses effects via changes in politicians' utility function in period 1. This main term must be negative in equilibrium (so that the first, positive, element is overtaken by the other, negative, elements). The second main term expresses effects via changes in period 1 probability of staying in power. Only the latter expresses "persistent" effects (for periods beyond the first). This term is positive, at least as long as "populist" factors are at play.

Consider the effect of concern for a budget balance, represented by $H'(B)$, which is higher as the concern gets greater. A higher budget concern contributes to a less positive (or more negative right-hand side expression in (5.9), thus reducing the subsidy (e.g., reduction drives H' down).

To interpret (5.9), we may write it alternatively as

$$H'(B)\frac{dS}{ds} = \{U_s - e[V_s + V_N N'(s)] - q[C_N N'(s) + C_s]\}$$

$$+ \frac{Z_2}{1-\delta\Phi}\left(\frac{El_s(\Phi)}{s} + \frac{El_N(\Phi)}{N}N_s\right) \qquad (5.9a)$$

$$= \frac{dZ_{-S}}{ds} + \frac{Z_2}{1-\delta\Phi}\left(\frac{El_s(\Phi)}{s} + \frac{El_N(\Phi)}{N}N_s\right).$$

The left-hand side can be considered as the marginal cost of fuel subsidies, and the right-hand side the overall marginal gain from paying additional subsidies. dZ_{-S}/ds denotes any change in politicians' immediate welfare from increased s, when ignoring the direct subsidy cost (moved to the left-hand side). dZ_{-S}/ds could be positive or negative. It tends to be negative for a "responsible" government that appropriately considers both inefficiency costs and excessive carbon costs of fuel subsidies. It can be positive when the direct utility to politicians from own or associates' fuel consumption is high, more likely for a nonrepresentative government or one with a smaller tightly knit selectorate. Less ambiguously, dZ_{-S}/ds decreases in s.

The second main term on the right-hand side expresses gains due to higher likelihood of staying in power in the current period as a result of higher fuel subsidies today. There is no effect of changes in s_1 on the probability of staying in power in future periods, as s is set period by period and there are no political persistence effects. There are still effects on future periods, since a higher probability of staying in power now makes it more likely to enjoy power in the future. Also this main term is likely to be a decreasing function of s.

Based on the discussion above, the factors that contribute to a high level of fuel subsidy can be identified as follows:

1. *N low*   The right-hand side of (5.9a) is then high. The fiscal cost of subsidizing gasoline is small when relatively few people have cars. This effect is, however, countered by the fact that $d\Phi/ds$ is likely to be small when N is small (so that few voters are affected by the gasoline subsidy; see point 3). This leaves this factor overall somewhat uncertain, although lower emphasis on points 1 and 3 may make point 2 dominate more.

2. *dZ_s/ds high at "moderate" s levels*   The sitting government might raise the current utility level to a high level when paying out subsidies, since there is usually little emphasis among politicians on the moderating factors (which are inefficiencies caused by subsidies; and excess carbon emissions). However, this derivative could easily be negative for all values of s, thus contributing to less fuel subsidy when factors 1 and 3 are small (as when N is small).

3. *$d\Phi/ds$ high at "moderate" s levels*   A large political gain from additional fuel subsidies could be effected where the selectorate is small, or election outcomes depend heavily on targeting groups sensitive to fuel subsidies.

4. *$U'(H)$ is small at "moderate" s levels*   There is then little concern for additional budget deficits caused by fuel subsidies (either because such deficits are quite small or the government does not choose to worry much about them).

5.3   Endogenizing Additional Public-Good Supplies

The model studied so far ignores effects of growth on future reelection probabilities. It can often be relevant to assume that such effects are present. A recent study by   Mundaca (2015) shows the impacts of imposing additional fiscal energy costs (energy subsidy removal, or energy taxes) on growth. She finds strong such effects for the Middle East and North Africa (MENA) region of the World Bank (where the level of energy subsidies tends to be high). A comparator study for the Europe and Central Asia (ECA) region, where energy taxes are more prevalent, finds that imposing additional fiscal energy costs may by contrast be harmful to growth.

Consider a simple extension of the model above that considers growth effects on a country that at the outset subsidizes fossil energy.

Assume that the government in question is "more active" in its determination of resources on current expenditures on a range of public goods, P, to attract voters, and that may also affect growth, at least in the long run. We may here think of services such as education and health that are likely to have growth-enhancing effects in the long run but that may still be discouraged when a government takes mainly short-run positions. We assume that P does not require any up-front investments.

Assume that P enters into the government's decision process in four ways:

1. As expenditure for the sitting government, via (5.3a).
2. As a potential utility element for government, entering into the utility function U (where it may also represent altruistic valuation of the effect on the general public).
3. By affecting the voting propensity of voters who may be swayed by these expenditures.
4. By affecting the rate of growth of the economy. Considering, in particular, P as educational expenditures, these are likely to raise the productive capacity of workers over time. This effect could be small, but it could also be sizable down the line.

These four pathways for effects are reflected in the following new formulation of the government's utility function:

$$
\begin{aligned}
EW_1 &= G + U(T,P,s) - eV(T,N,s) - qC(N,s) + H(B) \\
&\quad + (1+g(P_1))\delta\Phi Z_2 + (1+g(P_1))(1+g)\delta^2\Phi^3 Z_3 + \dots \\
&= +Z_1 + (1+g(P_1))\delta\Phi Z + (1+g(P_1))\frac{(1+g)\delta^2\Phi^2}{1-\delta(1+g)\Phi} Z.
\end{aligned}
\tag{5.10}
$$

Here we start from period 1 as there are no up-front investments to consider in period 0. The right-hand side of (5.10) indicates that P_1 works via four channels in this case:

1. By affecting the immediate reelection probability Φ. This has repercussion effects by affecting the level of the absolute value function also from period 2 on.
2. By affecting the level of Z_1 through its effect on U.
3. By affecting Z_1 through its effect on $H(B_1)$, the government budget balance in period 1.

4. By affecting the growth rate from period 1 to period 2 (thus appearing in period 2); this also has repercussion effects in the same way as factor 1.

Factors 1, 2, and 4 are positive while 3 (the public sector cost of the service evaluated at the current budget balance) is negative. The main effects of T and s should here be little impacted by introducing P. We, however, get an additional first-order condition with respect to P, as follows (where we need to explicitly consider only P_1, as decisions regarding P are sequential):

$$\frac{dEW_1}{dP_1} = \frac{1}{\Phi}\frac{\Phi_P}{1-(1+g)\delta\Phi}Z + g_P\frac{1}{\Phi}\frac{\delta\Phi^2}{1-(1+g)\delta\Phi}Z + U_P - H'(B) = 0. \qquad (5.11)$$

Effects on policy enter only as perceived by politicians; this also applies to the effect on growth, although with rational expectations g would correspond to its true expected value. Politicians may, however, be imperfectly informed about these effects. In particular, when considering a utility-maximizing, non-altruistic politician whose U_P may be close to zero, and perceives no effect on growth ($g_P = 0$), the only concern will be the effect on reelection (the first term in equation 5.9) against the fiscal cost (the last term). Such a politician who may also feel a budget squeeze (high H'), and little immediate political benefit from these types of public-goods supply (Φ_P small), may tend to opt for a low level of P.

Let us now consider, more formally, factors that might contribute to making P high, in the context of this model. For this purpose we rewrite (5.9) as follows:

$$H'(B) = U_P + \left\{\frac{El_P(\Phi)}{P_1} + g_P\delta\Phi\right\}\frac{Z}{1-(1+g)\delta\Phi}. \qquad (5.11a)$$

$H'(B)$ here indicates the immediate marginal budgetary cost of P_1. The terms on the right-hand side represent marginal benefits of increasing P_1. There are three such benefits (represented by the three terms):

1. The immediate utility to politicians (or the public when this factor reflects politicians' altruistic concerns).
2. The impact of P_1 on the immediate reelection probability. This has further effects in subsequent periods by increasing the probability of further staying in power.

3. Effects via the increased growth rate induced by higher P_1. In our model this effect works in the way that positive growth effects, induced by growth-enhancing policies, are favorable by their own to politicians, by increasing the overall value of politicians' benefits for all periods over which that politician is reelected (but, we assume, not for other periods). We see that this effect becomes small if δ (politicians' subjective discount factor) and/or Φ (the equilibrium reelection probability in any future period) are small.

5.4   Impacts of Corruption

Corrupt activity can be modeled in several ways in the context of this model. I will here consider a simple case where bribes can be paid to government officials in charge of energy pricing, in return for setting energy prices low. It then seems relevant to assume that a more "focused" group of recipients or beneficiaries of energy subsidies makes such bribes more viable.

I further assume that corruption can be risky for politicians. One way to model this is to assume that corruption, once discovered, can lead to the overthrow or ousting of power of the respective corrupt politician. I am particularly interested in studying how the benefits from corruption can depend on parameters such as the fraction of the public that own cars. To incorporate these effects, consider the following simpler version of the government budget balance:

$$B_t = R_t - rT_0 - Ns_t - P_t. \tag{5.3a}$$

Now, for simplicity, assume that the fraction of households that have vehicles, N, is exogenous. This fraction could still be important in determining the level of corruption. Call the level of bribes Y, while the probability that a politician gets caught in the following period as a consequence of receiving bribes, is called σ. Assume that the politician's utility function can thus be rewritten as

$$\begin{aligned}
EW_1 &= G + \lambda Y(N, s_1) + U(T, s_1) - eV(T, N, s_1) - qC(N, s_1) - H(B_1(s_1)) \\
&\quad + (1 - \sigma(Y; Y_M))\{[\delta\Phi(T, s, N]Z_2 + [\delta\Phi(T, s, N)]^2 Z_3 + \ldots\} \\
&= Z_1 + (1 - \sigma)\frac{\delta\Phi(2)}{1 - \delta\Phi(2)} Z_2.
\end{aligned} \tag{5.12}$$

Again, Z_t is assumed constant for all $t = 2, 3, \ldots$. Then, for simplicity, take the magnitude of bribes paid to be an exogenous function $Y(N, s)$ of the number of car owners, N, and the fuel subsidy rate, s. Lambda is here a scaling parameter that makes it possible to compare bribes to budget allocations. Thus, if $\lambda > 1$, a politician is more occupied with bribes than with budgetary improvements. For corrupt politicians, we could have λ orders of magnitude greater than unity, and for noncorrupt politicians, λ could be close to zero (or = 0 in the limit for a politician that is completely averse to corruption).

In the current period (period 1) bribes will here affect (increase) the politician's utility only by raising Z_1 accordingly. For future periods, bribe taking has two effects: future values of Z (here, for simplicity, represented by a stationary future value Z_2) are increased accordingly for as long as the politician stays in office. But there is an offsetting effect from the fact that bribing may be (successfully) reported and the politician prosecuted as a result, σ; in this case the politician, by assumption, forfeits his or her bribes.

The parameter σ is a function of two magnitudes: it increases in the amount of bribes received by this politician, Y, and decreases in the average amount of bribes successfully received by all politicians in the economy, Y_M. When all bribers and all politicians behave identically, $Y_M = (1 - \sigma)Y$. Then the equilibrium effect of simultaneous changes in bribing propensities is given by (with subscript S denoting simultaneous changes in the overall equilibrium bribing levels)

$$\left(\frac{d\sigma}{dY} \right)_S = \frac{\sigma_Y}{1 + \sigma_{YM}Y}, \tag{5.13}$$

where all general equilibrium effects are taken into consideration, and $\sigma_Y > 0$ and $\sigma_{YM} < 0$ denote partial derivatives. The effect on the probability that a given politician is indicted after discovered to having received bribes, σ_Y, is assumed to be a negative function of average bribing, Y_M. Thus

$$\left(\frac{d\sigma}{dY} \right)_I = \sigma_Y(Y; Y_M). \tag{5.14}$$

When optimizing (5.10a), any given politician will view Y_M as exogenously given and only consider Y to be variable, and given as function of (here, the exogenous) N and (the endogenous) s. In this case

$$\frac{dEW_1}{ds_1} = \frac{d(Z_1 - Y_1)}{ds_1} + \lambda Y_s + \frac{1}{1 - \delta\Phi}\left[\frac{1}{\Phi}(\Phi_s + \Phi_N N_s) - \sigma_Y Y_s \delta\Phi\right]Z_2 = 0, \quad (5.15)$$

where $Z_1 - Y_1$ denotes period 1 nonbribe income (equivalent to the politician's period 1 utility in equation 5.7). There are two new terms relative to (5.9), namely λY_s (the value of additional bribes paid to the politician resulting from higher fuel subsidies) and the last term in the square bracket (the discounted utility loss due to the increased probability of being fired when bribes are increased). The additional concerns, raised by the possibility of corruption, thus imply that these two terms are traded off against each other.

There are here several mechanisms by which the fuel subsidy rate can be affected by the possibility of, or actual, bribing, considered in turn:

1. Value of lambda (the marginal utility value of bribes to the politician from receiving them). A higher lambda raises the marginal value to the politician of paying fuel subsidies. Thus s_1 increases.
2. Fuel subsidy increase. A given increase in fuel subsidies is rewarded more in terms of bribes, so that Y_s increases (independent of N). This has two offsetting effects on the subsidy rate: a positive effect via an increased amount of bribes received and a negative effect via an increased probability that the politician is removed due to corruption.
3. Higher N (more households have cars). This affects bribing revenue as the marginal value of s in terms of Y increases. But there are two offsetting factors: the budget cost (the negative of B) increases, which works in the opposite direction, and the fact that higher N tends to increase the detection probability σ for given subsidy rate. The overall effect on corruption is unclear. Nevertheless, this effect is generally less conducive to bribe taking, as compared to a pure increase in Y_s (as under point 2), due to the moderating effect via the negative budget balance (resulting from more households that are car owners and must be subsidized).
4. Higher than average bribing and corruption in society, Y_N. I assume that more bribing by a particular politician leads to a reduced marginal effect of more bribing in the detection probability, so σ_Y is reduced.

There could further be added anticipated effects of higher infrastructure investment T in period 0, on incentives for corruption. A greater T would, however, change little in the model except the budget balance

B (interest payments on the associated loan are assumed to be paid in perpetuity); otherwise, the current utility of government is increased, and reelection probabilities are correspondingly increased. While *T* is not explicitly modeled, it is easy to think that increased *T* may increase the public's value of the transport infrastructure, and of their cars, and thereby increase the incentives of the public (possibly represented by their lobbyists) to bribe politicians into providing more fuel subsidies. (Note that motor fuel subsidies are worthless where there are no roads, but have high value to motorists where a road system exists.) Politicians' revenues from receiving bribes may allow us to extend our current model to more complex case where improvements in the transport infrastructure are made gradually over time, and possibly influenced by bribe taking.[7]

5.5 Concluding Remarks

This chapter presented a very stylized model of government behavior focusing on its propensity to subsidize motor fuel. The model used extended the analysis in Strand (2013) and served principally as a basis for follow-up empirical work on political determinants of fuel subsidies as introduced in Beers and Strand (2013). The objective of the analysis is to provide as a guide for empirical applications as well as a guide as to the choice of variables in a political-economy analyses of energy subsidies.

The basic message concerns trade-offs between the short and the long run. The long run is here represented by factors that affect politicians' reelection probabilities over time, mainly through the permanent welfare impacts of investments in transport infrastructure in the initial period (but with no additional such investments in subsequent periods), and the returns from such investments. Indeed, increased government emphasis on long-term transport infrastructure investment is often warranted for efficiency reasons but is discouraged as government leaders take short-sighted views owing to a combination of high discounting and low reengagement probabilities. Bids to improve infrastructure do often tempt politicians to take bribes, as fuel subsidies become more valuable to vehicle owners. Overall, however, politicians tend to be welfare enhancing.

Nevertheless, the nature of corruption is that "corruption may breed corruption," as is well documented in the literature (e.g., by Shleifer and Vishny 1993). Moreover rates at which corruption is punished (corrupt politicians are prosecuted) may be negatively related to overall corruption and bribing rates. This is not a new idea, but multiple "bribing equilibria" (e.g., no bribing in some instances with positive or incessant bribe taking in other instances) can easily make fuel subsides the target of corrupt politicians.

Some of the main conclusions from my analysis are listed in table 5.1. The left-hand column contains all the key variables that influence the outcome of the model, and presumably the real world, for a number of hypothetical cases. Chances are that when politicians gain personally from fuel subsidies, their reelection prospects are improved, and when politicians are myopic, the result is higher fuel subsidy rates. The impact of a large fraction of the public having cars is ambiguous: in a democracy, it tends to raise subsidies (as a wide electorate gains from the subsidies), but under autocracy, it can reduce the subsides (as the political base then is narrowed; the main effect of many cars in the road is then that the fiscal cost of subsidies is high). The reduction of subsidies tends to discourage corruption, but more corruption tends to spur subsidy growth, in particular, due to politicians' short-sightedness. The table also indicates impacts on infrastructure investments and budget balance; with unsurprising results.

Table 5.1
Overview of some important impacts of model assumptions on key variables

Key variable or model variant	Effect in fuel subsidies	Effect in infrastructure investment	Effect on budget balance
Many have cars	Negative in autocracy Positive in democracy	Negative	Ambiguous
Politicians gain personally from subsidies	Higher	Neutral	Negative
Subsidies positive for politicians' reelection	Higher	Lower	Negative
Politicians have small budget concern	Higher	Higher	Negative
Politicians are myopic	Higher	Lower	Negative
Growth effect added to basic model	Reduced	Higher	Negative early, but positive later
Corruption added to basic model	Mostly higher	Mostly lower	Negative

Appendix: Symbols Used in the Chapter

EW_t = discounted utility of government starting in period t
T = collective transport investment in period 0
N = number of private vehicles, number between 0 and 1 (= fraction of the public that has cars)
s = fuel subsidy rate
S = total fuel subsidies amount = $sN(s)$, where $N'(s) > 0$
B = budget surplus
$H(B)$ = utility to sitting government from current budget surplus
C = carbon emissions per period
G = (gross) utility to sitting government officials, due to being in power
Z = net flow utility to the sitting government
U = utility to government officials from transport infrastructure and fuel subsidies (may incorporate fully or partly the utility to the general public)
V = marginal externality cost in private transport in the country
q = carbon price
e = subjective disutility to government, related to the economic costs resulting from subsidizing fuels, valued from 0 (disinterested government) to 1 (fully internalizing fuel externalities)
Φ = probability that the government remains in power until the next period
δ = discount factor of government
r = interest rate facing government
P = government current spending on other public goods
Y = bribes paid to politicians in return for setting low energy prices.
Y_M = average bribe taking level of politicians in the country
σ = probability that a politician gets caught and is fired as a result of receiving bribes
λ = marginal utility of bribe money for politicians

Notes

1. Car stock data have been subject to serious empirical scrutiny in previous research. See, for example, Dargay (1991, 2001, 2002), Fridstrøm (1998), Lescaroux and Rech (2008), Medlock (2002), who focus on high-income countries, and Dargay et al. (2007) and Storchmann (2005), who include lower income countries.

2. For a more precise definition, and discussion of the concept of a selectorate, see Gelbach and Keefer (2011), and Keefer and Vlaicu (2008).

3. See also the appendix for a list of symbols used in the chapter.

4. We assume, for simplicity, that even when some principal needs to be serviced, payments are required forever (or as a minimum for the length of the incumbency of the current government).

5. This effect can also go the other way, as better public transport is likely to reduce motorists' externality costs of driving (i.e., less congestion). This effect may, in principle, spur the demand for cars.

6. We assume that politicians care about such utilities, even private ones, only as long as they stay in office.

7. There is, of course, a further issue of corruption occurring in infrastructure contract procurement, which is not pursued further here.

References

Beers, Cees v., and Jon Strand. 2013. Political determinants of fossil fuel pricing. Policy Research Working Paper 6470. World Bank.

Coady, David, Ian Parry, Louis Sears, and Baoping Shang. 2015, How large are global energy subsidies? Working Paper 15/105. IMF.

Commander, Simon, 2011. The political economy of energy subsidies. Consultancy Report. World Bank.

Dargay, Joyce M. 1991. *The Irreversible Demand Effects of High Oil Prices Motor Fuels in France, Germany and the UK*. Oxford: Oxford Institute of Energy Studies.

Dargay, Joyce M. 2001. The effects of income on car ownership: Evidence of asymmetry. *Transportation Research* 35: 807–21.

Dargay, Joyce M. 2002. Determinants of car ownership in rural and urban areas: A pseudo-panel analysis. *Transportation Research* 38: 351–66.

Dargay, Joyce M., D. Gately, and M. Sommer. 2007. Vehicle ownership and income growth, worldwide, 1960–2030. *Energy Journal* 28 (4), 163–90.

Fredriksson, Per G., and Daniel L. Millimet. 2004. Comparative politics and environmental taxation. *Journal of Environmental Economics and Management* 48: 705–22.

Fridstrøm, Lasse. 1998. An econometric model of aggregate car ownership and road use. Presented at the 8th World Conference on Transport Research, Antwerp.

Gelbach, S., and P. Keefer. 2011. Investment without democracy: Ruling-party institutionalization and credible commitment in autocracies. *Journal of Comparative Economics* 39: 123–39.

Hammar, Henrik, Åsa Löfgren, and Thomas Sterner. 2004. Political economy obstacles to fuel taxation. *Energy Journal* 25: 1–17.

IMF. 2013. *Energy Subsidy Reform. Lessons and Implications*. Washington, DC: International Monetary Fund.

IMF. 2014. *Getting Energy Prices Right: From Principle to Practice*. Washington, DC: International Monetary Fund.

Keefer, Philip, and Rezvan Vlaicu. 2008. Democracy, credibility and clientism. *Journal of Law Economics and Organization* 24: 271–306.

Kojima, Masami, 2012a. *Petroleum Product Pricing and Complementary Policies: Experience from 65 Developing Countries since 2009.* Washington, DC: World Bank.

Kojima, Masami. 2012b. Oil price risks and pump price adjustments. Policy Research Working Paper 6227. World Bank.

Kojima, Masami, and Doug Koplow. 2015. Fossil fuel subsidies. Policy Research Working Paper 7220. World Bank.

Kotsogiannis, Christos. 2011. Determinants of fuel subsidies: A global study. Seminar presentation. DECEE.

Lescaroux, F., and O. Rech. 2008. The impact of automobile diffusion on the income elasticity of motor fuel demand. *Energy Journal*, 29: 41–60.

Medlock III, K. B. and R. Soligo. 2002. Car ownership and economic development with forecasts to the year 2015. *Journal of Transport Economics and Policy* 26: 163–88.

Mundaca, Gabriela. 2015. Energy subsidies, public investment, and endogenous growth. Unpublished paper. World Bank.

Shleifer, Andrei, and Robert W. Vishny. 1993. Corruption. *Quarterly Journal of Economics* 108: 599–617.

Storchmann, Karl. 2005. Long-run gasoline demand for passenger cars: The role of income distribution. *Energy Economics* 27: 25–58.

Strand, Jon. 2011. Political economy of fuel subsidies and their reform. Project Note. DECEE.

Strand, Jon. 2013. Political economy aspects of fuel subsidies: A conceptual framework. Policy Research Working Paper 6392. World Bank.

Vagliasindi, Maria. 2012 a. Implementing energy subsidy reforms: An overview of key issues. Policy Research Working Paper 6122. World Bank.

Vagliasindi, Maria. 2012 b. *Implementing Energy Subsidy Reforms. Evidence from Developing Countries.* Washington, DC: World Bank.

World Bank, 2010. Subsidies in the energy sector: An overview. Background paper for the WBG Energy Strategy.

6 Fuel-Price Subsidies and the Control of Corruption: A First Approach

Christos Kotsogiannis and Leonzio Rizzo

6.1 Introduction

Government fuel-price subsidies[1] (deviations of domestic actual prices from specified benchmark prices) are pervasive around the world to the extent that international organizations, such as the IMF, the World Bank, and the OECD, have called for their phasing out.[2]

In perfectly competitive markets, price subsidies misallocate resources, since actual prices deviate from marginal-cost pricing, thereby generating economic efficiency losses.[3] Price subsidies are also undesirable from a distributional perspective, since any desired redistribution can be achieved with more efficient instruments. They also have important spillover effects;[4] put a strain on public finances with detrimental effects on public sector debts;[5] and encourage socially wasteful activities, such as smuggling and black-market transactions. All this can exacerbate energy volatility, since market demand is not very responsive to international prices and, perversely, benefit the rich (as they are significant users of energy) far more than the poor.[6]

The inefficiencies due to fuel-price subsidies are widespread, but they have recently come to the fore[7] as countries realize that these are inefficient instruments to achieve the desired outcomes (a concern amplified by recent increases in food and energy prices and the ongoing economic crisis). But phasing out subsidies is an exceedingly difficult task (see OECD 2010; IMF 2013). The justification that is typically given for the existence of fuel-price subsidies is that this is the only instrument that can be used to alleviate energy poverty and provide a safety net for the poor. However, this is rarely the case, as the benefits typically accrue to middle- and high-income consumers, and poor households are unable to afford even subsidized energy.

So given that subsides are inefficient instruments what explains their prevalence? No doubt there are potentially complex considerations behind this question but intuition will also suggest—as subsidies tilt consumption, through a change in the relative price, towards the subsidized good—that there are important political economy considerations related to the "capture" (taken to mean, broadly, the political corruption in which private interest influence a state's decision-making process to their own benefit) of the state by interest groups.[8] It is this issue that this short paper aims to address.

Work on this issue is surprisingly limited, one of the reasons being the paucity of reliable data on fuel subsidies. To overcome this obstacle, this analysis focuses on gasoline (and diesel) prices and on the variable "corruption control,"[9] by which we attempt to comprise the "perceptions of the extent to which public power is exercised for private gain, including both petty and grand forms of corruption, as well as 'capture' of the state by elites and private interests" (Kaufmann et al. 2010: 4).[10]

6.2   Preliminary Analysis

Fuel-price subsidies are typically calculated by the price-gap method (see Kosmo 1987; Larsen and Shah 1992; Koplow 2004; Coady et al. 2010; Beers and Strand 2013). The price gap is obtained as the difference between a benchmark price and the actual fossil-fuel price paid at the pump.[11] We use as the benchmark the US average fuel pump price in US\$ cents per liter. For oil-importing countries, the subsidy is computed by subtracting the domestic price and taking into account the cost of shipping the fuel from the hub to the country and then further reducing the total amount by US\$0.10 (Beers and Strand 2013). For oil-exporting countries, the subsidy is computed as for the oil-importing countries but with an additional US\$0.10 per liter being subtracted to account for the internal distribution and retailing costs in the domestic market (Beers and Strand 2013).

These price gaps are identified as subsidies per liter of gasoline, or diesel, in US\$ cents and given by

$$PG^{imp} = P^{usa} - P^{dom} - 10 \qquad \text{(for importing countries),}$$
$$PG^{exp} = P^{usa} - P^{dom} - 20 \qquad \text{(for exporting countries),}$$

where PG^{imp} is the price gap for net energy-importing countries, PG^{exp} is the price gap for net energy-exporting countries, P^{usa} is the retail pump price of a unit of energy in the US market, and P^{dom} is the retail pump price of a unit of energy in the domestic market.

Figure 6.1 plots the average diesel price against the (average) control of corruption (a variable that takes values between 0 and 100, with higher values indicating higher control for corruption) over a period of 12 years. With the median value for control of corruption being 50.49, what figure 6.1 shows is that countries above the median value have higher, on average, diesel prices than the countries that are below the median value. Yet, interestingly, countries below and above the median differ in the diesel-price responsiveness (to a change in the control of corruption): with countries above the median having a diesel-price response higher to the countries below the median.

The same picture emerges when we plot gasoline prices against control of corruption. What figures 6.1 and 6.2 therefore reveal is that fuel prices (diesel and gasoline) are much more sensitive to the change in the control of corruption when the control of corruption level is already relatively high.

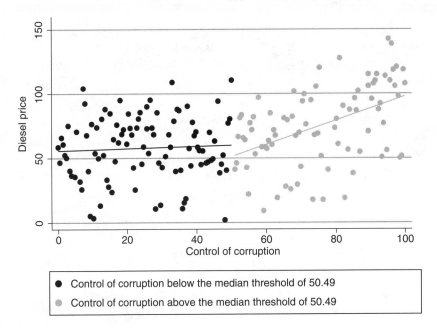

Figure 6.1
Diesel price and control of corruption. Both diesel price and control of corruption are averaged over 1991, 1992, 1995, 1998, 2000, and 2002–2008.

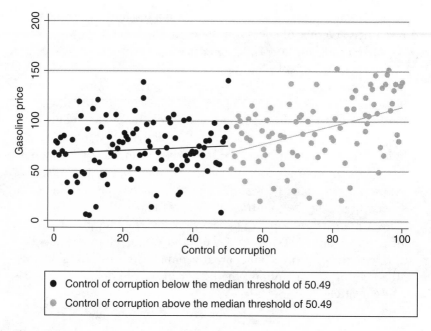

Figure 6.2
Gasoline prices and control of corruption. Both gasoline price and control of corruption
are averaged over 1991, 1992, 1995, 1998, 2000, and 2002–2008

What this seems to be pointing to is that the use of a subsidy for
political gain becomes less effective when there is already in place
significant control of corruption (taken here to mean—as noted at the
outset—the control of capture of the state by interest groups). Thus, if
this hypothesis is valid, the relationship between fuel prices and the
level of control of corruption is nonlinear and depends on the initial
control of corruption.

6.3 Empirical Analysis

To test for the impact of corruption control on fuel prices and/or subsidies, we estimate a reduced form equation of fuel subsidies by using
a panel dataset for the years 1991, 1992, 1995, 1998, 2000, and 2002–
2008. Summary statistics are reported in the appendix A, table 6A.1,
while data description and data sources of the variables are reported
in the appendix B.

The analysis considers the following specification:

$$s_{jt} = \varphi_t + \gamma\theta_{jt} + \rho\theta_{jt}n_{jt} + \delta n_{jt} + \beta'X_{jt} + \epsilon_{jt},$$ (6.1)

where s_{jt} is the subsidy rate and j and t are, respectively, country and time indicators; φ_t is a year effect; θ_{jt} is the variable control of corruption that takes values from 0 to 100, and reflects the degree to which citizens in country j are aware of the corruption level of their own country[12]; n_{jt} is a dummy equal to 1 when the variable θ_{jt} is above its median; X_{jt} is a vector of state-specific time-varying regressors; and is a mean zero, normally distributed random error.

Candidates for inclusion in X are variables that affect the level of subsidies. Drawing on the literature (see Beers and Strand 2013), we include both economic and demographic variables, such as population, per-capita income, and per-capita land. We also control for a terms-of-trade effect (capturing the possibility that importers of fuel have the incentive to reduce demand of fuel by reducing the subsidy rate) by using the net supply of fuel (production minus consumption) and a general openness measure (exports plus imports of goods as quota of GDP). The specification further allows for a measure of road gasoline consumption when we estimate the gasoline subsidy and road diesel consumption when we estimate the diesel subsidy. To address potential endogeneity issues, these variables are introduced with a one-year lag.

In a reduced form equation, the fuel subsidy is normally linked to the population size, as this variable influences the use of fuel. Moreover the level of income can influence the level of subsidies (since subsidies can be used as a redistributive device), and an oil-exporting (oil-importing) country has the incentive to raise (reduce) the international price of oil. Also the difference between total exports and imports can affect the fuel subsidies, as it is also the case for road gasoline/diesel consumption (the higher gasoline/diesel consumption is the more effective a subsidy on a consumption unit will be). Last, the size of a country can affect the level of the subsidy, as the larger the size of the country, the higher is the need to travel and the higher is the consumption of fuel, and thus the benefit from subsidies.

Changes in the macroeconomic or in the legal and institutional environment can likewise affect the countries' fiscal position, and therefore ability to provide subsidies. To account for this in the estimation, we include a set of time dummies.

6.4   Results

We regress gasoline subsidies against *control of corruption* using a
random effect model.[13] All regressions reported control for year effects.
We estimate both for diesel and gasoline subsidies the impact of *control
of corruption* by using the subsidy definition provided in section 6.2.
Consistent with the discussion at the outset, an increase in the *control
of corruption* decreases subsidies. In fact the coefficient *control of corruption* (table 6.1 columns 2 and 5) is negative both for diesel (–0.426) and
gasoline (–0.565), and significant at 1 percent level.

We then control, as indicated in table 6.1, columns 3 and 6, for a
dummy (n_{jt}) equal to 1 if the variable *control of corruption* is above its
median and interact the dummy with the variable *control of corruption*
($n_{jt} * \theta_{jt}$). The coefficient (P) of this interaction for diesel subsidy is
–0.576 and significant at the 5 percent level (column 3). The coefficient
(γ) of the variable *control of corruption* that is not interacted is –0.216
(column 3), but not statistically significant. What this suggests is that
an increase in the control of corruption is effective in decreasing the
diesel subsidy only if the initial control of corruption is above the
median level. Interestingly, the impact on the diesel subsidy of increasing the control of corruption is almost three times the one emerging
when the starting level of the control of corruption is below the median;
the same results hold for the gasoline subsidy (column 6). It is worth
noting that if prices are used as the dependent variable, the results do
not change—only the signs change (table 6.2).

For example, in a country with a *control of corruption* equal to
40 (a value below the median), the impact on the diesel subsidy (column
3, table 6.1) of a unit increase in the *control of corruption* is –0.216
– 0.576 * 0 = –0.216, but not significant; the same happens for the gasoline subsidy (column 6, table 6.1) whose coefficient is –0.247 –0.990 * 0
= –0.247, significant at 5 percent level.

Take now a country whose *control of corruption* is, for example, 70
(and above the median). Then the impact on the diesel subsidy (column
3, table 6.1) of a unit increase in the control of corruption is –0.216 –
0.576 * 1 = –0.792, which is significant at 1 percent level, and so strongly
negatively affects the diesel subsidy; the same happens for gasoline
(column 6, table 6.1) whose coefficient would be –0.247 – 0.990 * 1
= –1.237, which is also significant at 1 percent level and so strongly
negatively affects the gasoline subsidy.

Table 6.1
Random effects regressions of diesel and gasoline subsidies

Variables	Diesel subsidy			Gasoline subsidy		
	(1)	(2)	(3)	(4)	(5)	(6)
Control of corruption		-0.426*** (0.112)	-0.216 (0.132)		-0.565*** (0.116)	-0.247** (0.122)
Control of corruption * Dummy control of corruption			-0.576** (0.287)			-0.990*** (0.260)
Dummy control of corruption (= 1 if control of corruption above median)			27.209* (15.996)			50.053*** (14.573)
10^{-5} * Population	0.031*** (0.012)	0.032*** (0.011)	0.028** (0.011)	0.033** (0.013)	0.033*** (0.010)	0.027** (0.010)
US deflator – Domestic deflator	-0.099 (0.067)	-0.223*** (0.078)	-0.239*** (0.077)	0.032 (0.065)	-0.093 (0.073)	-0.108 (0.072)
Lag 10^{-2} * GDPPPP/ Population	-0.750** (0.353)	-0.171 (0.403)	0.053 (0.423)	-1.156*** (0.338)	-0.653* (0.354)	-0.428 (0.346)
10^{-2} * (Lag of oil supply – Oil consumption)	0.309 (0.276)	0.244 (0.265)	0.191 (0.253)	0.468** (0.231)	0.385** (0.172)	0.301** (0.136)
10^2 * Area/ Population	0.009 (0.014)	0.027* (0.014)	0.032* (0.017)	0.007 (0.024)	0.020 (0.023)	0.025 (0.020)
(Exports + Imports)/GDP	0.098*** (0.031)	0.125*** (0.034)	0.134*** (0.033)	0.095** (0.042)	0.121*** (0.044)	0.135*** (0.044)
Lag of road diesel/ Gasoline fuel consumption per million inhabitants	0.001 (0.008)	-0.001 (0.010)	-0.003 (0.010)	0.064*** (0.018)	0.081*** (0.019)	0.091*** (0.020)
Constant	-31.479*** (4.980)	-24.601*** (5.149)	-31.392*** (5.979)	-61.333*** (5.629)	-49.299*** (6.201)	-60.085*** (6.546)
Observations	1,206	1,086	1,086	1,219	1,098	1,098
R-squared within	0.145	0.166	0.168	0.200	0.228	0.235

Note: Robust standard errors are shown in parentheses; ***significant at 1 percent; **significant at 5 percent; *significant at 10 percent.

Table 6.2
Random effects regressions of diesel and gasoline prices

Variables	Diesel price			Gasoline price		
	(1)	(2)	(3)	(4)	(5)	(6)
Control of corruption		0.444*** (0.108)	0.260** (0.124)		0.588*** (0.113)	0.292** (0.115)
Dummy control of corruption (= 1 if control of corruption above median)			-23.786 (15.793)			-47.495*** (14.616)
Control of corruption * Dummy control of corruption			0.508* (0.281)			0.938*** (0.260)
10^{-5} * Population	-0.032** (0.013)	-0.033*** (0.012)	-0.029** (0.012)	-0.034** (0.014)	-0.034*** (0.011)	-0.028** (0.011)
Domestic deflator	-0.084 (0.064)	-0.202*** (0.074)	-0.216*** (0.073)	0.048 (0.062)	-0.069 (0.069)	-0.083 (0.069)
Lag 10^{-2} * GDPPPP/ Population	0.732** (0.362)	0.148 (0.410)	-0.047 (0.431)	1.125*** (0.331)	0.635* (0.347)	0.427 (0.339)
10^{-2} * (Lag of oil supply − Oil consumption)	-0.380 (0.294)	-0.319 (0.280)	-0.272 (0.270)	-0.543** (0.250)	-0.467** (0.184)	-0.387** (0.151)
10^{2} * Area/ Population	-0.013 (0.014)	-0.035** (0.016)	-0.039** (0.018)	-0.011 (0.024)	-0.026 (0.022)	-0.031 (0.020)
(Exports + Imports)/GDP	-0.100*** (0.032)	-0.125*** (0.035)	-0.133*** (0.035)	-0.097** (0.042)	-0.120*** (0.045)	-0.135*** (0.045)
Lag of road diesel/ Gasoline fuel consumption per million inhabitants	-0.001 (0.009)	0.001 (0.010)	-0.003 (0.010)	-0.066*** (0.018)	-0.084*** (0.020)	-0.095*** (0.021)
Constant	108.668*** (9.523)	113.387*** (10.085)	120.791*** (10.661)	102.875*** (9.733)	102.034*** (10.589)	113.578*** (10.935)
Observations	1,206	1,086	1,086	1,219	1,098	1,098
R-squared within	0.650	0.650	0.651	0.582	0.586	0.589

Note: Robust standard errors are shown in parentheses; ***significant at 1 percent; **significant at 5 percent; *significant at 10 percent.

6.5   Robustness Check

We explore further by investigating whether it is the income level of countries that drives the results. To do so, we classify—using the World Bank classification—countries into low-income, lower middle-income, upper middle-income, and high-income countries. We then pull together the two high-income classes and the two low-income classes and split the sample in low- and high-income countries (table 6.3). The former contains 548 observations, with the average per-capita income being US$1,277.19, and the latter contains 555 observations with the average per-capita income being US$19,986.58.

In 2003, for example (see table 6A.2 in appendix A), 58 countries where included in the high-income sample and 66 in the low-income sample; in the same year the high-income per-capita sample accounted for a bit more of 1,300 million people and almost 30,500 billion dollars of GNI, whereas the low-income per-capita sample accounted for almost 4,600 million people and for US$4,900 billion of GNI.

We did run regressions to estimate the impact of *control* of *corruption* in the two subsamples of low- and high-income per-capita countries. We found that the coefficients for both the diesel and gasoline (for low- and high-income per-capita countries) are significant at 1 percent level and that they are significantly different in both the diesel and gasoline regressions.

We further introduced a low- and high-income coefficient for the *control of corruption* interacted with the dummy equal to 1 when *control of* corruption is higher than its median value. In the low-income case, the coefficient of the countries with a control of corruption lower than the median (−0.215) does not significantly affect the diesel subsidy (column 2, table 6.4); also in the high-income case (−0.172), the coefficient is not significant (column 2, table 6.4). It also follows that we

Table 6.3
High and low per-capita income countries

Variable	Observations	Mean	Std. dev.	Min	Max
GNI of High + Upper high income per capita	555	19,986.58	16,155.42	3,050.00	85,580.00
GNI of Low + Lower middle income per capita	548	1,277.19	913.39	90.00	3,850.00

Table 6.4
Control of corruption on subsidies and the per-capita income of the countries

Variables	Diesel subsidy (1)	(2)	Gasoline subsidy (3)	(4)
Low * Control of corruption	-0.314*** (0.115)	-0.215 (0.137)	-0.361*** (0.108)	-0.213* (0.122)
Low * Control of corruption * Dummy control of corruption		-0.331 (0.400)		-0.512 (0.443)
Low * Dummy control of corruption (= 1 if control of corruption above median)		17.699 (20.404)		27.905 (24.089)
High * Control of corruption	-0.464*** (0.113)	-0.172 (0.164)	-0.643*** (0.118)	-0.300* (0.154)
High * Control of corruption * Dummy control of corruption		-0.562* (0.339)		-0.855*** (0.289)
High * Dummy control of corruption (= 1 if control of corruption above median)		20.634 (20.413)		39.703** (17.334)
10^{-5} * Population	0.029*** (0.011)	0.027** (0.011)	0.028*** (0.010)	0.025** (0.010)
US deflator – Domestic deflator	-0.217*** (0.078)	-0.222*** (0.079)	-0.078 (0.070)	-0.084 (0.072)
Lag 10^{-2} * GDPPPP/Population	-0.038 (0.416)	0.088 (0.431)	-0.515 (0.342)	-0.386 (0.342)
10^{-2} * (Lag of oil supply – Oil consumption)	0.247 (0.263)	0.193 (0.256)	0.393*** (0.151)	0.319** (0.130)
10^2 * Area/Population	0.027* (0.016)	0.029 (0.018)	0.015 (0.022)	0.018 (0.021)
(Exports + Imports)/GDP	0.120*** (0.034)	0.128*** (0.034)	0.118*** (0.045)	0.129*** (0.045)
Lag of road diesel/gasoline fuel consumption per million inhabitants	-0.001 (0.010)	-0.002 (0.010)	0.092*** (0.021)	0.097*** (0.021)
Constant	-25.791*** (5.146)	-30.571*** (6.120)	-51.768*** (6.254)	-58.977*** (6.659)
Observations	1,072	1,072	1,084	1,084
R-squared within	0.167	0.170	0.241	0.246

Note: Robust standard errors are shown in parentheses; ***significant at 1 percent; **significant at 5 percent; *significant at 10 percent.

cannot reject the null hypothesis that the low- and high-income coefficients are not different (p-value = 0.73 of chi-squared test). The implication of this is that the result does not depend on the income level of the country.

Looking at countries with a control of corruption above the median in the group of low-income countries, the coefficient of the diesel subsidy (column 2, table 6.4) is $-0.215 - 0.331 = -0.546$ and not significant, whereas for the high-income countries (column 2, table 6.4) it is $-0.172 - 0.562 = -0.734$ and significant at 5 percent level. But the hypothesis that the low- and high-income coefficients are not different cannot be rejected (p-value = 0.64 of chi-squared test), which implies that the higher impact on diesel subsidies of an increase in the control of corruption, when the initial *control of corruption* is above the median, does not depend on the income level of the country.

For low-income countries the coefficient of the countries with a control of corruption lower than the median is -0.213, and is significant at 10 percent level for the gasoline subsidy (column 4, table 6.4), whereas for the high-income countries the coefficient is -0.300, and significant at 10 percent level (column 4, table 6.4). Moreover we cannot reject the hypothesis that the low- and high-income coefficients are not different (p-value = 0.46 of chi-squared test), which implies that the impact on gasoline subsidies due to an increase in the *control of corruption*, when the initial *control of corruption* is below the median, does not depend on the income level of the country.

Turning now to the low-income countries with a *control of corruption* above the median one observes that the coefficient of the gasoline subsidy (column 4, table 6.4) is $-0.213 - 0.512 = -0.725$ and significant at 10 percent, whereas for the high-income countries (column 4, table 6.4), it is $-0.300 - 0.855 = -1.155$ and significant at 1 percent level. However, we cannot reject the hypothesis that the low- and high-income coefficients are not different (p-value = 0.36 of chi-squared test), which also implies that the higher impact on gasoline subsidies, due to an increase in the control of corruption, when the initial control of corruption is above the median, does not depend on the income level of the country.

What emerges from the preceding discussion is that when the initial *control of corruption* is high (above the median), the negative impact on diesel and gasoline subsidies, due to a further increase in the *control of corruption* is almost threefold larger for diesel and fivefold larger for gasoline than in the below-of-the-median case and the result is independent of whether the country belong to the low- or the high-income country group. When the *control of corruption* is initially low (below the median), in the diesel-price case, a further increase in the *control of corruption* leaves diesel subsidies unaltered independently of the income group the country belongs to (low or high). In the gasoline case, a further increase in the *control of corruption* decreases slightly the subsidy: a result that holds independently of the income group the country belongs to (low or high).

6.6   Concluding Remarks

Are fuel subsidies affected by the control of corruption? Using a panel for the years 1991 to 2008, it has been shown that the answer to this question is in the affirmative, but only if a country has experienced some level of *control of corruption*.

More specifically, it has been shown that an increase in the control of corruption decreases diesel and gasoline subsidies if the initial level of corruption control is sufficiently high to start off with; otherwise, improving matters (in terms of increasing the control of corruption) has no effect on diesel subsidies—but has a small effect only on gasoline subsidies.

The analysis has been very partial, in the sense it has focused only on just one variable (which captures the weaknesses of the political institution) that might explain the behavior of subsidies, and there are clearly many others. It has served nonetheless to illustrate the potential value of the emphasis on an important aspect, that of *control of corruption*, which impacts on the inefficiencies of fuel subsidies—but it does so (as the analysis has shown) when the level of corruption control is initially high enough.

Acknowledgments

Much of this work was initiated while Kotsogiannis was a visiting scholar in the DECRG: Environment and Energy of the World Bank working on the project "Fuel subsidies and decentralization." Views expressed here should not be attributed to the World Bank, its Executive Board, or its management. We thank Jon Strand for introducing the topic to us, and for many insightful discussions, Massimiliano Ferraresi for excellent assistance with the data, and Lin Shi for early assistance with the World Bank dataset. An earlier (and substantially different) version of this chapter was presented at the CESIfo 2014 Venice Conference "The Economics and 'Political Economy of Energy

Subsidies." We thank the participants of the conference, the discussant Carolyn Fischer, and three anonymous referees, for comments and advice.

Appendix A: Statistical Appendix

Table 6A.1
Summary statistics for years 1991 to 2008

Variable	Obs	Mean	Std. dev.	Min	Max
Diesel price	1086	66.35	42.32	1.00	326.90
Diesel subsidy	1086	-24.34	35.25	-260.84	67.00
Gasoline price	1098	80.63	43.82	2.00	358.71
Gasoline subsidy	1098	-40.87	38.45	-291.95	61.24
Control of corruption	1118	51.86	29.37	0.00	100.00
10^{-5} * Population	1118	47.93	152.99	0.27	1324.66
US deflator – Domestic deflator	1118	94.82	24.61	0.18	252.63
Domestic deflator	1118	2.42	19.59	-144.75	85.64
Lag 10^{-2} * GDPPPP/Population	1118	12.89	13.48	0.22	84.41
10^{-2} * (Lag of oil supply – Oil consumption)	1118	-0.07	16.34	-124.80	91.33
10^{2} * Area/Population	1118	45.99	91.66	0.14	666.25
(Exports + Imports)/GDP	1118	90.78	53.47	15.87	438.09
Lag of road gasoline fuel consumption per million inhabitants	1118	185.89	226.16	1.08	1300.89
Lag of road diesel fuel consumption per million inhabitants	1118	172.18	292.58	0.00	3710.57
Dummy for high per-capita GNI countries	1103	0.50	0.50	0.00	1.00
Dummy for low per-capita GNI countries	1103	0.50	0.50	0.00	1.00

Notes: For diesel price and subsidy the number of observations is lower than the number of observations for gasoline price and subsidy since for the following countries and years data on diesel price are missing: Albania 2005; Canada 2005; Chile 2005; Haiti 2005 and 2007; Panama 2005; Qatar 2008; Thailand 2005; Uruguay 2005; Venezuela 2005 and Trinidad; and Tobago 2005 and 2008. Additionally the number of observations for other control variables is 1118, but for gasoline price and gasoline subsidy, it is 1098 because data on gasoline prices are missing for the following years and countries: Belarus 2005; Brunei 2005; Bulgaria 2005; China Hong Kong 2005; Costa Rica 1998 and 2000; Georgia 2000; Haiti 2006; Iceland 2005; Macedonia 2005; Moldova 1998, 2000, 2002, 2004, 2005 and 2006; Nepal 2005; Qatar 2002; Slovenia 2005; and Zambia 2000. Finally, there are 15 missing observations for GNI: Argentina 2007 and 2008; Czech Republic 1998 and 2000; Estonia 1998 and 2000; Haiti 1998, 2000, 2002, and 2003; Libya 2000; Qatar 2002 and 2003; and United Arab Emirates 1998 and 2000.

Table 6A.2
Population, per-capita GNI and control of corruption in 2003

High-income per-capita countries				Low-income per-capita countries			
Country	Population in millions	Per-capita GNI	Control of corruption	Country	Population in millions	Per-capita GNI	Control of corruption
Argentina	38.02346	3,670	43.2	Albania	3.086736	1,580	23.3
Australia	19.8954	21,140	93.69	Algeria	31.88544	1,890	36.41
Austria	8.1178	27,020	97.09	Angola	15.64683	730	6.8
Bahrain	0.695896	13,060	73.3	Armenia	3.059964	950	32.52
Belgium	10.37608	26,380	90.78	Azerbaijan	8.234039	820	14.56
Botswana	1.79362	3,190	83.5	Bangladesh	148.2813	400	3.4
Brunei	0.355509	17,790	63.11	Belarus	9.873968	1,630	16.5
Canada	31.676	24,640	94.66	Benin	7.358142	400	24.76
Chile	15.9547	4,570	86.89	Bolivia	8.835442	900	21.84
China, Hong Kong	6.7308	26,340	92.23	Bosnia and Herzegovina	3.783067	1,970	46.12
Costa Rica	4.18027	4,150	74.76	Brazil	181.5374	2,950	59.71
Croatia	4.44	6,390	57.77	Bulgaria	7.823	2,300	55.34
Cyprus, South	0.817104	15,480	85.44	Cambodia	13.43208	350	19.9
Czech Republic	10.20736	7,730	70.87	Cameroon	17.01773	660	20.87
Denmark	5.387174	33,940	99.51	China, P.R.	1288.4	1,270	44.17
Estonia	1.35352	5,790	80.1	Colombia	41.74129	2,350	46.6
Finland	5.212996	27,640	100	Congo (Brazzaville)	3.260769	700	16.02
France	60.15485	25,130	91.26	Congo, Democratic Rep. of	55.59062	110	2.91
Gabon	1.315994	3,590	45.15	Dominican Republic	9.252034	2,560	41.75
Germany	82.541	25,400	94.17	Ecuador	12.77349	2,130	22.33
Greece	11.02355	14,790	72.82	Egypt	74.29632	1,340	35.92
Hungary	10.12955	6,550	74.27	El Salvador	6.016772	2,410	40.29
Iceland	0.289548	32,110	98.06	Ethiopia	70.88066	110	33.98
Ireland	3.9957	28,680	91.75	Georgia	4.573208	910	18.45
Israel	6.6897	17,370	83.98	Ghana	20.95456	320	47.57
Italy	57.60465	22,310	75.24	Guatemala	12.09096	1,750	31.07
Japan	127.718	34,010	85.92	Honduras	6.621657	1,200	26.21
Korea, South	47.859	12,680	67.48	India	1064.399	530	44.66
Kuwait	2.396417	23,080	82.52	Indonesia	213.6555	910	15.53
Latvia	2.325342	4,510	65.05	Iran	67.04429	1,910	48.06
Lebanon	3.965419	4,470	42.72	Ivory Coast	18.45336	660	15.05
Libya	5.68481	4,890	28.16	Jordan	5.164	2,000	65.53
Lithuania	3.45424	4,650	66.02	Kazakhstan	14.909	1,800	8.74

Table 6A.2 (continued)

Country	High-income per-capita countries Population in millions	Per-capita GNI	Control of corruption	Country	Low-income per-capita countries Population in millions	Per-capita GNI	Control of corruption
Luxembourg	0.45163	42,110	92.72	Kenya	33.99161	410	21.36
Malaysia	24.71466	4,130	66.99	Kyrgyzstan	5.0386	340	24.27
Malta	0.3986	11,300	81.07	Macedonia	2.028451	1,940	33.5
Mexico	101.0209	6,870	54.37	Moldova	3.887928	570	22.82
Netherlands	16.22527	28,800	95.63	Mongolia	2.484456	610	51.94
New Zealand	4.0272	16,720	99.03	Morocco	29.82078	1,480	53.4
Norway	4.5649	44,010	96.12	Mozambique	19.78363	230	32.04
Oman	2.525751	8,610	68.93	Namibia	1.934616	2,170	58.74
Panama	3.119453	3,780	47.09	Nepal	26.12256	260	51.46
Poland	38.20457	5,480	70.39	Nicaragua	5.317982	990	40.78
Portugal	10.44105	13,090	86.41	Nigeria	134.2699	410	4.85
Saudi Arabia	22.04248	9,100	59.22	Pakistan	148.4388	540	30.1
Singapore	4.1148	22,790	98.54	Paraguay	5.681974	1,040	2.43
Slovakia	5.37965	6,810	68.45	Peru	27.13072	2,160	53.88
Slovenia	1.9957	12,470	82.04	Philippines	82.34397	1,030	41.26
Spain	42.0045	17,490	90.29	Romania	21.74203	2,340	49.03
Sweden	8.956	30,680	97.57	Russian Federation	144.5995	2,590	29.13
Switzerland	7.338957	43,480	96.6	Senegal	10.70696	550	52.91
Trinidad & Tobago	1.309114	8,050	54.85	South Africa	46.11649	2,840	60.68
Turkey	69.32946	3,810	50	Sri Lanka	19.173	950	48.54
United Arab Emirates	3.765526	36,120	84.95	Sudan	37.14216	410	6.31
United Kingdom	59.56878	29,500	95.15	Syria	17.95188	1,240	36.89
United States	290.326	39,950	93.2	Tajikistan	6.379311	210	13.11
Uruguay	3.30354	4,240	80.58	Tanzania	36.92965	330	18.93
Venezuela	25.674	3,450	10.19	Thailand	64.52288	2,060	50.97
				Togo	5.698109	290	27.67
				Tunisia	9.8398	2,500	69.9
				Turkmenistan	4.703861	990	9.22
				Ukraine	47.81295	980	17.48
				Uzbekistan	25.5677	420	14.08
				Vietnam	80.9024	510	35.44
				Yemen	19.84343	540	29.61
				Zambia	11.21896	370	17.96

Appendix B: Data Sources and Definitions

Gasoline (diesel) subsidy is defined in section 6.2, where P^{usa} is the actual price of gasoline (diesel) in 1998 in US$ cents, taken from GTZ and IEA and P^{dom} is the current premium gasoline (diesel) prices measured in November of each year in US$ cents per liter.

Control of corruption Source: Kaufmann et al. (2010).

GDPPPP measures the gross domestic product converted to international dollars using purchasing PPP GDP is gross domestic product converted to international dollars using purchasing power parity rates. An international dollar has the same purchasing power over GDP as the US$ has in the United States. It is calculated without making deductions for depreciation of fabricated assets or for depletion and degradation of natural resources. Data are in current international dollars. Source: World Bank, International Comparison Program database.

Oil supply – Oil consumption is given by oil supply minus oil consumption. Oil supply is measured by annual data on total oil supply and the unit is thousand barrels per day. Oil consumption is measured by annual data on total petroleum consumption and the unit is thousand barrels per day. Source: Energy Information Administration (EIA).

Area/Population is the land area per km² divided by population. In particular, land area is a country's total area, excluding area under inland water bodies, national claims to continental shelf, and exclusive economic zones. Most definitions of inland water bodies include major rivers and lakes. Source: Food and Agriculture Organization.

Domestic deflator is given for each country by the ratio of GDP in current local currency to GDP in constant local currency. We use as base year 2005. Source: World Bank National Accounts data, and OECD National Accounts data files.

US deflator is given by the ratio of US GDP in current US$ to GDP in constant US$. We use as base year 2005. Source: World Bank National Accounts data, and OECD National Accounts data files.

(Exports + Imports)/GDP is the sum of exports and imports of goods and services measured as a share of gross domestic product. Source: World Bank National Accounts data and OECD National Accounts data.

Road gasoline fuel consumption is road sector gasoline fuel consumption (*kt* of oil equivalent. Gasoline is light hydrocarbon oil use in internal combustion engine such as motor vehicles, but excluding aircraft). Source: International Road Federation, World Road Statistics, and International Energy Agency.

Road diesel fuel consumption is road sector diesel fuel consumption (*kt* of oil equivalent. Diesel is heavy oils used as fuel for internal combustion in diesel engines). Source: International Road Federation, World Road Statistics, and International Energy Agency.

Population is the total population based on the de facto definition of population, which counts all residents regardless of legal status or citizenship except for refugees not permanently settled in the country of asylum, as these individuals are generally considered part of the population of their country of origin. Source: United Nations Population Division and World Population Prospects.

Notes

1. There are, of course, many types of subsidies. Here we are mainly concerned with price (gasoline and diesel) subsidies.

2. Approximately, about 13 percent of the countries in our dataset, and for which data are available, have been subsidizing gasoline, and about 22 percent diesel.

3. The total global deadweight loss from fuel subsidies (gasoline and diesel) in 2012 has been estimated to be around $44 billion; see Davis (2014).

4. There are many externalities associated with fuel subsidies (because of the excessive use of fuel). These include soil salinization (due to excessive irrigation), poor water quality (due to excessive use of fertilizers), and increases in global pollution (due to excessive emissions). International energy prices have increased substantially over the past few years (natural gas being an exception). Despite this, many low- and middle-income economies have been reluctant to adjust their domestic energy prices to reflect these increases. The resulting fiscal costs have been substantial and pose even greater fiscal risks for these countries if international prices continue to increase and put immense pressure on fiscal budgets. See also IMF (2013).

5. In a number of countries fuel subsidies can be as large as public education and health expenditures. See Coady et al. (2006) for some evidence.

6. Mayer, Banerjee, and Trimble (2015) find, for instance, that in India, electricity subsidy payments are received by the nonpoor and that more than half of the subsidy payments are directed to households that account for the top 40 percent of the income distribution (whereas 87 percent of all subsidies are directed to households living above the poverty line).

7. The G20 group of leading economies has recently called for an end to fuel subsidies because of concerns about their impact on wasteful oil consumption.

8. For elements of this, and additional references, see Strand (2013) and Beers and Strand (2013). See also Coate and Morris (1995). A classic example, but by no means the only one, of an interest group that is known to be lobbying for protection (which include fuel

subsidies) is the transport sector. See Romero and Etter (2013) for an application to Colombia.

9. Corruption and capture are words in common usage but can mean different things in different contexts. For a discussion of "capture" and o some of the alternative denotations of the problem of corruption, see Bardhan (1997), Klitgaard (1988), and Rose-Ackerman (1999).

10. These indexes are not of course problem free. For a discussion, see Dreher, Kotsogiannis, and McCorriston (2007).

11. Consumer subsidies arise when the prices (paid by consumers), including both firms (intermediate consumption) and households (final consumption), are below a benchmark price. Producer subsidies arise when prices received by suppliers are above this benchmark. Where an energy product is internationally traded, the benchmark price for calculating subsidies is based on the international price. This approach to measuring subsidies is often referred to as the price-gap approach and is used widely in analyses by international agencies. (Kojima 2012a, b).

12. For more on the construction of this variable, see Kaufmann et al. (2010).

13. Estimations are performed using a random effect model because the within variability of the control of corruption variable is extremely low.

References

Beers, C. van, and J. Strand. 2013. The political determinants of fossil fuel pricing. Mimeo. World Bank.

Bardhan, P. 1997. Corruption and development: A review of issues. *Journal of Economic Literature* 3: 1320–46.

Coady, D., M. El-Said, R. Gillingham, K. Kpodar, P. Medas, and D. Newhouse. 2006. The magnitude and distribution of fuel subsidies: Evidence from Bolivia, Ghana, Jordan, Mali, and Sri Lanka. Working Paper 247. IMF.

Coady, D., R. Gillingham, R. Ossowski, J. Piotrowaski, S. Tareq., and J. Tyson. 2010. Petroleum product subsidies: Costly, inequitable and rising. Staff Position Note SPN/10/05. IMF.

Coate, S., and S. Morris. 1995. On the form of transfers to special interest. *Journal of Political Economy* 103 (6): 1210–35.

Davis, L. 2014. The economic cost of global fuel subsidies. *American Economic Review* 104 (4): 581–85.

Dreher, A., C. Kotsogiannis, and S. McCorriston. 2007. Corruption around the world: Evidence from a structural model. *Journal of Comparative Economics* 35: 443–66.

IMF. 2013. *Energy Subsidy Reform in Sub-Saharan Africa. Experiences and Lessons*. Washington, DC: International Monetary Fund

Kaufmann, D., A. Kraay, and M. Mastruzzi. 2010. The worldwide governance indicators: Methodology and analytical issues. Policy Research Working Paper 5430. World Bank, Development Research Group.

Klitgaard, R. 1988. *Controlling Corruption*. Berkeley: University of California Press.

Kojima, M. 2012a. Petroleum product pricing and complementary policies: Experience from 65 developing countries since 2009. Policy Research Working Paper 6396. World Bank.

Kojima, M. 2012b. Oil price risks and pump price adjustments. Policy Research Working Paper WPS6227. Washington, DC: World Bank.

Kosmo, M. 1987. *Money to Burn? The High Cost of Energy Subsidies*. Washington, DC: World Resources Institute.

Koplow, D. 2004. Subsidies to energy industries. In C. J. Cleveland, ed., *Encyclopedia of Energy*, vol. 5, 749–64. Amsterdam: Elsevier.

Larsen, B., and A. Shah. 1992. Carbon taxes, the greenhouse effect and developing countries. Policy Research Working Paper 957. World Bank.

Mayer, K., S. G. Banerjee, and C. Trimble. 2015. *Elite Capture: Residential Tariff Subsidies in India*. Washington, DC: World Bank. doi:10.1596/978-1-4648-0412-0.

OECD. 2010. The scope of fossil-fuel subsidies in 2009 and a road map for phasing-out fossil-fuel subsidies. IEA, OECD, and World Bank Joint Report. Prepared for the G20 Summit, Seoul, November 11–12.

Romero, G., and C. Etter. 2013. The political economy of fuel subsidies in Colombia. Environment Working Paper 61. OECD

Rose-Ackerman, S. 1999. *Corruption and Government: Causes, Consequences and Reform*. Cambridge: Cambridge University Press.

Strand, J. 2013. Political economy aspects of fuel subsidies: A conceptual framework. Policy Research Working Paper 6392. World Bank.

7 Fuel Subsidies and Governance in Sub-Saharan Africa

Christina Kolerus and Albert Touna-Mama

7.1 Introduction

There is a broad consensus that various kinds of political pressures are the main reason behind failures to adjust fuel prices or to phase out fuel subsidies in many sub-Saharan African (SSA) countries (e.g., see IMF 2013). For instance, the Nigerian government's attempt to raise gasoline prices in early 2012 triggered violent protests across the country. After a week-long national strike led by various stakeholders, the government decided to roll back the price adjustment from 140 naira ($0.86) to 97 naira ($0.60) per liter. This price is 50 percent above the old subsidized price of 65 naira ($0.40) but still significantly below the world price (Nossister 2012).

There are, however, few studies that shed light on how political pressures and institutions in SSA influence fuel subsidies. This chapter approaches fuel subsidies by studying the price-setting process of gasoline, diesel, and kerosene and the influence of political factors therein. Looking at case studies in Cameroon and Rwanda as well as performing a quantitative analysis for a sample of sub-Saharan countries, this study shows that successful price adjustments or reforms of fuel subsidies should be based on two main elements: first, building a coalition with gasoline and diesel stakeholders, reaching beyond the typically targeted low-income stakeholders and including urban middle classes, and second, bolstering government governance, in particular its effectiveness to credibly commit to policies—including possible compensation packages.

Political pressures can emerge from consumers of fuel products that are subject to subsidy reform. In SSA, fuel consumers can be broadly assigned to the socioeconomic groups associated with the three main fuel products. Kerosene, for example, is used by low-income households and in rural areas where electricity is not available, especially for lighting, cooking, and heating. Diesel is an important input to commercial transport, agriculture, and industry and for captive power generation. And gasoline is used for urban transport, including private vehicles mainly driven by the urban upper classes. Given these relatively clear distinctions, policy makers can have an incentive to influence subsidies on selected fuels in order to please stakeholders behind those products, with objectives other than the overall social benefit. Hence specific benefits can accrue to the socioeconomic groups behind certain products, depending on the political weights these groups have. It follows that the nuances of public interventions in fuel markets should be apparent in the differential treatment the various fuel products receive.

Ultimately, whether or not the government can exploit differences across stakeholder groups for political gains depends on the country's governance. Where poor governance or weak checks and balances exist, it is likely that the differential treatment of fuel prices is tilted toward groups with more political leverage. This support can take different forms, including transfers from the central government to state-owned enterprises or nonpayment of bills (customs or taxes) to other public entities. Even for countries with largely liberalized fuel markets, the government can still influence domestic prices indirectly, for example, through moral suasion or threats. Moreover weak capacity in policy making decreases the likelihood that stakeholders buy into subsidy reform, for instance, by accepting compensatory policies.

In this chapter we exploit variations across prices of fuel products (gasoline, diesel, and kerosene) and governance to isolate the influence of political and governance factors on fuel price setting.[1] First, looking at case studies, we show that improvements in government over time, as in the case of Rwanda, have been accompanied by higher relative fuel prices. In the case of Cameroon, we argue that attempts to reform subsidies only succeeded after the government had secured support from key stakeholders behind gasoline and diesel consumers. Second, combining these two observations, we perform a simple regression analysis and find evidence of a differential treatment of the main fuel products used in SSA given the responses of their prices to governance indicators, such as government effectiveness, rule of law, voice and accountability, and corruption. Countries with better governance institutions have, on average, higher gasoline and diesel prices. The effect of governance is particularly important at times of higher world prices and for oil exporters. Political pressures from the poor and rural population that makes up most of the kerosene consumers do not seem to be effective via governance institutions. An important contribution to the literature is that reform packages should go beyond low-income groups in order to generate a "reform coalition" that appeals to the urban middle classes and provides improved service delivery to "compensate taxpayers" as well.

7.2 Related Literature

Interest in government intervention into fuel markets re-surfaced in the late 2000s, triggered by the sharp upturn of international fuel prices and the subsequent slippage of public expenditures due to fuel subsidization (for cross-country evidence, see Coady et al. 2006, 2010; Kpodar and Djiofack 2009; World Bank 2011). Building on the traditional political economy literature and their analyses of policies being shaped by the struggle among stakeholders (e.g., Alesina and Drazen 1991; La Porta et al. 1999; Persson and Tabellini 2000), a broad consensus exists that political circumstances matter for the process of setting fuel prices in most countries where the government has a discretionary role in the fuel market.

Victor (2009) argues that failures to reform subsidies fully lie in the political economy of subsidies. In some countries the fear of instability—including by governments that do not face popular referenda—pushes governments to offer highly visible services to avoid unrest. Therefore it becomes difficult to phase out fuels subsidies. In addition governments with poor effectiveness are likely to offer subsidies because they are a readily available instrument that requires little administrative capability (IMF 2013). In this context, phasing out subsidies requires a political strategy that compensates those powerful interests that consent to a policy change. In this chapter we argue that in SSA countries these powerful interests tend to be stakeholders to the gasoline and diesel market.

Bacon et al. (2010) argue that coalitions of public support are needed to offset opposition from interest groups who benefited from the status quo. This can be accomplished by tailoring compensation packages for key stakeholders to secure their support. The poor always represent a key constituency regarding equity considerations as well as a possible source of unrest after price increases. The authors acknowledge, however, that in practice it is difficult to find a subsidy that targets only poor households and avoids leakages through diversion of kerosene to other markets. In this chapter, while we do not test for equity considerations, we argue that there is little support from the data that the supposedly power of the poor to generate unrest and instability matter for fuel price setting in sub-Saharan Africa.

The IMF (2013) study also looks at the many failures of energy subsidy reforms. This study argues that well-targeted measures to mitigate the impact of energy price increases on the poor are critical for building public support for reform. Ultimately, successful and durable reforms require a depoliticized instrument for setting energy prices, such as an automatic pricing mechanism with responsibility given to an independent body to reduce the chances of reform reversal.

Overall, systematic evidence of political influence on subsidy reform—including a threat to political and economic stability by unrest of the poor—is yet to be established. This chapter attempts to contribute to the debate by looking at how government institutions influence the fuel price-setting process across countries and over time.

7.3   Case Studies

Numerous case studies based on SSA countries suggest a prominent role of two main factors, governance and the influence of gasoline and diesel stakeholders. This chapter presents two examples, Rwanda and Cameroon, which represent both angles. In the case of Rwanda, an improvement in governance was accompanied by higher relative fuel prices. In the case of Cameroon, failed attempts to reform fuel subsidies led to a new strategy with mitigating measures now mostly directed toward stakeholders behind gasoline and diesel.

7.3.1   Rwanda

Rwanda has experienced strong improvements in governance since the mid-2000s (figure 7.1a and b, LHS chart). These improvements followed an ambitious program of economic management, structural policies, and business regulatory environment. Government effectiveness, for instance, has clearly surpassed other countries, and Rwanda is now among the top performers in SSA. Concomitantly, fuel prices have become considerably higher than average prices in other SSA countries (figure 7.1a and b, RHS chart). Precisely, the decoupling started in the mid-2000s around the same time as the improvements in governance.

Throughout our sample period Rwanda—as most other SSA countries—has been using an ad hoc pricing mechanism where the pump price is determined by the Ministry of Commerce and Ministry of Finance in conjunction with fuel dealers. Subject to substantial discretion, the mechanism allowed for increases in world fuel prices to not be fully passed through to domestic retail prices. As a consequence the government's fiscal accounts have absorbed part of the increase in world fuel prices through forgone revenues, similar to other SSA economies. However, unlike many countries in the region, the authorities have not abandoned price adjustments altogether even during the year 2008. Also, albeit the pricing mechanism per se has not changed, the government seems to have changed the way world price changes were incorporated, even after the oil price spike.

With respect to the pricing mechanism, the policy has been such that the government sets maximum prices for gasoline and diesel in Kigali with some specific rules for certain fuel products introduced over time. For instance, the retail diesel and gasoline prices are set equal if the international diesel price is higher than the international gasoline price, and the retail diesel price is lower otherwise. Despite a reduction in fuel taxes in July 2011 (at a cost equivalent to 0.4 percent of GDP), gasoline prices kept increasing—at least in parallel to the rest of SSA countries. Moreover the decision seems to have been less driven by powerful lobby groups. The government tried to bring fuel taxes more in line with those in the neighboring countries as well as to curb inflation. Through it all, political pressures seem to have played less of a role in the pricing policy.

While this case study does not establish causality between stronger governance and higher fuel prices, it illustrates the fact that both can go together and strong governance is likely to have played a role especially during the high pressure period of year 2008.

7.3.2 Cameroon

Cameroon is an oil exporter and its fuel prices are among the lowest of our sample—albeit higher than most other oil exporters. The country's fuel-pricing mechanism is based on ad hoc pricing decisions and while Rwanda ranked 6th in 2011 among all SSA countries on government effectiveness indicator, Cameroon ranked 24th.

In February 2008, an attempt to increase fuel prices marginally triggered violent anti-government protests from a population that was already unhappy over the increasing cost of living as well as other

(a)

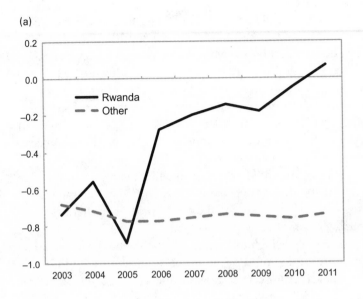

(b)

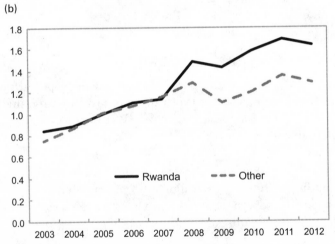

Figure 7.1
Rwanda versus SSA: decoupling of governance and fuel prices in the mid-2000s
Source: IMF Fuel Subsidies Database, World Bank WGI, staff calculations

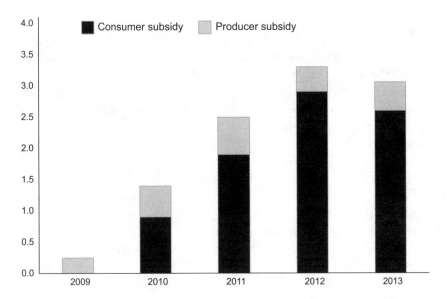

Figure 7.2
Fuel subsidies in Cameroon, 2009 to 2013

political issues. In particular, major urban transportation organizations called for a national strike, which was largely followed and quickly spilled over to other tranches of the population (mostly young and unemployed) beyond the sole urban transport professionals. After weeks of violent protests, the authorities rolled back part of the increase and raised civil servant salaries by 15 percent.

Since then the authorities had resisted calls from both the IMF and the World Bank to raise fuel prices, but the ever growing burden on the budget started creating major cash flows problems in early 2014. The government estimated that between 2008 and 2013 approximately CFAF 1,200 billion (7.7 percent of GDP) was spent on fuel subsidies (see also figure 7.2).

On June 30, 2014, the government finally decided to raise retail prices of gasoline (by 14 percent) and diesel (by 15 percent). The authorities also announced a series of accompanying measures such as (1) maintaining the price of kerosene unchanged, (2) reducing by 50 percent both the small business tax and the parking tax, (3) increasing civil servant wages by 5 percent, (4) increasing the minimum salary, and (5) increasing the urban and interurban transportation fare. These measures targeted interest groups with the most disruptive power (transportation organizations) rather than the rural households and poor. The government scrambled to convince various unions and organizations to call off any strike in order to preserve social peace and to share the burden of the increased world fuel prices.

This case study illustrates that it is indeed possible to manufacture a reform coalition around stakeholders behind gasoline and diesel— even in an environment where governance has not shown major improvements.

7.4   Estimating the Influence of Governance on Fuel Prices

Following the insights from the two case studies above, we test econometrically to which extent governance institutions and consumer groups affect fuel prices. We perform a basic fixed-effects panel estimation and regress retail prices of each fuel product on governance indicators and various controls. The methodology and data sources are detailed in box 7.1.

7.4.1   Identification
The identification strategy is based on two main assumptions. First, SSA countries are price takers and too small to influence fuel world market prices. Any deviation from (changes in) the world price would therefore be attributed either to transaction costs (e.g., when a country is landlocked), which we capture through country fixed effects, or to influence by policy makers—hence the existence of fuel subsidies.

Second, policy makers who influence the domestic fuel price are motivated by pleasing their stakeholders, which are represented in the consumer groups of the three different fuel types. Gasoline consumers represent mostly urban elites, and diesel is used by public transportation, industry and power generation. Kerosene consumers are mostly low-income households and in rural areas. These groups (or subgroups) can exercise pressures on policy makers to maintain constant fuel prices. At rising world prices, a constant domestic retail price would lead to higher fuel subsidies.

Yet the strength and intensity of pressures from consumer groups on policy makers is difficult to measure. However, we do have measures of various aspects of governance, as described in box 7.2. And, in order to affect retail prices, policy makers have to exert power through the existing institutions. Where poor governance or weak checks and balances exist, it is likely that the differential treatment of

Box 7.1

Methodology and data

The analysis is based on an unbalanced panel with annual observations over the period 2003 to 2011 for 42 SSA countries. Since the data cover a broad range of SSA countries as well as the oil price spike in 2008 and the subsequent decline during the global financial crisis, there are substantial variations across countries and over time that allow us to isolate the effect of governance on fuel prices and thus on subsidies.

For each fuel product—gasoline, diesel and kerosene—we run regressions of the domestic retail price on the world fuel price, indicators of governance, and fiscal and monetary policy variables. Data for the three fuel types come from the IMF database on fuel subsidies. The world price is taken from the US Energy Information Administration (EIA) and governance indicators are from the World Bank Governance Database. Macroeconomic policy variables come from the IMF IFS database. For each fuel product j, the specification for estimation takes the following form:

$$P_{jit} = \alpha_{0t} + \alpha_1 WP_{jt} + \beta_1' X_{it} + \beta_2' Governance_{it}$$
$$+ \gamma_1 WP_{jt} * Governance_{it} + \gamma_2 Oil Exporter_i * Governance_{it} + \varepsilon_{it},$$

where P_{jit} is the log of the domestic retail price of country i in year t; WP_{jt} is the log world price of fuel j; $Governance_{it}$ is a set of indicators reflecting the institutional quality of the country's governance and thus the exposure or vulnerability to political pressures, including government effectiveness, voice and accountability, political stability, corruption control, rule of law and regulatory quality; X_{it} is the set of macro policy controls that includes external debt to GDP (reflecting an exogenous fiscal policy stance) and the M2 to GDP ratio to proxy for monetary policy.

We estimate the above equation with time and country fixed effects, and robust standard errors clustered on the country level. We also include an interaction term between the world price and each governance variable—to test the influence of these variables under different world price pressures—and between a dummy for oil exporters and each governance variable—to test for the role of oil exporters.

fuel prices is tilted toward groups with more political leverage. Moreover weak capacity in policy making decreases the likelihood that stakeholders buy into subsidy reform, for instance, by accepting compensatory policies. So ultimately, whether or not the government can exploit differences across stakeholder groups for political gains depends on the country's governance.

Box 7.2
Governance indicators

The World Bank Governance Indicators (see also Kaufman et al. 2010) cover six broad aspects of governance reflecting the country's institutional quality of policy making. The indicators assume values between -2.5 and 2.5, with larger values representing better governance. The six indicators are as follows:

• *Government effectiveness* Capturing perceptions of the quality of public services, the quality of the civil service and the degree of its independence from political pressures, the quality of policy formulation and implementation, and the credibility of the government's commitment to such policies.
• *Regulatory quality* Capturing perceptions of the ability of the government to formulate and implement sound policies and regulations that permit and promote private sector development.
• *Voice and accountability* Capturing perceptions of the extent to which a country's citizens are able to participate in selecting their government, as well as freedom of expression, freedom of association, and a free media.
• *Political stability and absence of violence/terrorism* Capturing perceptions of the likelihood that the government will be destabilized or overthrown by unconstitutional or violent means, including politically-motivated violence and terrorism.
• *Rule of law* Capturing perceptions of the extent to which agents have confidence in and abide by the rules of society, and in particular the quality of contract enforcement, property rights, the police, and the courts, as well as the likelihood of crime and violence.
• *Control of corruption* Capturing perceptions of the extent to which public power is exercised for private gain, including both petty and grand forms of corruption, as well as "capture" of the state by elites and private interests.

Source: World Bank (http://info.worldbank.org/governance/wgi/index.aspx#home)

Finally, we allow for a different role for oil exporters. As a stylized fact, these countries feature considerably lower fuel prices than nonexporters (figure 7.3). While this can partly be explained by rentier behavior, oil exporters also show significantly worse governance outcomes than nonexporters.[2]

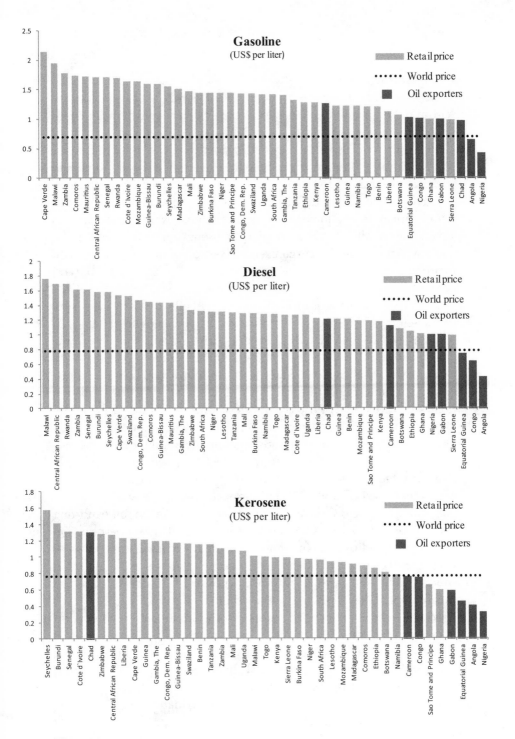

Figure 7.3
Fuel retail prices by country

7.4.2 Findings

The two main findings can be summarized as follows. First, countries with stronger governance (i.e., where public policies are more independent from political pressures) tend to have higher domestic retail prices.[3] Those are also countries with higher quality of policy formulation and implementation, and where the government's commitment to such policies is more credible. Moreover the effect on prices is stronger at higher world prices. Second, gasoline and diesel are the fuel types whose prices policy makers try to affect most when governance is weak. Our results clearly show that kerosene consumers seem to be less powerful or less well organized to exert pressures on prices—with the only exception of non–oil exporters with strong voice and accountability.

The first governance indicator, government effectiveness, has a very consistent, positive effect on the prices of gasoline and diesel (table 7.1, columns 1–3). While the effect is mainly driven by oil exporters in the case of gasoline, both fuel types show significant interaction terms with world prices. This implies that for all countries (oil and non–oil exporters), government effectiveness is even more relevant for adjusting domestic prices (to world price developments) when world prices are high. But a country's governance must be particularly strong to adjust prices upward—as it becomes more and more painful for its stakeholders. Figure 7.4 displays the marginal effects of government effectiveness on retail prices depending on the world price in the case of oil exporters (based on table 7.1). For instance, at average world prices, a one unit increase in government effectiveness in an oil-exporting country would lead to a 35 percent increase in its gasoline price—at "average" world prices. Note that a one unit increase in governance is very high. For instance, Rwanda, as described above, is the only SSA country that successfully improved government effectiveness by roughly one unit—albeit over a period of six years.

Most other governance indicators show a similar pattern as government effectiveness. At high world prices, there is a significant positive effect on the retail price of gasoline (mainly driven by oil exporting countries) and diesel when the rule of law is stronger (table 7.1, columns 4–6) and when corruption is better controlled (table 7.1, columns 7–9). Surprisingly, political stability does not seem to matter except for diesel at high world prices (table 7.2, columns 1–3). A priori, social unrest would be among the main reasons for policy makers to lower fuel prices, making it a natural indicator for the influence of fuel consumers

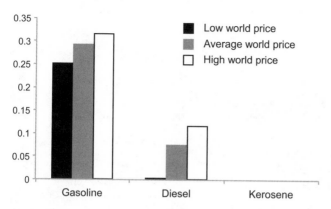

Figure 7.4
Impact of government effectiveness for oil exporters

on policy makers. At a second glance, the result still seems compelling for diesel though, as diesel stakeholders are among the group with the strongest potential for disruption of the economic activity: urban, lower middle-class workers who are employed in public transportation as well as in industrial sites. Overall, this finding contradicts the belief that fuel prices are influenced by the perception that the government will be destabilized by the poor.

Regulatory quality (i.e., the ability of the government to formulate and implement sound policies) influences fuel price setting in oil-exporting countries (table 7.2, columns 4–6). The strongest effect is on gasoline prices, but diesel and even kerosene are weakly significant. This finding supports the widely held view that the lack of alternative policy instruments in place to target some group households contributes to the persistence of fuel subsidies as those are easy to implement.

Finally, the indicator reflecting freedom of expression, freedom of association, and a free media seems to be an outlier in the usual impact of governance—at least for non–oil exporters (table 7.2, columns 7–9). First, for non–oil exporters, there is no effect on gasoline and diesel prices. Second, better governance in this indicator can actually lead to lower prices of kerosene. That is, kerosene consumers in non–oil-exporting countries seem to be empowered by more freedom of expression and association. With this, the mostly poor and heterogeneous stakeholders of kerosene are more able to voice their concerns, reach policy makers, and exert pressure to keep prices low. This finding

Table 7.1
Impact of governance on retail fuel prices (I)

	(1) Gasoline	(2) Diesel	(3) Kerosene	(4) Gasoline	(5) Diesel	(6) Kerosene	(7) Gasoline	(8) Diesel	(9) Kerosene
World price	0.606***	0.674***	0.688***	0.586***	0.656***	0.662***	0.593***	0.668***	0.684***
	(0.0286)	(0.0344)	(0.0699)	(0.0312)	(0.0324)	(0.0640)	(0.0333)	(0.0339)	(0.0626)
Government effectiveness	0.0967	0.141**	0.0527						
	(0.0802)	(0.0695)	(0.132)						
Effective × World price	0.0567**	0.0915**	-0.00432						
	(0.0245)	(0.0374)	(0.0699)						
Effective × Exporter	0.338**	0.116	0.331						
	(0.145)	(0.152)	(0.221)						
Rule of law				-0.0285	-0.0355	-0.126			
				(0.0985)	(0.0802)	(0.134)			
Law × World price				0.0605**	0.0879**	-0.0111			
				(0.0282)	(0.0362)	(0.0707)			
Law × Exporter				0.666*	0.339	0.552			
				(0.343)	(0.296)	(0.473)			
Corruption control							0.0601	0.0286	-0.127
							(0.0699)	(0.0626)	(0.118)

Table 7.1 (continued)

	(1) Gasoline	(2) Diesel	(3) Kerosene	(4) Gasoline	(5) Diesel	(6) Kerosene	(7) Gasoline	(8) Diesel	(9) Kerosene
Corrupt × World price							0.0597	0.102**	0.000505
							(0.0362)	(0.0435)	(0.0793)
Corrupt × Exporter							0.263*	0.252	0.305
							(0.148)	(0.200)	(0.238)
M2	0.000160**	0.000119*	0.000306***	0.000154**	0.000117*	0.000312***	0.000148**	0.000109	0.000319***
	(6.87e-05)	(6.43e-05)	(9.30e-05)	(7.47e-05)	(6.56e-05)	(8.90e-05)	(7.19e-05)	(7.02e-05)	(9.52e-05)
External debt	-6.01e-05	-0.000119	0.000301	-0.000148	-0.000194	0.000229	-8.93e-05	-0.000165	0.000249
	(0.000217)	(0.000214)	(0.000296)	(0.000229)	(0.000207)	(0.000296)	(0.000217)	(0.000226)	(0.000283)
Constant	0.627***	0.478***	0.206*	0.584***	0.389***	0.104	0.576***	0.420***	0.0791
	(0.0576)	(0.0535)	(0.103)	(0.0786)	(0.0611)	(0.1000)	(0.0477)	(0.0499)	(0.0843)
Observations	359	359	341	359	359	341	359	359	341
R-squared	0.764	0.820	0.745	0.766	0.822	0.746	0.759	0.820	0.744
Number of clusters	42	42	40	42	42	40	42	42	40

Note: Robust standard errors in parentheses
***$p < 0.01$, **$p < 0.05$, *$p < 0.1$.

Table 7.2
Impact of governance on retail fuel prices (II)

	(1) Gasoline	(2) Diesel	(3) Kerosene	(4) Gasoline	(5) Diesel	(6) Kerosene	(7) Gasoline	(8) Diesel	(9) Kerosene
World price	0.563***	0.629***	0.662***	0.577***	0.644***	0.654***	0.575***	0.637***	0.661***
	(0.0355)	(0.0318)	(0.0480)	(0.0309)	(0.0380)	(0.0641)	(0.0298)	(0.0326)	(0.0534)
Political stability	0.0249	0.0213	-0.0467						
	(0.0336)	(0.0292)	(0.0499)						
Stability × World price	0.0192	0.0492*	-0.0178						
	(0.0197)	(0.0250)	(0.0431)						
Stability × Exporter	0.0107	-0.0662	0.160						
	(0.0877)	(0.122)	(0.154)						
Regulatory quality				-0.0353	0.0300	0.0624			
				(0.132)	(0.131)	(0.157)			
Quality × World price				0.0227	0.0548	-0.0471			
				(0.0405)	(0.0543)	(0.0816)			
Quality × Exporter				0.511***	0.364*	0.434*			
				(0.146)	(0.209)	(0.247)			
Voice accountability							-0.106	-0.0904	-0.278**
							(0.0757)	(0.0705)	(0.130)

Table 7.2 (continued)

	(1) Gasoline	(2) Diesel	(3) Kerosene	(4) Gasoline	(5) Diesel	(6) Kerosene	(7) Gasoline	(8) Diesel	(9) Kerosene
Voice × World price							0.00268	0.0437	-0.0539
							(0.0289)	(0.0361)	(0.0655)
Voice × Exporter							1.097***	0.675***	1.191***
							(0.160)	(0.122)	(0.338)
M2	0.000150**	0.000122*	0.000312***	0.000169**	0.000126*	0.000288***	0.000183***	0.000136**	0.000331***
	(7.19e-05)	(6.06e-05)	(9.35e-05)	(7.55e-05)	(7.16e-05)	(0.000102)	(6.30e-05)	(5.46e-05)	(8.93e-05)
External debt	-7.59e-05	-0.000113	0.000250	-6.46e-05	-0.000106	0.000318	-2.60e-05	-0.000105	0.000238
	(0.000229)	(0.000195)	(0.000290)	(0.000225)	(0.000217)	(0.000281)	(0.000186)	(0.000168)	(0.000290)
Constant	0.505***	0.360***	0.0857	0.552***	0.430***	0.214*	0.641***	0.429***	0.176**
	(0.0370)	(0.0281)	(0.0518)	(0.0720)	(0.0836)	(0.117)	(0.0560)	(0.0428)	(0.0776)
Observations	359	359	341	359	359	341	359	359	341
R-squared	0.754	0.817	0.744	0.761	0.817	0.749	0.782	0.826	0.767
Number of clusters	42	42	40	42	42	40	42	42	40

Note: Robust standard errors in parentheses

*** $p < 0.01$, ** $p < 0.05$, * $p < 0.1$.

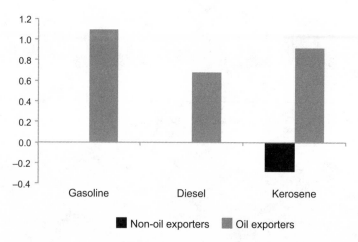

Figure 7.5
Marginal effects of voice and accountability on retail prices

complements the results from other indicators that show gasoline and diesel stakeholders to be exerting pressures while kerosene stakeholders seem not influential enough.

However, in oil-exporting countries, we see the opposite effect happening—in line of the previous role of governance. With high significance, more voice and accountability leads to higher prices (figure 7.5). Also the effect does not depend on the world fuel price.

Overall, when looking at all governance indicators, the most striking regularity from our estimations is that governance matters most to balance pressures from gasoline and diesel stakeholders, meaning from the urban elites and from industry and transportation workers, while the poor seem to lack channels to pressure policy makers. This can also be seen when looking at the coefficients of fuel world prices. For all specifications, the impact of a 1 percent change in the world price is lowest for gasoline—and highest for kerosene. Only around 60 percent of this increase is passed on to domestic gasoline prices, while in the case of kerosene, this ratio tends toward 70 percent. Given that overall the retail price is lowest for kerosene, these findings suggest that most countries keep the price low on equity considerations—or at least considerations that are not directly linked to political pressures on decision makers.

Finally, oil exporters stand out. Lower prices in oil-producing countries are likely to reflect the perceived entitlement by the population to receive a rent from national oil resources, throughout all socioeconomic groups. However, the full difference between the (very low) fuel prices in oil-producing countries and others observed in the data cannot be attributed to rentier attitude alone—political pressures play an important role, as shown in the regressions analysis: urban elites seem to be particularly influential in oil-exporting countries.

7.5   Concluding Remarks and Discussion

Political factors seem to play an important role in the price-setting process on domestic fuel markets, as suggested by numerous anecdotes for various countries. Our analysis provides qualitative and quantitative evidence that political factors influence domestic fuel price setting in sub-Saharan Africa. We find that countries with better governance tend to have, on average, higher domestic retail prices. Moreover the high sensitivity of gasoline and diesel retail prices to political factors suggests that urban elites and transportation lobbies are most influential in affecting the price-setting process in their favor.

From our analysis it also emerges that the kerosene price is the least influenced by political factors. This is consistent with the fact that the bulk of fuel subsidies in SSA are used to sustain gasoline and diesel prices at relatively low levels despite the fact that this, supposedly, benefits a numerical minority. This phenomenon is also known as a "pork-barrel program" in the political economy literature, a collectively financed program whose benefits are concentrated in a small group, and it is thought to have social costs that exceed the social benefits (Drazen 2000). Such a program is likely to persist because of the lack of (or missing) information on those people who benefit least. The results highlight the need for fuel subsidy reforms to make known the social costs of the status quo. In most SSA countries this cost is substantial and diverts resources away from priority sectors such as education, health, and infrastructure.

In light of the recent experience with energy subsidies in SSA, these findings suggest several policy options under political constraints. First, countries with low levels of public policy effectiveness tend to choose easy-to-implement subsidization of fuel prices. In fact subsidies are popular because their benefits are easily observable and perceived immediately, unlike, for example, education. In addition the subsidies are used on a regular basis, unlike health facilities, for example, and their availability is transparent, unlike targeted means-tested transfers.

All these factors make it hard to phase out fuel subsidies—especially in the presence of weak policy credibility or lack of trust in the government's willingness and capacity to compensate vulnerable groups—and use the savings from subsidy reform for social needs. This finding clearly supports reform packages that include targeted mitigating measures. However, such measures should go beyond low-income groups in order to generate a "reform coalition." In order to generate enough traction, reform strategies could identify tax or expenditure measures that appeal to the urban middle classes such as improved service delivery so as to "compensate taxpayers" as well.

We also find that the pressure on policy makers to intervene in fuel price setting is particularly important when world prices are relatively high. This was the case in the late 2000s during the fuel and food crisis when tensions escalated in street protests in several SSA cities. The finding underscores the need for fuel subsidy reforms to include a strategy for periods of price spikes. As any reform package should establish an automatic pricing formula in order to depoliticize fuel pricing, such a formula could also accommodate a mechanism for periods of high fuel prices. In addition price increases prior to moving to a formula could be phased and sequenced differently for each fuel product, acknowledging political implications.

Overall, this study lends support to subsidy reform strategies that are politically sensible and mindful of government shortcomings beyond energy subsidies.

Notes

1. A different approach would have been to consider difference in institutional setting that structure the approval of policy changes in order to capture check and balances (e.g., see van Beers and Strand 2013).

2. Our sample includes seven oil-exporting countries, albeit we drop Nigeria in the estimations due to very strong outlier characteristics.

3. In Kolerus and Touna-Mama (2013), we find that countries with stronger institutions also feature a higher pass-through of world prices to domestic fuel prices.

References

Alesina, Alberto, and Allan Drazen. 1991. Why are stabilizations delayed? *American Economic Review* 81: 1170–88.

Bacon, Robert, Eduardo Ley, and Masami Kojima. 2010. Subsidies in the energy sector: An overview. In *Background Paper for the World Bank Group Energy Sector Strategy*. Washington, DC: World Bank.

Coady, David, Moataz El-Said, Robert Gillingham, Kangni Kpodar, Paulo Medas, and David Newhouse. 2006. The magnitude and distribution of fuel subsidies: Evidence from Bolivia, Ghana, Jordan, Mali, and Sri Lanka. Working Paper 06/247. IMF.

Coady David, Robert Gillingham, and Javier Arze del Granado. 2010. The unequal benefits of fuel subsidies: A review of evidence for developing countries. Working Paper 10/202. IMF.

Drazen, Allan. 2000. *Political Economy in Macroeconomics*. Princeton: Princeton University Press.

IMF. 2013. Energy subsidy reform: Lessons and implications. In *Board Paper*. Washington, DC: IMF.

Kaufmann, Daniel, Aart Kraay, and Massimo Mastruzzi. 2010. The worldwide governance indicators: Methodology and analytical issues. Policy Research Working Paper 5430. World Bank.

Kolerus, Christina, and Albert Touna-Mama. 2013. The political economy of fuel price policies: Evidence from sub-Saharan Africa. Mimeo. IMF.

Kpodar, Kangni, and Djiofack Calvin. 2009. The distributional effects of oil price changes on household income: Evidence from Mali. *Journal of African Economies* 19 (2): 205–36.

La Porta, Rafael, Florencio Lopez-de-Silanes, Andrei Shleifer, and Robert Vishny. 1999. The quality of government. *Journal of Law Economics and Organization* 15 (1): 222–79.

Nossister, Adam. 2012. Under pressure, Nigerian leader relents on gas price. *New York Times*, January 16.

Perrson, Torsten, and Guido Tabellini. 2000. *Political Economics: Explaining Economic Policy*. Cambridge: MIT Press.

Van Beers, Cees, and Jon Strand. 2013. Political determinants of fossil fuel pricing. Policy Research Working Paper 6470. World Bank.

Victor, David. 2009. Untold billions: The politics of fossil-fuel subsidies. International Institute for Sustainable Development/Global Subsidies Initiative, Winnipeg and Geneva.

World Bank. 2011. *Petroleum Markets in Sub-Saharan Africa: Comparative Efficiency Analysis of Twelve Countries*. Washington, DC: World Bank.

8 Effects of Releasing Subsidies on the Wage Rates and the Gender Wage Inequality

Mohammad Habibpour and Neda Seiban

8.1 Introduction

Among the resource-rich developing countries, Iran is a pioneer in releasing petroleum and natural gas subsidies and forwarding part of the released funds directly and equally to the public. This scheme has been implemented since December 18, 2010, in Iran as a national subsidy reform plan, which was a part of the National Economic Reform Plan. The policy is expected to affect the economic sectors and the labor market due to the magnitude of the subsidies. In this chapter, we use a series of the national income-expenditure surveys, before and after the releasing subsidies, to investigate the policy effects on the wage rates and the gender wage inequality.

Based on the Word Bank development indicators, the natural resources rents in Iran were 29.5 percent of the total GDP in 2009. This huge amount of rents was distributed to the public by the government. Some of the rents as wages were paid to employees in the public sector. Some were distributed in the private sector in the form of government expenditures and investments. Because government expenditures in the private sector raise the revenue of corporations and foundations, the rents at least partly could be translated into wages. In fact, in several specific product industries some of the rents translated into employment opportunities, since the money could be partly transmitted as wages to employees in the subsidized industries. These channels would transfer the rents to wages of men and women on a discriminative basis, however. As a result, any major policy changes on the distribution process of the rents would significantly affect the wage rates and the wage gap. We were not be able to study precisely how these channels work or how the wage rates were contrived, but we could determine any changes caused by policy and evaluate their effects by comparing alternative transition channels. We found that the combination of policies, release of subsidies and the distribution of the released funds, had significant positive effects on the wage rates but negative effects on the gender wage inequality.

After releasing subsidies and dividing the released funds to the government (20percent), industrial organizations (30percent), and the public (50percent), we investigated how allocated funds change the wage rates and whether they are less discriminative compared to the wages before the policy. Our results show the scheme was relatively less discriminating than the allocator channels before implementation of the policy. In the following, we first estimate the magnitude of the gender wage gap in Iran and we measure the extent of the problem in the Iranian labor market. Next, we use a rich survey on the household levels before and after the policy to determine the short-run effects of the releasing subsidies and allocating the funds to different economic sectors on the gender wage gap. We further evaluate the policy effects for different wage quantiles in Iran.

8.1.1   Gender Wage Inequality

According to the UN Economic Commission for Europe, lack of access to top-paying jobs, lack of paid work opportunities, lack of benefit supports, and inability in obtaining rights will lead to a gender wage gap. Therefore ending the gender wage gap not only benefits the employers and workers but also advances social justice and equal opportunities. Although since the 1970s notable efforts were made to promote policies and strategies to narrow the gender wage gap, the female labor force still suffers from a significant gender inequality in wage pay (UNECE 2012).

Warth and Koparanova (2012) suggest that widening the gender wage gap increases the probability of women lapsing into extreme poverty and diminishes the total welfare of society by allocating higher economic dependency to men. Thus, it is important to study the changes in the wage gap after an economic structural change or an economic reform. In this chapter we examine the gender wage gap in Iran and the effect of releasing rent subsidies from natural resources as part of a national economic reform plan. We begin with the general facts on the gender wage gap in Iran.

According to the International Trade Union Confederation, in 2001 the gender wage gap was 19.5 percent in Iran (ITUC 2008). The magnitude of gender pay gap in Iran for years 2002 and 2005 comes from

Razavi and Habibi (2014) who examine the gender wage gap using the Oaxaca decomposition model. They find that in 2002, the total gender wage gap was 14.5 percent in the public sector and 121 percent in the private sector, and that in 2005, it was 5.7 percent in the public sector and 117 percent in the private sector. Moreover our univariate analysis of the gender wage inequality in the urban area in 2009 (table 8A.3 in the appendix) and rural area (table 8A.4 in the appendix) shows meaningful wage differences between males and females in different economic sectors in Iran.

More precisely, in the urban area (table 8A.3), women on average receive higher salary wages than men in the public sector and lower salary wages in the private sectors. Results indicate wage inequalities against women in self-employed wages in both the agriculture sector and the non-agriculture sector. The overall wage inequality of salary and self-employed wages shows wage discrimination against women such that men's wages are higher in the private sectors than women's wages in the public sector. Additionally education is a key factor in determining wage inequality against women, as the inequality is much higher for illiterate women (compared to illiterate men) than educated women (compared to educated men). Moreover there is higher wage inequality against married women than single women in three sources of incomes (except public). Nevertheless, in the public sector married women are receiving higher wages than single women (compared to single men). Besides, the gender inequality is higher among self-employed earnings where salary earnings and wage inequalities increase as workers age (and thus used as a proxy for experience).

In the rural area (table 8A.4), gender wage inequality against women persists in all sectors except the public sector. Again, in the agriculture sector, education is a key factor of the magnitude of the wage inequality against women, as the inequality is much higher for illiterate women (compared to illiterate men) than educated women (compared to educated men). As in the urban area, the wage inequality against married women is higher than for single women (except the public sector) and it increases with increasing age.

8.1.2 Subsidy Reform Plan

Under the Iranian's subsidy reform plan, in December 2010 the government started to reduce the subsidies of energy products in different steps and transfers a portion of its proceeds to the public (Guillaume et al. 2011). During the first phase of the reform, the government transferred, on the one hand, a monthly amount of 445,000 rials ($45) per family members to the head of family's bank account (starting in January 2011). This was authorized by the Parliament by the "Targeted Subsidies Reform Act" in January 2010, which not only refers to increasing the energy prices, but to the prices of some goods and services such as "wheel, rice, milk, postal services ..." that had increased as well.[1] On the other hand, to manage the income derived from this action, the government would allocate 50 percent to the public in the form of "in-cash and social security system," 30 percent to "the producers and industries," and the rest of this income to improve the government infrastructures (Hassanzadeh 2012).

What was the impact of this reform on the labor market? The policy will change the allocation strategy of natural resource rents from subsidizing to direct transfers. The latter suggested decreasing the income inequality (Farzanegan and Habibpour 2014) while the former would benefit special industries. In addition Ross (2008) suggests that oil rents [or generally natural resource windfalls] in the resource-rich developing countries can exclude a part of female labor force and decrease their political representation. The rents affect the labor supply by increasing the women's unearned income and the labor demand by closing part of the jobs for the women due to the Dutch disease. He argued this as another aspect of the resource curse that affects the core of social structure[2] However, he does not mention any reduction in wages of those who remain in the labor market.

Following Ross's arguments, one likely consequence of the exclusion of women from the labor force is a decrease in their negotiation power, resulting in a relative wage reduction compared to men's wages. Instead of women's exclusion from the labor force, we can envision women in the work force taking lower paid career paths or accepting positions of lower social standing. Hence, the wage gap between female and male in the lower wage positions will be higher than the higher-paid jobs. However, Farzanegan and Habibpour (2014) suggest that transferring the rents of the resources to the public may alleviate the resource curse. Therefore releasing subsidies together with resource dividends might narrow the gender wage gap in a resource-rich developing country and prevent the occurrence of a resource curse.

To evaluate the implemented policy in Iran, we used national income expenditures surveys from 2007 to 2013. The data cover four years before the policy implementation and three years after that. The results are discussed in the following sections.

8.1.3 Transmission Channels

National surveys cannot be used to study the channels that transmit the financial resources to the labor market. Therefore, we studied the wage rates that are the result of the demand and supply interactions. We suggest four possible transmission channels:

First, some of the funds after releasing subsidies were placed at the disposal of the government. We refer to the stylized facts (tables 8A.3 and 8A.4). Working in the public sector proved advantageous in increasing women's wages (we will show the evidence based on regression results). Clearly, higher funds directed to the public sector can raise women's wages more than those of men.

Second, the money transfers did facilitate access to necessary job information and job agencies for women. The funds also enabled flexible working hours for women so that they had time to search for a better and higher paid job and yet meet their work obligations within the required hours. Before receiving the funds, and because of budget constraints, women were subjected to longer working hours.

Third, the funds provided women with financial credits, which facilitated their access to the labor market, and to developing or setting up their own businesses. Enough funding was provided especially for those women who wanted to set up their own business in rural areas, where there are lower fixed setup costs, and the funds filled the gaps between the money needed to set up a business and the credit the household already had. Because the funds were transferred to every individual, a family of four members could, on average, accumulate a reasonable amount of money over a number of months. They would then be eligible for joining the Family Loan Funds that are popular among Iranian families. In 2009, Iranian families organized about six thousand Family Loan Funds.[3]

Fourth, Ross (2008) discussed the negative effects of the natural resource rents on the female labor force as one of the resource curses. More recently Farzanegan and Habibpour (2014) suggest that a direct transfer of the rents as resource dividends (RD) might alleviate the resource curse effects.[4] Hence we can presume that allocating the natural resource rents to the public sector raises female labor force participation and prevents their wage reduction.

8.2   Data, Methodology, and Results

We used seven national surveys from 2007 to 2013, which totaled 493,502 individuals in the urban Iran and 468,764 individuals in rural Iran before and after releasing subsidies. The data are provided by the National Statistic Center of Iran annually and are available online.[5]

To investigate the gender wage inequality in the data and the effects of releasing subsidies on wages, we did a series of cross-sectional OLS regressions, a pooled regression using all surveys together, and a quantile regression to study the effects of different wage groups. Moreover we tracked about 30 thousand individuals during 2010 to 2012 to examine the policy effects on the same households over time.

We ran OLS regressions using the log of the labor force wage as a dependent variable[6] while controlling for literacy, age, marital status, and their interactions, as well as other control variables. Based on the data we divided earned incomes into salary income and non-salary incomes (self-employed income). For the latter, we controlled for the agricultural and non-agricultural sectors and being an entrepreneur or not, and for the former we controlled for being in the public or private sectors. The job experience was not included in the dataset. Therefore, we used the age as a proxy for job experience. The descriptive statistics for both rural and urban areas are provided in the tables 8A.1 and 8A.2 in the appendix. Moreover we added a Female dummy variable, being one if yes, as our main variable of interest. Ceteris paribus, a significant negative sign of the Female dummy indicates the gender wage inequality in the labor market.

In our pooled regression, we utilized a dummy for the years that the policy is implemented and its interaction with the Female dummy. We tested a quantile regression to see if the policy effects differ for the different wage groups. For the years 2010 to 2012, we tracked about 30,000 of households in the national survey, and we estimated if the dividends received from the government after releasing the subsidies had an effect on the wages rates. Then we tested if the effects of the transfers on the wages rates were equal for both genders.

8.2.1   Cross-sectional Comparison

From 2007 to 2013 we estimated for each year a cross-sectional OLS regression on the logarithm of salary and non-salary (self-employed) incomes. The analysis is divided to the rural and urban area. For each year four tables with six specifications were estimated.[7] Specifications are different for salary income and self-employed incomes because they have different related variables in the dataset. Whether being in the public, private, or corporate sector was asked of those surveyed in the salary income questionnaire, and whether being a worker or entrepreneur was asked of those with self-employed incomes. The specifications are quite the same for different years and different regions so as to allow the coefficients to be compared.

The results in table 8.1 and 8.2 show that the wage discrimination, on average, decreased in the urban area for salary income, from −0.32 before the policy to −0.25 after the policy (in years 2011 to 2013). In addition, the Female dummy coefficient, on average, decreased from −0.73 to −0.61 in the rural area after the subsidies were released. Respectively, for self-employed income, the coefficient decreased, on average, from −0.86 to −0.66 in the urban area and from −0.77 to −0.62 in the rural area. We show the changes graphically in the Female dummy coefficient for four years before the subsidies and three years after in figure 8A.1.

As the figure shows, before subsidies were released, literacy and working in the public sector, on average, increased with the salary wage. These increases are also higher for women. In contrast, on average, lower wages are offered in the private sector and were even lower for women compared to men's wages. Marriage positively affects men's wages, as a married woman will receive low wages.

For the self-employed there are positive effects on earnings of literacy and being an entrepreneur and women who are entrepreneurs relatively receive higher wages than men. Again, being married is expected to result in higher wages, but married women will receive lower wages. The wages in the agriculture sector are, on average, lower than in the non-agriculture sectors.

Based on the interaction terms in our results we suggest that education (literacy) and being an entrepreneur do benefit women in the labor market, allowing them to overcome gender income inequality. The most income discrimination is against married women in the private sectors especially if they are additionally illiterate.

We can thus infer from the cross-sectional OLS regressions that after release of the subsidies, gender wage discrimination is lower based on lower coefficients as compared with the years before subsidies were released. Similar to the results before the subsidies' implementation, the interfaces among the dummy variables female, marital status, literacy, and the different economic sectors suggest that, on average,

Table 8.1

Determinants of the wage (log) for males and females in urban and rural areas for salary wages, 2007 to 2013

Urban	2007	2008	2009	2010	2011	2012	2013
Literacy	0.38***	0.23***	0.30***	0.31***	0.32***	0.37***	0.34***
	(0.03)	(0.02)	(0.025)	(0.027)	(0.025)	(0.027)	(0.029)
Female	-0.38***	-0.28***	-0.32***	-0.29***	-0.22***	-0.26***	-0.26***
	(0.05)	(0.04)	(0.052)	(0.046)	(0.045)	(0.042)	(0.046)
Public	0.11	0.26***	0.18**	0.13**	0.25***	0.32***	0.37***
	(0.11)	(0.1)	(0.09)	(0.068)	(0.099)	(0.106)	(0.116)
Private	-0.34***	-0.18*	-0.31***	-0.34***	-0.019**	-0.04	-0.06
	(0.1)	(0.1)	(0.09)	(0.067)	(0.098)	(0.106)	(0.115)
Age	0.12***	0.11***	0.11***	0.12***	0.11***	0.10***	0.09***
	(0.005)	(0.004)	(0.005)	(0.005)	(0.004)	(0.004)	(0.005)
Age^2	-0.001***	-0.001***	-0.001***	-0.001***	-0.001***	-0.001***	-0.0009***
	(0.00005)	(0.00005)	(0.00006)	(0.00006)	(0.00006)	(0.00005)	(0.00006)
Marry	0.35***	0.24***	0.31***	0.28***	0.27***	0.25***	0.26***
	(0.02)	(0.02)	(0.026)	(0.025)	(0.024)	(0.023)	(0.023)
Female_ Marry	-0.17***	-0.22***	-0.21***	-0.19***	-0.21***	-0.16***	-0.23***
	(0.06)	(0.05)	(0.057)	(0.05)	(0.051)	(0.049)	(0.052)
Female_ Public	0.74***	0.63***	0.63***	0.60***	0.52***	0.57***	0.61***
	(0.06)	(0.05)	(0.056)	(0.048)	(0.05)	(0.46)	(0.05)
Number of obs	10,459	11,131	10,681	10,889	10,573	10,774	10,990
R^2	0.36	0.32	0.36	0.36	0.34	0.30	0.30

Rural	2007	2008	2009	2010	2011	2012	2013
Literacy	0.23***	0.29***	0.27***	0.27***	0.26***	0.24***	0.20***
	(0.02)	(0.02)	(0.025)	(0.024)	(0.023)	(0.025)	(0.024)
Female	-0.75***	-0.72***	-0.67***	-0.72***	-0.56***	-0.62***	-0.65***
	(0.06)	(0.05)	(0.06)	(0.064)	(0.061)	(.059)	(0.075)
Public	0.39***	0.21*	0.51***	0.71***	0.48***	0.57***	0.60***
	(0.12)	(0.12)	(0.143)	(0.178)	(0.153)	(0.159)	(0.169)
Private	-0.13	-0.38***	-0.15***	0.06	-0.09	0.009	0.15
	(0.12)	(0.12)	(0.14)	(0.176)	(0.151)	(0.157)	(0.166)
Age	0.09***	0.07***	0.08***	0.09***	0.08***	0.07***	0.06***
	(0.005)	(0.005)	(0.005)	(0.004)	(0.004)	(0.004)	(0.004)
Age^2	-0.001***	-0.0008***	-0.0008***	-0.001***	-0.0008***	-0.0007***	-0.0007***
	(0.00006)	(0.00006)	(0.00006)	(0.00006)	(0.00005)	(0.00005)	(0.00005)
Marry	0.27***	0.19***	0.21***	0.19***	0.16***	0.16***	0.21***
	(0.03)	(0.02)	(0.026)	(0.026)	(0.025)	(0.025)	(0.024)
Female_ Marry	-0.57***	-0.40***	-0.37***	-0.15*	-0.29***	-0.34***	-0.31***
	(0.08)	(0.077)	(0.08)	(0.086)	(0.083)	(0.081)	(0.09)
Female_ Public	1.36***	1.04***	0.92***	0.84***	0.90***	0.99***	1.12***
	(0.08)	(0.09)	(0.09)	(0.088)	(0.087)	(0.076)	(0.081)
Number of obs	8,468	8,734	8,354	8,932	8,567	8,333	8,772
R^2	0.28	0.28	0.26	0.25	0.24	0.24	0.20

Note: * Significant at 10 percent, ** significant at 5 percent, *** significant at 1 percent.

Table 8.2
Determinants of the wage (log) for males and females in urban and rural areas for self-employed wages, 2007 to 2013

Urban	2007	2008	2009	2010	2011	2012	2013
Literacy	0.20***	0.26***	0.28***	0.19***	0.22***	0.24***	0.22***
	(0.03)	(0.04)	(0.038)	(0.04)	(0.04)	(0.038)	(0.04)
Female	-0.88***	-0.91***	-0.82***	-0.82***	-0.70***	-0.62***	-0.66***
	(0.05)	(0.06)	(0.054)	(0.062)	(0.061)	(0.059)	(0.053)
Agriculture	-0.46***	-0.46***	-0.41***	-0.44**	-0.44***	-0.41***	-0.30***
	(0.04)	(0.05)	(0.044)	(0.049)	(0.046)	(0.043)	(0.038)
Entrepreneur	0.56***	0.53***	0.62***	0.54***	0.52***	0.56***	0.58***
	(0.03)	(0.03)	(0.034)	(0.032)	(0.033)	(0.036)	(0.034)
Age	0.05***	0.04***	0.04***	0.05***	0.04***	0.04***	0.03***
	(0.005)	(0.005)	(0.005)	(0.005)	(0.005)	(0.005)	(0.005)
Age^2	-0.0006***	-0.0004***	-0.0004***	-0.0005***	-0.0004***	-0.0003***	-0.0003***
	(0.00005)	(0.00005)	(0.00005)	(0.00006)	(0.00005)	(0.00005)	(0.00005)
Marry	0.07 *	0.09 **	0.08**	0.08**	0.11***	0.11***	0.09**
	(0.04)	(0.04)	(0.038)	(0.04)	(0.04)	(0.038)	(0.036)
Female_Ent	0.46**	0.63***	0.41**	0.54**	0.33	0.43**	0.47*
	(0.18)	(0.23)	(0.208)	(0.269)	(0.224)	(0.174)	(0.248)
Number of obs	5,926	5,775	5,869	5,718	5,614	5,674	5,844
R^2	0.18	0.16	0.18	0.16	0.15	0.14	0.14
Rural	2007	2008	2009	2010	2011	2012	2013
Literacy	0.13***	0.19***	0.15***	0.14***	0.16***	0.15***	0.18***
	(0.03)	(0.03)	(0.032)	(0.03)	(0.03)	(0.03)	(0.029)
Female	-0.91***	-0.67***	-0.73***	-0.77***	-0.60***	-0.58***	-0.68***
	(0.04)	(0.05)	(0.050)	(0.049)	(0.048)	(0.048)	(0.048)
Agriculture	-0.30***	-0.44***	-0.45***	-0.41***	-0.43***	-0.39***	-0.19***
	(0.02)	(0.02)	(0.025)	(0.024)	(0.024)	(0.023)	(0.022)
Entrepreneur	0.40***	0.37***	0.50***	0.29***	0.38***	0.35***	0.35***
	(0.03)	(0.03)	(0.034)	(0.037)	(0.035)	(0.034)	(0.036)
Age	0.05***	0.04***	0.04***	0.04***	0.03***	0.03***	0.03***
	(0.004)	(0.004)	(0.005)	(0.004)	(0.004)	(0.004)	(0.004)
Age^2	0.0005***	-0.0004***	-0.0003***	-0.0003***	-0.0002***	-0.0002***	-0.0002***
	(0.00004)	(.00005)	(0.00005)	(0.00004)	(0.00004)	(0.00004)	(0.00004)
Marry	-0.09**	0.02	0.02	-0.06	-0.06*	0.005	0.02
	(0.04)	(0.04)	(0.044)	(0.042)	(0.042)	(0.042)	(0.041)
Female_Ent	-0.10	0.12	0.09	0.25*	-0.13	-0.38*	-0.0005
	(0.16)	(0.16)	(0.162)	(0.158)	(0.17)	(0.209)	(0.158)
Number of obs.	8,814	8,219	8,008	8,070	8,086	8,354	8,418
R^2	0.10	0.08	0.10	0.08	0.08	0.08	0.07

Note: * Significant at 10 percent, ** significant at 5 percent, *** significant at 1 percent.

women receive lower wages in the private sectors when they marry. In contrast, there are benefits due to education and working in the public sector for women receiving salary incomes. The results from the self-employed suggest that being an entrepreneur or taking a job in a non-agriculture sector can lower the wage gap.

8.2.2 Pooled Regression

As is clear in the previous section, we can conclude that the gender wage inequality exists and that discrimination lessened somewhat after the release of subsidies. Last, to the previous regressions, we added a pooled OLS regression with a time dummy variable for the years before and after the release of subsidies (ReSub) and interfaced this dummy variable with the Female variable (Female_ReSub) to see how the released subsidies affected the wages of women in the labor force. The Female coefficient indicates the wage gap between women and men while the sum of the Female and Female_ReSub coefficient shows the wage differential after the policy. Therefore, by using a difference-in-difference estimator, we can test the null hypothesis that the wage gap remains the same, that is, H_0: Female_Resub = 0, or the alternative that the wage gap has reduced after releasing subsidies, H1: Female_Resub > 0. Results in table 8.3 suggest that releasing subsidies had, on average, positive effects on the wage rates and this increase was, on average, advantageous for the women's wage rates.

Table 8.3
Pooled regression, 2007 to 2013

	Log salary		Log self-employed	
	Rural	Urban	Rural	Urban
Female	-0.73***	-0.30***	-0.66***	-0.67***
	(0.026)	(0.020)	(0.034)	(0.041)
ReSub	0.61***	0.56***	0.54***	0.54***
	(0.006)	(0.005)	(0.009)	(0.008)
Female_ReSub	0.12***	0.01	0.12***	0.17***
	(0.03)	(0.016)	(0.034)	(0.043)
N	60,160	75,497	57,969	40,420
R^2	0.34	0.39	0.14	0.22

Note: Robust standard deviations are reported in parenthesis. * Significant at 10 percent, ** significant at 5 percent, *** significant at 1 percent. The results are summarized. Joint control variables for both dependents are Literacy, Age, Age2, Marry, and Female_Marry. For salary wages Public, Female_Public, and Private, and for self-employed wages Agriculture, Entrepreneur, and Female_Ent are added in the specifications.

8.2.3   Quantile Regression

Using quantile regression, we analyzed the determinants of wage for different income groups. While table 8.4 shows the presence of gender wage discrimination in the Iran's labor market, the negative Female's coefficient is bigger in the lower quantiles and in the rural area. Clearly, the poor in the rural area have the highest level of the wage gap between females and males. In contrast, the highly paid wage groups in the urban area have the lowest gender wage gap. The released subsidies' (ReSub) coefficient is positive and significant for all quantiles, which shows positive effects of the releasing subsidies on the wage rates. Unlike the Female coefficient, ReSub is almost the same for all wage quantiles. This shows all wage groups (and probably all income groups) experience similar effects from the policy. Farzanegan and Habibpour (2014) mention releasing subsidies as a universal scheme that is more probable to influence income inequality than poverty indexes. The interaction of Female and ReSub is positive and significant in the rural area and so proves the policy to be advantageous for women.

Comparison of different quantiles in table 8.4 indicates that the lower wage groups suffer more from the wage discrimination than the higher wage groups. Moreover the positive effects of the releasing subsidies for female in the rural for salary wages are higher for lower quantiles. Figures 8A.2 and 8A.3 show quantile functions in the rural and urban areas by variables. The dashed lines show the OLS regression and the vertical line is the coefficient of every independent variable, which differ for different quantiles. The figures show that females with higher wages experience a lower wage increase than the females in the lower wage groups (ReSub_FE) after the policy implementation.

Table 8.5 shows the quantile regression results of the self-employed wages. Results suggest that the lower wage groups suffer more discrimination in both regions. The policy has increased the wage rates and this increasing effect was more an advantage for females. Figures 8A.4 and 8A.5 show that wage discrimination is higher in the lower wage groups. Furthermore releasing subsidies has positive effects for income groups, and this increasing effect was almost the same for different wage groups.

Table 8.4
Quantile regression, 2007 to 2013, for salary wages

	Rural					Urban				
	Q.10	Q.25	Q.5	Q.75	Q.90	Q.10	Q.25	Q.5	Q.75	Q.90
Female	-1.02***	-1.00***	-0.87***	-0.56***	-0.030***	-0.41***	-0.53***	-0.32***	-0.10***	-0.04
	(0.06)	(0.03)	(0.02)	(0.02)	(0.02)	(0.04)	(0.02)	(0.01)	(0.01)	(0.01)
ReSub	0.68***	0.62***	0.61***	0.57***	0.57***	0.58***	0.56***	0.54***	0.53***	0.54
	(0.01)	(0.009)	(0.006)	(0.006)	(0.007)	(0.01)	(0.007)	(0.005)	(0.005)	(0.006)
Female_ReSub	0.16**	0.14***	0.11***	0.10***	0.06**	0.02	-0.001	-0.01	-0.04***	-0.04**
	(0.07)	(0.03)	(0.02)	(0.02)	(0.02)	(0.04)	(0.02)	(0.01)	(0.01)	(0.01)
N	60,160	60,160	60,160	60,160	60,160	75,497	75,497	75,497	75,497	75,497
R^2	0.17	0.20	0.22	0.22	0.23	0.26	0.26	0.26	0.26	0.25

Note: Robust standard deviations are reported in parenthesis. * Significant at 10 percent, ** significant at 5 percent, *** significant at 1 percent. The results are summarized. Control variables are Literacy, Age, Age2, Marry, Female_Marry, Public, Female_Public, and Private.

Table 8.5
Quantile regression, 2007 to 2013, for self-employed wages

	Rural					Urban				
	Q.10	Q.25	Q.5	Q.75	Q.90	Q.10	Q.25	Q.5	Q.75	Q.90
Female	-0.90***	-0.83***	-0.71***	-0.57***	-0.45***	-1.01***	-0.91***	-0.66***	-0.44***	-0.44***
	(0.07)	(0.04)	(0.03)	(0.03)	(0.04)	(0.07)	(0.04)	(0.03)	(0.03)	(0.05)
ReSub	0.53***	0.57***	0.55***	0.53***	0.51***	0.57***	0.52***	0.52***	0.52***	0.51***
	(0.02)	(0.01)	(0.01)	(0.01)	(0.01)	(0.01)	(0.01)	(0.008)	(0.009)	(0.01)
Female_ReSub	0.09	0.10**	0.14***	0.15***	0.10**	0.09	0.21***	0.21***	0.17***	0.12**
	(0.07)	(0.04)	(0.03)	(0.03)	(0.04)	(0.07)	(0.04)	(0.03)	(0.03)	(0.05)
N	57,969	57,969	57,969	57,969	57,969	40,420	40,420	40,420	40,420	40,420
R^2	0.09	0.10	0.09	0.08	0.07	0.16	0.14	0.13	0.13	0.13

Note: Robust standard deviations are reported in parenthesis. * Significant at 10 percent, ** significant at 5 percent, *** significant at 1 percent. The results are summarized. Control variables are Literacy, Age, Age2, Marry, Female_Marry, Agriculture, Entrepreneur, and Female_Ent.

8.2.4   Tracked Households

In the three years of our datasets, from 2010 to 2013, we found that a significant number of households were registered at a same address: 161,376 individuals out of 415,748 (39 percent). However, the main purpose of the Statistical Center of Iran was not tracking the households (at least not declared officially); it is possible that some households remained not exactly the same during these three years. We made two modifications to be sure that we tracked identical households. First, we tested if the gender of each observation remained unchanged. This resulted in an elimination of 35,115 of individuals. Second, we followed the age of each person, since age increased by one year in each survey, which resulted in the elimination of 63,363 observations.

Last, we came up with 62,898 individuals over three years, which is about 15percent of the original sample. Although the extracted sample can be biased due to the elimination of several observations, it enables us to study a panel of thirty thousand households in Iran for the first time. We compared the extracted sample and the main sample in table 8A.9. The table shows that the gender dummy in the extracted sample is very close to the main sample.

Moreover, instead of ReSub, we used RD (resource dividends) that indicates how much every household received after releasing subsidies as dividends of natural resources in 2011 and 2012. By removing the time dummy, we used the real value of wages as the dependent variable. The results in table 8.6 show the positive effects of funds on the wage rates. In addition, the interaction of dividends with Female indicates the decreasing effects of the transfers on the wage gap.

8.3   Conclusions

In this chapter we present the results of our study of the effects of released subsidies on the wage rates in Iran over seven-year period of income-expenditures national surveys. The policy suggests a new channel of transmitting the windfall revenues from natural resources to the economic sectors and directly to the households instead of subsidizing special products. Due to the magnitude of the released funds, the policy can significantly affect the economic sectors, and as a result the labor market and the wage rates. However, the data are insufficient

Table 8.6
Tracked data, 2010 to 2012

	Salary			Self-employed		
Dependent	Log Nominal	Log Real	Log Nominal	Log Nominal	Log Real	Log Nominal
Female	-1.73	-1.44	-0.49***	-3.54**	-3.32**	-0.56***
	(1.37)	(1.4)	(0.07)	(1.4)	(1.54)	(0.1)
RD	0.07***	0.03***		0.07***	0.02	
	(0.01)	(0.01)		(0.01)	(0.01)	
RD_Female	0.07	0.05		0.20**	0.19**	
	(0.08)	(0.08)		(0.09)	(0.09)	
ReSub			0.27***			0.28***
			(0.01)			(0.02)
ReSub_ Female			0.009			0.16*
			(0.06)			(0.09)
N	6,282	6,282	10,192	6,032	6,032	9,325
R^2	0.34	0.34	0.36	0.12	0.12	0.14

Note: Robust standard deviations are reported in parenthesis. * Significant at 10 percent, ** significant at 5 percent, *** significant at 1 percent. The results are summarized. We control for Literacy, Age, Age2, Marry, Female_Marry, Public, Female_Public, and Private in salary income. Control variables are Literacy, Age, Age2, Marry, Female_Marry, Agriculture, Entrepreneur, and Female_Ent for self-employed income.

for studying the transmission channels of the changes in the wage rates directly.

We suggest that after releasing subsidies and dividing the released funds to the public sector, industrial organization, and the public, the wage rates increased significantly. Besides, our results show a high level of gender wage gap in the Iranian labor market. The quantile analyzes show that the wage gap is higher in the lower wage groups. Although the wage gap persists after releasing the subsidies, increasing effects of the policy on the wage rates were not discriminative for the salary wages and that results in an overall decrease of the wage gap. In addition, the policy increased females' self-employed wages more than the males' wage, which decreases the wage gap more significantly.

Appendix

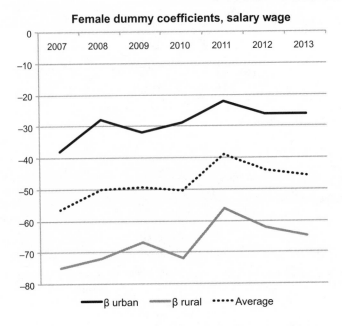

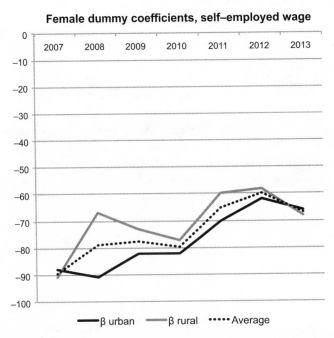

Figure 8A.1
Female coefficient changes, 2007 to 2013

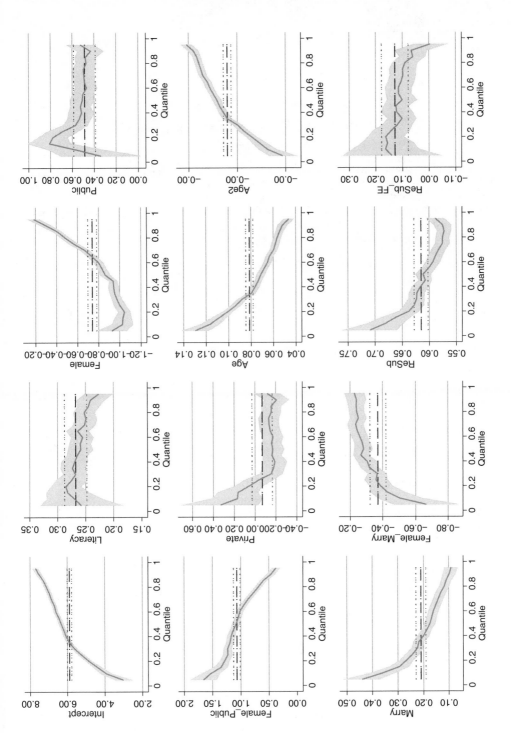

Figure 8A.2
Salary wages in rural area, 2007 to 2013

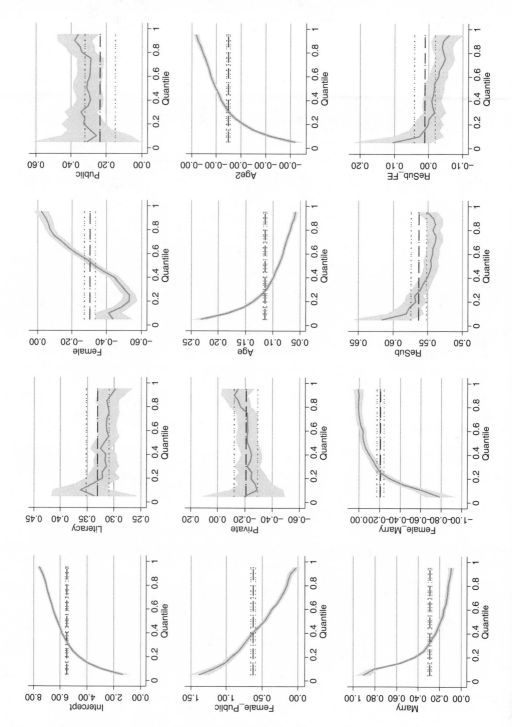

Figure 8A.3
Salary wages in urban area, 2007 to 2013

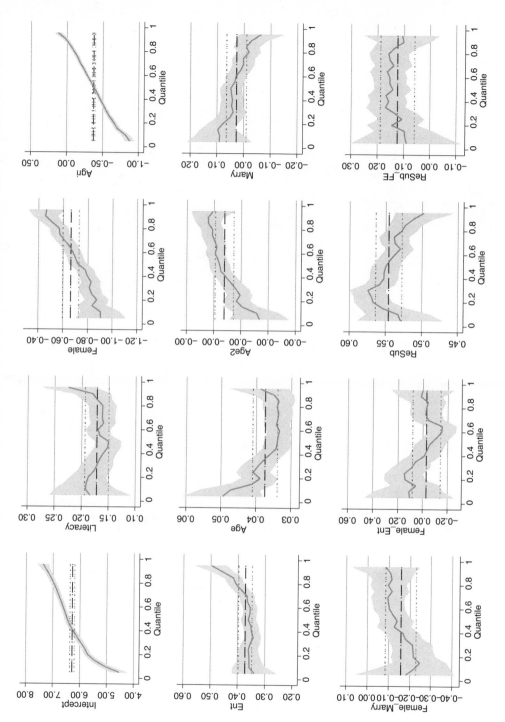

Figure 8A.4
Self-employed wages in rural area, 2007 to 2013

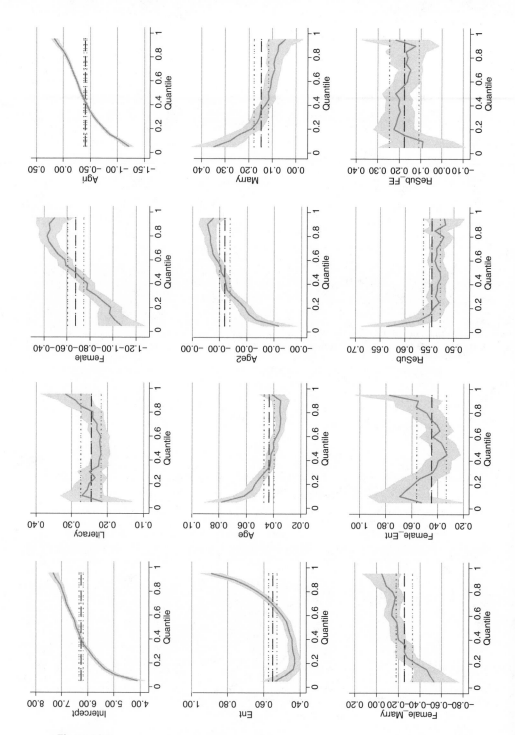

Figure 8A.5
Self-employed wages in urban area, 2007 to 2013

Table 8A.1
Descriptive statistics in rural area, 2007 to 2013

Variable	Obs.	Mean	Std. dev.	Min	Max
ID	493,502				
Ln (salary wage)	71,691	8.083919	0.9531164	1.88974	12.22401
Ln (self-employed wage)	68,793	7.345601	1.113939	0.3485449	13.06298
Age	458,719	30.21723	20.48402	0	99
Literacy	416,417			0	1
Female	458,743			0	1
Public	83,717			0	1
Private	83,717			0	1
Marry	387,529			0	1
Entrepreneur	110,060			0	1
Agriculture sec.	110,060			0	1
Female_Marry	387,528			0	1
Female_Public	70,323			0	1
Female_Private	70,323			0	1
Female_Literacy	416,416			0	1
Female_Agri	94,751			0	1
Female_Ent	94,751			0	1

Table 8A.2
Descriptive statistics in urban areas, 2007 to 2013

Variable	Obs.	Mean	Std. dev.	Min	Max
ID	468,764				
Ln (salary wage)	82,413	8.538093	0.9306675	1.886887	13.07131
Ln (self-employed wage)	43,754	7.782125	0.9596026	0.7742127	13.13444
Age	453,833	30.45665	19.17854	0	99
Literacy	416,456			0	1
Female	453,870			0	1
Public	88,840			0	1
Private	88,840			0	1
Marry	390,939			0	1
Entrepreneur	51,138			0	1
Agriculture sec.	51,138			0	1
Female_Marry	390,938			0	1
Female_Public	81,539			0	1
Female_Private	81,539			0	1
Female_Literacy	416,455			0	1
Female_Agri	47,333			0	1
Female_Ent	47,333			0	1

Table 8A.3
Univariate analysis of gender wage inequality in urban area, 2009

Sector	Control for	Sa/Se	Age all	Age 15–19	Age 20–24	Age 25–29	Age 30–34	Age 35–39	Age upper 40s
All			-7663[a]	-850[a]	-4001[a]	-10173[a]	-14777[a]	-17005[a]	-13586[a]
Public/Private		Sa	5112[b]	-2257	2667[b]	751	4855[b]	9511[b]	5374[b]
Public/Private	Single	Sa	5466[b]	-1962	1772[b]	981	-97	10032[b]	-344
Public/Private	Married	Sa	7418[b]	-7001	5378[b]	1502	8689[b]	10549[b]	8310[b]
Public/Private	Illiterate	Sa	-9089[a]	-8059	-8535[a]	-8874[a]	-5065	-9106[a]	-9220[a]
Public/Private	Literate	Sa	5602[b]	-1841	3066[b]	878	4657[b]	10207[b]	6516[b]
Public		Sa	1456[b]		12780[b]	2151	-479	3636[b]	1255[b]
Public	Single	Sa	10823[b]		9488[b]	5780[b]	-5841[a]	807	873
Public	Married	Sa	2050[b]		1911[b]	439	3003[b]	4316[b]	2413[b]
Public	Illiterate	Sa	-1102						-11506
Public	Literate	Sa	1307[b]		12836[b]	2151	-479	3533[b]	915
Private		Sa	-5479[a]	-2456[a]	-2611[a]	-5102[a]	-3477[a]	-4768[a]	-9957[a]
Private	Single	Sa	-425	-2144	-1688[a]	-2839[a]	-2144	3439	-6900[a]
Private	Married	Sa	-7446[a]	-7662	-5103[a]	-7220[a]	-3207[a]	-6628[a]	-10759[a]
Private	Illiterate	Sa	-8788[a]	-8059	-8396[a]	-8874[a]	-5065	-9066[a]	-8838[a]
Private	Literate	Sa	-4881[a]	-2038	-2316[a]	-4958[a]	-3542[a]	-3159[a]	-8679[a]
Agri/non-Agri		Se	-8706[a]	-917	-4788[a]	-6778[a]	-7915[a]	-6700[a]	-10755[a]
Agri/non-Agri	Single	Se	-2430	-715	-2964[a]	-6343[a]	-528	-3049[a]	-4244[a]
Agri/non-Agri	Married	Se	-10089[a]	-2631	-8365[a]	-7018[a]	-9481[a]	-6812[a]	-11430[a]
Agri/non-Agri	Illiterate	Se	-7031[a]		-1253		-13264[a]	-5529[a]	-7081[a]
Agri/non-Agri	Literate	Se	-8678[a]	-772	-4856[a]	-6829[a]	-7620[a]	-6162[a]	-11106[a]
Agri		Se	-10924[a]	-810	-1602	-6466	-10786	-13602[a]	-13095[a]
Agri	Single	Se	-369	-842	-1406	-3495	-54		-1355
Agri	Married	Se	-13458[a]		-2643	-9438	-14618	-14380[a]	-13806[a]
Agri	Illiterate	Se						-2416[a]	-8017[a]
Agri	Literate	Se	-12168[a]	-826	-1634	-6542[a]	-10753	-14764[a]	-16565
non-Agri		Se	-7605[a]	-1069	-5560[a]	-6715[a]	-7283[a]	-4438[a]	-8871[a]
non-Agri	Single	Se	-2910[a]	-826	-3481[a]	-6874	-796	-3367[a]	-4656[a]
non-Agri	Married	Se	-8508[a]		-9108[a]	-6591[a]	-8753[a]	-4060[a]	-9362[a]
non-Agri	Illiterate	Se	-6052[a]	-2510	-1556	-13716[a]	-5737[a]	-5766[a]	-5766[a]
non-Agri	Literate	Se	-7606[a]	-864	-5637[a]	-6757[a]	-6902[a]	-4009[a]	-8909[a]

Note: The table is reporting Salary (Sa) and Self-employed (Se) wages in urban area. Differences in the wages are reported in rials per hour.
a. Indicates on average significant higher male wage.
b. Indicates on average significant higher female wage.

Table 8A.4
Univariate analysis of gender wage inequality in rural area, 2009

Sector	Control for	Sa/Se	Age all	Age 15–19	Age 20–24	Age 25–29	Age 30–34	Age 35–39	Age upper 40
All			-5690[a]	-1098[a]	-4277[a]	-8694[a]	-11957[a]	-13711[a]	-9489[a]
Public/Private		Sa	-3666[a]	-4371[a]	-1363	-2417	-3207[a]	770	-7569[a]
Public/Private	Single	Sa	-1058[a]	-4606[a]	-1711[a]	-2643[a]	-2316	3200	-7295[a]
Public/Private	Married	Sa	-3001[a]	-3326	1128	-658	-2201	496	-6883
Public/Private	Illiterate	Sa	-7832[a]	-5298[a]	-3385	-7623[a]	-7578[a]	-9604[a]	-7939
Public/Private	Literate	Sa	-2206[a]	-4338[a]	-1226	-2220[a]	-2404[a]	4751[b]	-1439
Public		Sa	-1773		10948[b]	-3563	4719	-1648	-4739
Public	Single	Sa	6269[b]		7286	-8358[a]	5903	-2793	-22139[a]
Public	Married	Sa	-1401		17131[b]	735	4323	-1669	-2824
Public	Illiterate	Sa	-15667[a]						-16189[a]
Public	Literate	Sa	-1755		10948[a]	-3563	4719	-1955	-4072
Private		Sa	-7401[a]	-4679[a]	-4291[a]	-5768[a]	-9032[a]	-9736[a]	-9009[a]
Private	Single	Sa	-3513[a]	-4723[a]	-3343[a]	-3151[a]	-5452[a]	-3463[a]	-5208[a]
Private	Married	Sa	-9535[a]	-5100	-7390[a]	-8695[a]	-10164[a]	-10113[a]	-9658[a]
Private	Illiterate	Sa	-7495[a]	-5298[a]	-2059	-7623[a]	-7703[a]	-9462[a]	-7498[a]
Private	Literate	Sa	-7101[a]	-4678[a]	-4411[a]	-5636[a]	-8993[a]	-8464[a]	-7867[a]
Agri/non-Agri		Se	-6477[a]	-483[a]	-1912[a]	-4759[a]	-6979[a]	-8462[a]	-8024[a]
Agri/non-Agri	Single	Se	-829[a]	-478[a]	-1210[a]	-3500[a]	-2924[a]	-7924	-2010[a]
Agri/non-Agri	Married	Se	-8114[a]	-183	-4517[a]	-5529[a]	-7630[a]	-8591[a]	-8586[a]
Agri/non-Agri	Illiterate	Se	-6915[a]	-165	-1048[a]	-3106[a]	-3443[a]	-7128[a]	-7126[a]
Agri/non-Agri	Literate	Se	-6314[a]	-491	-1913[a]	-4768[a]	-7164[a]	-8384[a]	-8967[a]
Agri		Se	-5795[a]	-171	-1008[a]	-3734[a]	-5777[a]	-7165[a]	-7597[a]
Agri	Single	Se	44	-157	-570	-2480[a]	-2358[a]	-850	-2039[a]
Agri	Married	Se	-7598[a]		-2946[a]	-4713[a]	-6476[a]	-7554[a]	-8127[a]
Agri	Illiterate	Se	-6717[a]	-23	-472[a]	-2788[a]	-2575[a]	-5879[a]	-6946[a]
Agri	Literate	Se	-5415[a]	-173	-1016 [A]	-3767[a]	-6060[a]	-7262[a]	-8621[a]
non-Agri		Se	-7896[a]	-2588[a]	-5054[a]	-5605[a]	-7816[a]	-9006[a]	-8555[a]
non-Agri	Single	Se	-4231[a]	-2603[a]	-3934[a]	-5956[a]	-4410[a]	-30459	-1642
non-Agri	Married	Se	-8445[a]	-2287[a]	-7619[a]	-5149[a]	-8064[a]	-8598[a]	-9202[a]
non-Agri	Illiterate	Se	-7693[a]	-1151	-3486[a]	-4083[a]	-4544[a]	-9075[a]	-7747[a]
non-Agri	Literate	Se	-7940[a]	-2651[a]	-5048[a]	-5518[a]	-7950[a]	-8960[a]	-8762[a]

Note: The table is reporting Salary (Sa) and Self-employed (Se) wages in rural area. Differences in the wages are reported in rials per hour.
a. Indicates on average significant higher male wage.
b. Indicates on average significant higher female wage.

Table 8A.5
Determinants of the wage (log) in urban and rural areas for salary wages, 2009

Urban	1	2	3	4	5	6
Literacy	0.30***	0.43***	0.30***	0.30***	0.26***	0.26***
	(0.026)	(0.026)	(0.025)	(0.025)	(0.025)	(0.025)
Female	-0.11***	0.03	-0.43***	-0.32***	-0.34**	-0.72***
	(0.026)	(.048)	(0.046)	(0.052)	(0.107)	(0.097)
Public	0.28***	0.35***	0.18**	0.18**	0.25***	0.19**
	(0.086)	(0.086)	(0.09)	(0.09)	(0.086)	(0.09)
Private	-0.30***	-0.29***	-0.32***	-0.31***	-0.25***	-0.31***
	(0.085)	(0.086)	(0.089)	(0.09)	(0.085)	(0.089)
Age	0.11***	0.01***	0.11***	0.11***	0.11***	0.11***
	(0.005)	(0.0009)	(0.005)	(0.005)	(0.005)	(0.005)
Age^2	-0.001***		-0.001***	-0.001***	-0.001***	-0.001***
	(0.00006)		(0.00006)	(0.00006)	(0.00006)	(0.00006)
Marry	0.29***	0.54***	0.27***	0.31***	0.27***	0.31***
	(0.023)	(0.026)	(0.023)	(0.026)	(0.023)	(0.026)
Female_Marry		-0.15***		-0.21***		-0.19***
		(0.055)		(0.057)		(0.057)
Female_Public			0.57***	0.63***		0.56***
			(0.052)	(0.056)		(0.06)
Female_Private					-0.51***	
					(0.056)	
Female_Literacy					0.47***	0.44***
					(0.104)	(0.103)
Number of obs.	10,681	10,681	10,681	10,681	10,681	10,681
R^2	0.34	0.30	0.35	0.35	0.35	0.35

Table 8A.5 (continued)

Rural	1	2	3	4	5	6
Literacy	0.28***	0.33***	0.27***	0.26***	0.25***	0.25***
	(0.025)	(0.025)	(0.025)	(0.025)	(0.024)	(0.025)
Female	-0.64***	-0.45***	-0.84***	-0.67***	-0.24*	-0.76***
	(0.043)	(0.06)	(0.047)	(0.06)	(0.124)	(0.102)
Public	0.60***	0.64***	0.49***	0.51***	0.58***	0.51***
	(0.144)	(0.14)	(0.14)	(0.143)	(0.142)	(0.143)
Private	-0.16	-0.16	-0.17	-0.15***	-0.09	-0.16
	(0.14)	(0.13)	(0.14)	(0.141)	(0.139)	(0.141)
Age	0.08 ***	0.008***	0.08***	0.08***	0.08***	0.08***
	(0.005)	(0.001)	(0.004)	(0.004)	(0.005)	(0.004)
Age^2	-0.0009 ***		-0.0009 ***	-0.0008 ***	-0.0009 ***	-0.0008 ***
	(0.00006)		(0.00006)	(0.00006)	(0.00006)	(0.00006)
Marry	0.18***	0.41***	0.16***	0.21***	0.16***	0.20***
	(0.026)	(0.02)	(0.025)	(0.026)	(0.024)	(0.026)
Female_Marry		-0.29**		-0.37***		-0.35***
		(0.08)		(0.083)		(0.087)
Female_Public			0.84***	0.92***		0.89***
			(0.091)	(0.096)		(0.103)
Female_Private					-0.75***	
					(0.094)	
Female_Literacy					0.21**	0.10
					(0.098)	(0.102)
Number of obs.	8,354	8,354	8,354	8,354	8,354	8,354
R^2	0.25	0.22	0.26	0.26	0.26	0.26

Note: Robust standard deviations are reported in parenthesis. * Significant at 10 percent, ** significant at 5 percent, *** significant at 1 percent.

Table 8A.6
Determinants of the wage (log) in urban and rural areas for self-employed wages, 2009

Urban	1	2	3	4	5	6
Literacy	0.28***	0.28***	0.28***	0.28***	0.28***	0.28***
	(0.038)	(0.038)	(0.038)	(0.038)	(0.038)	(0.038)
Female	-0.78***	-0.63***	-0.65***	-0.82***	-0.67***	-0.72***
	(0.053)	(0.094)	(0.098)	(0.054)	(0.095)	(0.145)
Agriculture	-0.41***	-0.41***	-0.42***	-0.41***	-0.41***	-0.41***
	(0.044)	(0.044)	(0.044)	(0.044)	(0.044)	(0.044)
Entrepreneur	0.63***	0.63***	0.63***	0.62***	0.62***	0.62***
	(0.034)	(0.034)	(0.034)	(0.034)	(0.034)	(0.034)
Age	0.04***	0.04***	0.04***	0.04***	0.04***	.04***
	(0.005)	(0.005)	(0.005)	(0.005)	(0.005)	(0.005)
Age^2	-0.0004***	-0.0004***	-0.0004***	-0.0004***	-0.0004***	-0.0004***
	(0.00005)	(0.00005)	(0.00005)	(0.00005)	(0.00005)	(0.00005)
Marry	0.08**	0.12**	0.12***	0.08**	0.12***	0.12***
	(0.038)	(0.04)	(0.04)	(0.038)	(0.04)	(0.04)
Female_Marry		-0.21***	-0.20*		-0.22*	-0.22**
		(0.115)	(0.116)		(0.114)	(0.114)
Female_Agri			0.14			
			(0.233)			
Female_Ent				.41**	.42**	.41**
				(0.208)	(0.208)	(0.209)
Female_Literacy						0.06
						(0.133)
Number of obs.	5,869	5,869	5,869	5,869	5,869	5,869
R^2	0.17	0.17	0.17	0.17	0.17	0.17

Table 8A.6 (continued)

Rural	1	2	3	4	5	6
Literacy	0.15***	0.15***	0.15***	0.15***	0.15***	0.18***
	(0.032)	(0.032)	(0.032)	(0.032)	(0.032)	(0.033)
Female	-0.72***	-0.53***	-0.80***	-0.73***	-0.53***	-0.36***
	(0.048)	(0.078)	(0.084)	(0.050)	(0.079)	(0.095)
Agriculture	-0.45***	-0.45***	-0.49***	-0.45***	-0.45***	-0.46***
	(0.025)	(0.025)	(0.025)	(0.025)	(0.025)	(0.025)
Entrepreneur	0.50***	0.50***	0.50***	0.50***	0.50***	0.50***
	(0.034)	(0.034)	(0.034)	(0.034)	(0.034)	(0.034)
Age	0.04***	0.04***	0.03***	0.04***	0.03***	0.03***
	(0.005)	(0.005)	(0.005)	(0.005)	(0.005)	(0.005)
Age^2	-0.0003***	-0.0003***	-0.0003***	-0.0003***	-0.0003***	-0.0003***
	(0.00005)	(0.00005)	(0.00005)	(0.00005)	(0.00005)	(0.00005)
Marry	0.02	0.10**	0.12**	0.02	0.10**	0.12**
	(0.044)	(0.051)	(0.051)	(0.044)	(0.051)	(0.051)
Female_Marry		-0.3***	-0.24**		-0.30***	-0.26***
		(0.099)	(0.097)		(0.099)	(0.099)
Female_Agri			0.47***			
			(0.089)			
Female_Ent				0.09	0.06	0.04
				(0.162)	(0.160)	(0.157)
Female_Literacy						-0.34
						(0.091)
Number of obs.	8,008	8,008	8,008	8,008	8,008	8,008
R^2	0.10	0.10	0.10	0.10	0.10	0.10

Note: Robust standard deviations are reported in parenthesis. * Significant at 10 percent, ** significant at 5 percent, *** significant at 1 percent.

Table 8A.7

Determinants of the wage (log) in urban and rural areas for salary wages, 2012

Urban	1	2	3	4	5	6
Literacy	0.37***	0.51***	0.37***	0.37***	0.32***	0.32***
	(0.027)	(0.028)	(0.027)	(0.027)	(0.026)	(0.026)
Female	-0.08***	0.03	-0.33***	-0.26***	-0.45***	-0.82***
	(0.023)	(0.04)	(0.035)	(0.042)	(0.114)	(0.112)
Public	0.40***	0.40***	0.32***	0.32***	0.36***	0.32**
	(0.104)	(0.101)	(0.107)	(0.106)	(0.104)	(0.106)
Private	-0.05	-0.09	-0.04	-0.04	-0.006	-0.04
	(0.104)	(0.101)	(0.106)	(0.106)	(0.104)	(0.105)
Age	0.101***	0.01***	0.10***	0.10***	0.10***	0.10***
	(0.004)	(0.0008)	(0.004)	(0.004)	(0.004)	(0.004)
Age^2	-0.001***		-0.001***	-0.001***	-0.001***	-0.001***
	(0.00005)		(0.00005)	(0.00005)	(0.00005)	(0.00005)
Marry	0.24***	0.42***	0.22***	0.25***	0.22***	0.24***
	(0.021)	(0.023)	(0.021)	(0.023)	(0.021)	(0.023)
Female_Marry		-0.09**		-0.16***		-0.12***
		(0.046)		(0.049)		(0.048)
Female_Public			0.52***	0.57***		0.50***
			(0.042)	(0.46)		(0.047)
Female_Private					-0.47***	
					(0.043)	
Female_Literacy					0.64***	0.60***
					(0.112)	(0.112)
Number of obs	10,774	10,774	10,774	10,774	10,774	10,774
R^2	0.29	0.25	0.29	0.30	0.30	0.30

Table 8A.7 (continued)

Rural	1	2	3	4	5	6
Literacy	0.25***	0.33***	0.24***	0.24***	0.22***	0.23***
	(0.025)	(0.025)	(0.025)	(0.025)	(0.025)	(0.025)
Female	-0.55***	-0.38***	-0.78***	-0.62***	-0.12	-0.74***
	(0.042)	(0.058)	(0.050)	(0.059)	(0.12)	(0.114)
Public	0.69***	0.72***	0.58***	0.57***	0.68***	0.58***
	(0.159)	(0.16)	(0.159)	(0.159)	(0.166)	(0.159)
Private	0.02	0.02	0.01	0.009	0.108	0.01
	(0.158)	(0.159)	(0.15)	(0.157)	(0.165)	(0.157)
Age	0.07***	0.006***	0.07***	0.07***	0.07***	0.07***
	(0.004)	(0.0009)	(0.004)	(0.004)	(0.004)	(0.004)
Age^2	-0.0007***		-0.0007***	-0.0007***	-0.0007***	-0.0007***
	(0.00005)		(0.00005)	(0.00005)	(0.00005)	(0.00005)
Marry	0.14***	0.34***	0.13***	0.16***	0.13***	0.16***
	(0.024)	(0.024)	(0.024)	(0.025)	(0.024)	(0.025)
Female_Marry		-0.24***		-0.34***		-0.32***
		(0.083)		(0.081)		(0.085)
Female_Public			0.91***	0.99***		0.96***
			(0.07)	(0.076)		(0.083)
Female_Private					-0.83**	
					(0.075)	
Female_Literacy					0.23***	0.14
					(0.111)	(0.114)
Number of obs.	8,333	8,333	8,333	8,333	8,333	8,333
R^2	0.22	0.19	0.23	0.24	0.24	0.24

Note: Robust standard deviations are reported in parenthesis. * Significant at 10 percent, ** significant at 5 percent, *** significant at 1 percent.

Table 8A.8
Determinants of the wage (log) in urban and rural areas for self-employed wages, 2012

Urban	1	2	3	4	5	6
Literacy	0.25 ***	0.25***	0.25***	0.24***	0.25***	0.26***
	(0.038)	(0.038)	(0.038)	(0.038)	(0.038)	(0.039)
Female	-0.57***	-0.40***	-0.46***	-0.62***	-0.45***	-0.35**
	(0.056)	(0.098)	(0.098)	(0.059)	(0.101)	(0.163)
Agriculture	-0.41***	-0.41***	-0.43***	-0.41***	-0.41***	-0.41***
	(0.043)	(0.043)	(0.044)	(0.043)	(0.043)	(0.043)
Entrepreneur	0.58***	0.58***	0.58***	0.56***	0.55***	0.55***
	(0.035)	(0.035)	(0.035)	(0.036)	(0.036)	(0.036)
Age	0.04***	0.04***	0.04***	0.04***	0.04***	0.04***
	(0.005)	(0.005)	(0.005)	(0.005)	(0.005)	(0.005)
Age^2	-0.0003***	-0.0003***	-0.0003***	-0.0003***	-0.0003***	-0.0003***
	(0.00005)	(0.00005)	(0.00005)	(0.00005)	(0.00005)	(0.00005)
Marry	0.11***	0.16***	0.16***	0.11***	0.16***	0.16***
	(0.038)	(0.039)	(0.039)	(0.038)	(0.039)	(0.039)
Female_Marry		-0.27**	-0.24**		-0.27***	-0.27**
		(0.119)	(0.119)		(0.118)	(0.119)
Female_Agri			0.58**	0.43**		
			(0.256)	(0.174)		
Female_Ent					0.44**	0.46***
					(0.175)	(0.177)
Female_Literacy						-0.12
						(0.161)
Number of obs.	5,674	5,674	5,674	5,674	5,674	5,674
R^2	0.14	0.14	0.14	0.14	0.14	0.14

Table 8A.8 (continued)

Rural	1	2	3	4	5	6
Literacy	0.15***	0.15***	0.16***	0.15***	0.15***	0.16***
	(0.03)	(0.03)	(0.03)	(0.03)	(0.03)	(0.03)
Female	-0.60***	-0.60***	-0.82***	-0.58***	-0.55***	-0.47***
	(0.047)	(0.08)	(0.095)	(0.048)	(0.08)	(0.094)
Agriculture	-0.39***	-0.39***	-0.42***	-0.39***	-0.39***	-0.40***
	(0.023)	(0.02)	(0.023)	(0.023)	(0.02)	(0.02)
Entrepreneur	0.33***	0.33***	0.34***	0.35***	0.35***	0.35***
	(0.034)	(0.034)	(0.034)	(0.034)	(0.034)	(0.03)
Age	0.02***	0.02***	0.02***	0.03***	0.03***	0.02***
	(0.004)	(0.004)	(0.004)	(0.004)	(0.004)	(0.004)
Age^2	-0.0002***	-0.0002***	-0.0002***	-0.0002***	-0.0002***	-0.0002***
	(0.00004)	(0.00004)	(0.00004)	(0.00004)	(0.00004)	(0.00004)
Marry	0.01	0.02	0.03	0.005	0.01	0.02
	(0.042)	(0.047)	(0.047)	(0.042)	(0.047)	(0.047)
Female_Marry		-0.009	0.02		0.04	-0.01
		(0.101)	(0.101)		(0.102)	(0.103)
Female_Agri			0.34***			
			(0.09)			
Female_Ent				-0.38*	-0.39*	-0.41*
				(0.209)	(0.211)	(0.212)
Female_Literacy						-0.17*
						(0.094)
Number of obs.	8,354	8,354	8,354	8,354	8,354	8,354
R^2	0.08	0.08	0.08	0.08	0.08	0.08

Note: Robust standard deviations are reported in parenthesis. * Significant at 10 percent, ** significant at 5 percent, *** significant at 1 percent.

Table 8A.9
Comparison between extracted sample and the main sample

Variable	%Breadwinner	%Female	%Literate	%Worker	%Married	%Urban
Country main	25.41	49.89	79.91	32.85	55.54	48.78
Country extracted	34.92	47.02	76.64	38.35	65.11	44.58
Urban main	26.11	49.65	86.09	29.46	55.63	
Urban extracted	34.84	46.54	84.09	33.67	63.68	
Rural main	24.71	50.13	73.66	36.33	55.44	
Rural extracted	34.98	47.41	70.57	42.22	66.30	

Notes

We would like to express our special thanks and gratitude to Elisabeth Schulte for her useful comments.

1. Iranian parliament, "Targeted Subsidies Reform Act," http://www.parliran.ir/index.aspx?siteid=1&pageid=3070.

2. Other accounts detailing on the resource curse can be found in Van Wijenbergen (1984), Collier and Hoeffler (1998), Gylfason, (2001), Ross (2004), Collier and Hoeffler (2004), Mehlum et al. (2006), and Bjorvatn and Farzanegan (2013).

3. Quoted by the deputy of the Iranian central bank. http://banki.ir/ads/2960-bank-dari.

4. Several authors, including Sala-i-Martín and Subramanian (2003), Clemons (2003), Palley (2003), Sandbu (2006), and Segal (2011), suggest the Resource Dividend proposal as a direct transfer of resource rents to the public.

5. http://www.amar.org.ir/Default.aspx?tabid=111 (in Persian). English summary description without the data http://www.amar.org.ir/Default.aspx?tabid=1336.

6. The variable is in nominal values. It is not necessary to use values in real terms-since we have log dependent variables and an explanatory time dummy (Wooldridge 2006).

7. We display one specification for each year, which are specified alike. Full tables with more specifications are available on request. The results for the years 2009 and 2012 are provided in the appendix.

References

Bjorvatn, K., and M. R. Farzanegan. 2013. Demographic transition in resource rich countries: A blessing or a curse? *World Development* 45: 337–51.

Clemons, S. 2003. Sharing, Alaska-style. *New York Times*, April 9. Available at: http://www.nytimes.com/2003/04/09/opinion/sharing-alaska-style.html.

Collier, P., and A. Hoeffler. 1998. On economic causes of civil war. *Oxford Economic Papers* 50: 563–73.

Collier, P., and A. Hoeffler. 2004. Greed and grievance in civil war. *Oxford Economic Papers* 56: 563–95.

Farzanegan, M. R., and M. Habibpour. 2014. Direct distribution of rents and the resource curse in Iran: A micro-econometric Analysis. Working Paper Series 4824. CESifo.

Guillaume, D. M., M. R. Farzin, and R. Zytek. 2011. *The Chronicles of the Subsidy Reform*. Washington, DC: IMF.

Gylfason, T. 2001. Natural resources, education, and economic development. *European Economic Review* 45: 847–59.

Hassanzadeh, E. 2012. *Recent developments in Iran's energy subsidy reforms*. New York: Policy Brief. IISD.

International Trade Union Confederation. 2008. *The global gender Pay gap. ITUN Report*. ITUC.

Mehlum, H., K. Moene, and R. Torvik. 2006. Institutions and resource curse. *Economic Journal* 116: 1–20.

Palley, T. I. 2003. Combating the natural resource curse with citizen revenue distribution funds: oil and the case of Iraq. FPIF Special Report. Available at: http://www.thomaspalley.com/docs/articles/economic_development/natural_resources_curse.pdf.

Razavi, S. M., and N. Habibi. 2014. Decomposition of gender wage differentials in Iranian empirical study based on household survey data. *Journal of Developing Areas* 48 (2): 185–204.

Ross, M. L. 2004. What do we know about natural resources and civil war? *Journal of Peace Research* 41: 337–56.

Ross, M. L. 2008. Oil, Islam, and women. *American Political Science Review* 102 (1): 107–123.

Sala-i-Martín, X., and A. Subramanian. 2003. Addressing the natural resource curse: An illustration from Nigeria. Working Paper 9804. NBER.

Sandbu, M. E. 2006. Natural wealth accounts: A proposal for alleviating the natural resource curse. *World Development* 34: 1153–70.

Segal, P. 2011. Resource rents, redistribution, and halving global poverty: The resource dividend. *World Development* 39: 475–89.

United Nations Economic Commission for Europe. 2012. Promoting gender equity and women's economic empowerment on the road to sustainable development: Good practice from the UNECE region.

Van Wijenbergen, S. 1984. Inflation, employment, and the Dutch disease in oil exporting countries: A short-run disequilibrium analysis. *Quarterly Journal of Economics* 99: 233–50.

Warth, L., and M. Koparanova. 2012. Empowering women for sustainable development. Discussion Paper 2012.1. United Nations.

Wooldridge, J. 2006. *Introductory Econometrics: A Modern Approach*. Mason, OH: Thomson South-Western.

9 The Political Economy of Subsidy Reform in the Persian Gulf Monarchies

Jim Krane

9.1 Introduction

The political economy *Theory of the Rentier State*, as sketched by Mahdavy in 1970 and expanded by Beblawi and Luciani in 1987, holds that the massive influx of oil rent plays a large, perhaps dominant, role in shaping the political and social relationships between state and society.[1] Inflows of external rents allow governments to "purchase consent" of the governed without paying the political price of imposing taxes. This exchange of patronage for political acquiescence is enshrined within a social contract that, in turn, is said to bring rulers wide autonomy in decision making, while releasing them from the need to concede democratic participation in policy making. Citizens are portrayed as complacent and lacking in motivation for economic and educational self-improvement, since their incomes flow from citizenship rather than from hard work.[2]

Recent studies on the Gulf Arab monarchies (Saudi Arabia, United Arab Emirates, Kuwait, Oman, Qatar, and Bahrain) challenge some of these claims through close examination of state obligations, which might be described as the "supply" side of the social contract. These include work by Gray on the Gulf monarchies, Davidson on the UAE, Hertog on Saudi Arabia, and Jocelyn Mitchell on Qatar, all of which dispel some of the more caricatural notions of early theory while enriching conceptualization of the rentier bargain beyond a simple trade of petroleum rents for allegiance. These theoretical revisions also depict Gulf autocracies as increasingly deferential toward citizens.[3] However, other than Mitchell's portrayal of Qatari activism, these works neither ascribe much agency to citizens nor suggest that Gulf nationals can mobilize to pursue their interests. Rather they imply that regimes have maintained or increased benefit allocations in the interest of *avoiding* citizen mobilization. As in the early literature, the state–society social contract is portrayed as difficult to change.

In the chapter I illuminate a portion of the less explored "demand" side of the rentier social contract, which comprises the expectations of citizens. My results challenge the literature's monochrome view of the citizen by showing a more complex understanding of the interconnection between the state's natural resources and citizen welfare benefits. I gather public attitudes toward reform of energy subsidies, a topic with present-day policy relevance, and show that while many citizens do express notions of entitlement to welfare benefits and opposition to reform—in this case of subsidized energy—others are willing to consider the loss of those benefits under certain conditions.

One reason why the citizen "demand" side of the social contract has been relatively unexplored is lack of data. There have been few public surveys on attitudes toward energy in the Gulf and none (that I have found) that delve into matters comprising the foundations of ruling family support. To compensate, I gathered views of the general population by conducting a major public survey of 730 Gulf nationals that sought insights into their sense of entitlement to energy and attitudes toward higher retail prices. I use these responses to revise theoretical assumptions in three ways. First, by measuring citizen interpretations of the patronage distribution mechanism, to which scholars ascribe so much magnitude in generating regime support; second, by contrasting citizen interpretations with expectations in the literature; and third, by contrasting citizen views with those of elites and experts.

The data reveal a disparity that suggests commonly held assumptions—and academic theory—to be wide of the mark. Where theory and elite observers remain beholden to views of a rigid social contract that precludes "extraction" from the public, citizens reveal notions of a more flexible compact. While elites see citizens as fierce opponents of proposals that would erode public "rights" to cheap domestic energy, only a subset of the public conforms to this view. A substantial portion of the public appears more amenable to increases in subsidized electricity prices, especially when changes are portrayed as being in the national interest.

This disjuncture between views of citizens and those of scholars and elites is consistent with the "dictator's dilemma" problem, in which policy making in autocracies is insufficiently informed by public opinion.[4] Results of an expert elicitation reveal overestimation of public opposition that is symptomatic of this concept. Elites, policy makers among them, develop understandings and make policy under certain assumptions and conditions. Given their imperfect information on public opinion, those assumptions may be misguided, as this chapter will illustrate.

My survey results suggest that policy makers may have more scope than commonly understood for reducing high levels of per-capita resource consumption that characterize these monarchies. This chapter focuses on reform of residential electricity tariffs because of the large and growing amount of exportable energy consumed, and because the nature of electricity billing allows regimes leeway to impose discriminatory pricing in ways that reflect a customer's economic status or political clout. Electricity pricing thus provides more information on political entitlement than would be the case for transportation fuels, for example.

The reform challenges facing these regimes are of enormous significance for their countries, as well as for international energy markets and resource-importing states. As emphasized in a previous paper,[5] subsidies are fueling unrestrained growth in energy demand that threatens longstanding commodity exports from the Gulf, while driving regional per-capita carbon emissions to world-leading levels. Oil and gas exports remain the economic underpinning of these states, the chief source of government revenue, and the main source of distributional rents. The manner in which these societies confront domestic subsidies will provide clues about the longer term economic viability of these states and their role in energy markets, and, ultimately, about the longevity of the world's last remaining absolute monarchies.

9.2   Subsidy Reform and the Social Contract

The rentier state theory, which Herb describes as "the most influential theoretic paradigm in the study of the comparative politics of the eastern Arab world,"[6] presents the most relevant theoretical lens for an examination of the energy sector in the Gulf monarchies, the engine of the rents that support these political economies. Rentier scholarship affords little ambiguity on regime options vis-à-vis citizen subsidies. Welfare benefits are portrayed as vital components of citizenship that, collectively, comprise the citizen's most important inducement for acquiescence to his government's legitimacy.[7] This acquiescence is typically framed as a social contract or "ruling bargain." Authors declare that benefits cannot be retracted without offsetting their loss with a corresponding increase in democratic legitimacy.[8] To do otherwise would challenge the basis of the state.[9]

The concept of the social contract is thus central within the rentier state and in the theoretical works examining these states. Whereas in democratic settings, social contracts generally refer to collective bargains among representatives of labor, capital, and the state,[10] in more autocratic states the social contract becomes a redistributive "authoritarian bargain" enshrining the terms by which citizens legitimate governing regimes, and the constraints and incentives that apply to both parties. In the rentier Middle East these pacts assume the role of institutions that in more participatory polities confer government legitimacy through formal citizen input. Farsoun argues that rentier social contracts accord citizens with *political rights to economic security* that go beyond mere humanitarian aspirations. In so doing, Farsoun argued presciently that Arab regimes unwittingly created a bargain they could not maintain forever, ensuring that the growing expense of providing subsidy "rights" would someday become unaffordable.[11]

Benefit reforms have been amply covered in the political literature on democratic welfare states. These works also contain much of relevance for autocracies. As in democracies, government subsidy creates solidarity among beneficiaries who can rise up and threaten political leadership when their interests are jeopardized. Pierson argues that welfare societies thus maintain a constant *potential* for mobilization that raises the stakes of reform.[12] The highly centralized composition of the Gulf regimes poses an additional obstacle to subsidy reform, since it concentrates accountability. Reform-minded rulers are thus exposed to the full force of public reaction.

There is little doubt that Middle East social contracts are sheltered by formidable barriers to reform, despite their deleterious "effect on employment, productivity, foreign investment, trade, and macroeconomic performance."[13] Heydemann and others characterize reluctance to reform as an incumbent's rational response to circumstances in which costs of reform are immediate, while benefits are delayed and uncertain. Victor argues that subsidy provision is a well-understood technique for regimes to satisfy interest groups that underpin power. The outsized energy subsidies typical of oil-rich autocracies are sometimes described as a "populist paradox," since regimes that provide them have no need to buy votes. Regardless, the magnitude of these subsidies demonstrates the acute fear of unrest in petro-states. Most of these states lack the useful pressure-relief effects of elections that might otherwise offset threats from regional unrest, including (at the time of writing) the Arab Spring uprisings.[14]

9.2.1 Dangers of Abrogating Gulf Social Contracts

Gulf scholars have speculated for decades on how the public might react to government violations of the social contract, including in the area of energy pricing. Writing during the long oil bust of the 1980s and 1990s, Crystal saw the threatened (but mostly unimplemented) reduction of welfare benefits and imposition of taxes in Kuwait and Qatar as a source of instability that would drive demands for participation.[15] Gause argued that Gulf monarchies' failure to meet their ends of the social contract would jeopardize the future of their political systems.[16] More recently Davidson forecast in 2012 that an inability to maintain social contracts—along with a technology-empowered political opposition—would bring about the demise of all six Gulf monarchies by 2017.[17]

The electricity subsidies that are the focus of this research have long been understood as untouchable. Hertog and Luciani are among those arguing that higher prices would be helpful in reducing demand, while conceding that regimes would be unlikely to raise prices, especially on citizens' residential consumption.

Encouraging (residents) to change their electricity consumption pattern is much more difficult than pursuing a more rational use of energy in industry, and it is especially difficult if the price lever cannot be used. It is therefore expected that emphasis will be on increasing electricity production rather than reining in consumption and, if anything, savings efforts will be focused on industry rather than the residential sector.[18]

Kazim, in his 2007 study outlining energy conservation options for the UAE, stretches as far as to recommend that the Emirates cut consumption by reducing population growth, but does not even broach the possibility of raising residential electricity prices.[19] Perhaps the strongest reason for portraying subsidies and social contracts as so difficult to reform is the risk to the survival of the regimes that launch them. As Gurr writes, and as history shows, declines in state benefits and social welfare are common triggers for political violence and even overthrow of governments.[20]

9.2.2 Subsidy Reform in Energy Exporting States

What does history reveal about subsidy reform in oil exporting countries? The record is mixed. On the one hand, raising energy prices has been a prime driver of unrest. Examples include overthrown regimes in OPEC members Venezuela in 1993 and Indonesia in 1998. On the other, positive outcomes are also possible. All but five of 28 substantial energy subsidy reform efforts documented by the IMF in the past two decades met with some success.[21] Most reforms occurring in exporting states have come amid a decline in oil production.

Among energy exporters, Indonesia, after failed attempts in 1997 and 2003 successfully raised fuel prices in 2005 and 2008. Indonesia reduced its subsidy load from 3.5 percent of GDP in 2005 to 0.8 percent by 2009. Yemen also managed small reductions in fuel subsidies, which, however, still accounted for 7.4 percent of 2009 GDP. Mexico reduced gasoline subsidies in 2005 and 2006[22] after failing to reform electricity prices between 1999 and 2002. Malaysia underwent a series of attempts to reduce fuel subsidies (which stood at more than 1 percent of GDP in 2012) but most were reversed following public outcries.[23] Nigeria's fuel price reforms of 2011 and 2012 triggered anti-government unrest but still managed to reduce subsidy costs from 4.7 to 3.6 percent of GDP.[24] However, the most relevant example of subsidy reform has arisen in a neighboring OPEC member state in the Gulf, itself a former monarchy, and the country for which the term "rentier state" was coined.[25]

9.2.3   Iran's Subsidy Reform of 2010

In December 2010, Iran became the first major energy-exporting country to drastically cut indirect subsidies[26] as well as the first country in the world to replace energy handouts with a universal cash transfer program for households.[27] Iran's dramatic reform achieved positive welcomes from the IMF and, at least initially, the Iranian public.[28] The IMF and other observers credited the reform with initial reductions in domestic energy demand, including a 6 percent decrease in gasoline consumption,[29] while halving the world's largest energy subsidy burden, with a pre-reform value near $100 billion or a quarter of 2010 GDP. Demand reduction was sufficient to permit a temporary increase in oil exports, before Iran's oil trade was blocked by international sanctions.[30] The government built support for the reform by creating bank accounts for each household and depositing two monthly payments worth about $40 per person prior to the program's launch. Recipients could only access those payments after prices were raised.[31]

Iran's reform confronted a structure of energy underpricing similar to that in the Gulf monarchies but with more advanced harmful effects.

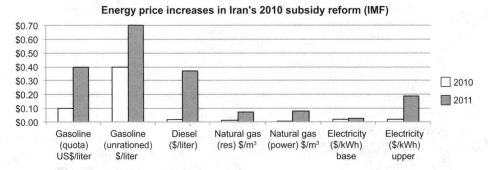

Figure 9.1
Comparison of energy prices in Iran, 2010 and 2011

Domestic demand was curtailing oil exports while forcing Iran to import market-priced gasoline at around US$2 per gallon, which it then sold domestically for 38 US cents.[32] Some 70 percent of these subsidies were said to accrue to the richest third of the population.[33] When subsidies were reduced, the largest increase in price affected smuggling-prone diesel fuel, which rose from US 1.6 cents to 37 cents per liter (an increase of more than 2,000 percent), followed by electricity for large residential consumers, where prices for consumption in excess of 600 kilowatt-hours per month jumped from US 1.6 cents to 19 cents per kWh (a rate nearly double the average US price in 2012). Rising price bands were designed to encourage conservation and protect the poor, with the first 100 kWh of electricity per month remaining available for 2.7 US cents.[34] (figure 9.1)

Although initial plans called for prices to be increased to 90 percent of international levels over five years, the subsidy reform was halted in 2012 by rising inflation and a lack of parliamentary support.[35] The tightening of international sanctions targeting Iran's nuclear program made it difficult to separate the macroeconomic effects of the subsidy reform from those triggered by the embargo. Whatever the cause, severe inflation undermined the measure, reducing energy prices in real terms as well as the value of the replacement cash transfers.[36] Dwindling political will also undercut the reform, since prices and payments were not adjusted for inflation. Although most goals were not achieved, the IMF in 2013 described the reform as "partially successful,"[37] while the Iranian government in 2015 was said to be preparing a new set of price increases.

Regardless, the Iranian reform and replacement stipends resonated within the six Gulf Cooperation Council (GCC) energy ministries. In Saudi Arabia, which operates amid similar levels of subsidy and budget dependence on oil exports, an adviser said Iran's actions represented a potential path toward more efficient resource consumption.[38] It thus bears asking: Would citizens in the Gulf monarchies accept reforms that reduce domestic pressure on exports, and, perhaps, compensate citizens for their loss in welfare?

9.3   Research Design

9.3.1   Hypotheses

Regime survival considerations are surely one of the chief inhibitors of subsidy reforms. If the literature's picture of the inelastic social contract is accurate, regimes are in a bind. In an expert elicitation conducted for this research, 80 percent of experts (61 of 76) agreed that citizens consider subsidies as "rights of citizenship," backing up the claims in the literature.[39] This consensus appears to conflict with moves toward reducing benefits. If energy subsidies are "rights," is it possible to reform them? Answering this question depends less on regime or expert concepts of the social contract, and more on the understandings of citizens. Policymakers contemplating a reduction in energy subsidies would therefore want to understand the boundaries of acceptable reform: Do citizens claim entitlement to energy resources? If so, does that mean they oppose higher prices? Would citizens require or even accept a replacement benefit in exchange for agreeing to pay more for energy? With this logic in mind, I designed three hypotheses that could be tested with public survey data.

First, I wanted to learn whether entitlement-minded citizens—those who express feelings of ownership over national resources—are more opposed to higher electricity prices. In numerous settings, including in Dubai in 2011, subsidized energy prices were raised with little warning or explanation. Given their sense of entitlement to energy, it should logically follow that the entitled group would oppose encroachment on that benefit, especially if no justification is given:

H1: Citizens exhibiting entitlement are less likely to support increased electricity prices

However, what if the national interest is invoked as the rationale for higher prices? If citizens are told that higher prices were needed to reduce waste so that their country's exports of oil and gas could be maintained, might entitlement-minded citizens be convinced to relinquish their problematic benefits? The second hypothesis tests the assumption that entitlement-minded citizens are still more inclined than others to oppose higher prices.

H2: Citizens exhibiting entitlement will express lower support for higher prices than the overall public, even if the national interest is invoked

As mentioned, Iran designed its subsidy reform to include a compensation payment for lost benefits, and citizens largely supported this strategy. It follows that even entitlement-minded GCC citizens would support such a benefit swap, since it would give them a greater amount of flexibility to choose benefits that corresponded more closely to their preferences.

H3: Citizens exhibiting entitlement will demonstrate more support for higher prices if offered an alternate benefit

I am also interested in measuring the relationship between demographic variables and support for higher prices. This is not because the rentier literature suggests certain categories of citizen are more prone to claiming subsidy rights, but to determine whether effects other than "entitlement" can better explain opposition to higher electricity prices. To test for these effects, I included demographic variables (presented in table 9.1) as part of a regression that seeks to correlate support for higher prices with socioeconomic status, education, gender, and age. One might expect in the patriarchal Gulf that women and younger citizens are less likely to control household finances or bear responsibility for paying bills and therefore could exhibit more support for higher electricity prices. Also more educated citizens might be expected to possess a greater understanding of the region's economic quandary and therefore might also support higher prices, while less educated citizens might be less willing to contemplate paying more.

9.3.2 Data and Methods

Data from the public survey provide the source for hypothesis testing. I also pursued a corresponding approach through an expert elicitation (EE) of Gulf energy experts to illuminate elite conceptions of energy subsidies and citizen entitlement. The two methods are logically complementary but statistically incompatible due to differences in selection of respondents and their available response categories. On the one hand, the public survey reflects an attempt to gather a representative sample of the public. On the other, the EE selects particular subject

Table 9.1
Frequency tables for three dependent and five independent variables

Dep 1	Freq.	Percent	Valid	Cum.	Dep 2	Freq.	Percent	Valid	Cum.
1 (v. willing)	49	9.06	10.54	10.54	1 (s. support)	64	11.83	14.1	14.1
2	90	16.64	19.35	29.89	2	117	21.63	25.77	39.87
3	90	16.64	19.35	49.25	3	110	20.33	24.23	64.1
4	94	17.38	20.22	69.46	4	114	21.07	25.11	89.21
5 (v. opposed)	142	26.25	30.54	100	5 (s. oppose)	49	9.06	10.79	100
Total	465	85.95	100		Total	454	83.92	100	
Missing	76	14.05			Missing	87	16.08		
Total	541	100			Total	541	100		

Dep 3	Freq.	Percent	Valid	Cum.	Share	Freq.	Percent	Valid	Cum.
1 (s. support)	53	9.8	11.32	11.32	0 No	312	57.67	57.67	57.67
2	113	20.89	24.15	35.47	1 Yes	**229**	**42.33**	42.33	100
3	126	23.29	26.92	62.39	Total	541	100	100	
4	130	24.03	27.78	90.17					
5 (s. oppose)	46	8.5	9.83	100	Female	Freq.	Percent	Valid	Cum.
Total	468	86.51	100		0 male	332	61.37	61.37	61.37
Missing	73	13.49			1 female	209	38.63	38.63	100
Total	541	100			Total	541	100	100	

Edu	Freq.	Percent	Valid	Cum.	Income	Freq.	Percent	Valid	Cum.
1	9	1.66	1.67	1.67	1	105	19.41	19.41	19.41
2	184	34.01	34.07	35.74	2	97	17.93	17.93	37.34
3	58	10.72	10.74	46.48	3	100	18.48	18.48	55.82
4	261	48.24	48.33	94.81	4	102	18.85	18.85	74.68
5	19	3.51	3.52	98.33	5	137	25.32	25.32	100
6	9	1.66	1.67	100	Total	541	100	100	
Total	540	99.82	100						
Missing	1	0.18			Age	Freq.	Percent	Valid	Cum.
Total	541	100			1 18 to 24	158	29.21	29.21	29.21
					2 25 to 29	149	27.54	27.54	56.75
					3 30 to 34	123	22.74	22.74	79.48
					4 35 to 39	59	10.91	10.91	90.39
					5 40+	52	9.61	9.61	100
					Total	541	100	100	

matter experts, and makes no attempt to be representative. Therefore I did not compare the two datasets statistically, but I instead provide the aggregated EE responses as an alternate view of the social contract to contrast with the citizen-participant view. These juxtapositions are useful in establishing whether prevailing views of elites, as well as those in the academic literature, reflect understandings held by citizens.

9.3.3 Public Survey

The polling firm YouGov conducted the public survey online, translating it into Arabic and providing it to its Middle East panel, which included 730 citizen respondents in the six GCC countries (Saudi Arabia, UAE, Kuwait, Oman, Qatar, and Bahrain).[40] The public survey responses were gathered between November 28 and December 4, 2011. The data are heavily skewed toward Saudi respondents and contain few responses from the smaller monarchies, which is due to the composition of the YouGov panel rather than the author's intent. All responses are from GCC citizens. However, YouGov warned that its panel was not representative of the citizen population as a whole and that it may be affected by errors in sampling and coverage. A company official said that, since the survey was conducted online, and Internet penetration remained less than universal in the Middle East in 2011, the results should be considered broadly illustrative of public opinion rather than statistically representative.

Because of small sample sizes in the smaller monarchies, I aggregated the GCC responses in the interest of statistical robustness. However, the dominance of Saudi responses means that the aggregated results are most strongly representative of Saudi opinion. While I had hoped to differentiate among countries, and I recognize the shortcomings of grouped responses, I believe the aggregated results can nevertheless guide the understanding of public opinion in the smaller monarchies given the close regional similarities in energy pricing, level of subsidy, and in political structure and culture. The terms of my agreement with YouGov limited me to six questions and did not allow for differentiating questions by country.

Given the urgency of reforming energy subsidies in five of the six monarchies (Qatar excepted), I wanted to learn how amenable citizens are to paying a cost-reflective price for electricity. How do citizens respond to a proposed loss of energy benefits? The survey allowed me to tease out perceptions of entitlement among citizens and evaluate levels of public opposition and support for a hypothetical retraction of citizen subsidies under conditions that might be useful in a policy-making context. Survey responses providing data for the three dependent variables were arrayed on five-point Likert scales.

- To test H1 and measure the first dependent variable (Dep 1), I asked how willing the citizen would be to paying the full cost of electricity without government assistance, explaining only that "the true cost without government subsidies is more than the average price that citizens in your country pay now." Respondents were offered five choices ranging from "very willing" to "very opposed."
- To test H2 and measure the second dependent variable (Dep 2), I asked how willingly citizens would pay higher prices to moderate consumption in the national interest. "Some people have said that since electricity is provided to citizens at an artificially low price some people waste it. This consumes oil and gas that could be exported." Responses on higher prices ranged from "strongly support" to "strongly oppose."
- To test H3 and measure the third dependent variable (Dep 3), I sought comment on what might be termed the "Iran model," asking whether the public would support a price increase if citizens were compensated with an alternate benefit of equal value. Responses ranged from "strongly support" to "strongly oppose."
- The main independent variable in my model is that which measures citizen entitlement to subsidized energy. To measure this variable, labeled "share" below, I used responses that agreed with the statement that government electricity subsidies were a manifestation of "my share of the country's energy wealth." I classified those who selected this response option as the "entitlement-minded" group, and used their aggregated responses to discern the effect of the main independent variable.
- Remaining independent variables are taken from demographic data from the YouGov survey panel. These predictors include respondents' reported gender ("female"), income ("income"), educational level ("edu"), and age group ("age").

Each of the three dependent variables measures a component of my theory. Dep 1 measures the impact of entitlement on willingness to pay, when prices are raised without an explanation. Dep 2 measures the impact of entitlement on willingness to support increased prices, when invoking the national interest in conserving natural resources for export. Dep 3 measures impact of entitlement on willingness to consider a benefit swap. I also sought to determine whether, as the rentier literature implies, a majority of citizens believe they are entitled to subsidized electricity as their "share" of the national resource patrimony. As depicted in the frequency tables (table 9.1), and discussed in subsequent sections, this assumption was not accurate.

9.3.4 Model Specification

The three dependent variables for this study contain five ordered categories measured on a scale from 1 to 5. Therefore I use ordinal logit as my main analytical technique.[41]

The basic regression model is as follows:

Support for higher electricity prices
$$= \alpha + \beta_1 \text{ (Entitlement)} + \beta_2 \text{ (age)} + \beta_3 \text{ (Education)} + \beta_4 \text{ (Income)} + \beta_5 \text{ (Female)} + \varepsilon,$$

where β_1 through β_5 are the parameters of interest in the study.

The results are shown in table 9.2, columns 1, 2, and 3. Each column presents results for the dependent variables aggregated for the six countries surveyed in the study. The tables present the coefficients from the multivariate model and the *p*-values to indicate the significance level of each variable. Standard errors are also given.

9.4 Results

What can the survey responses tell us about citizen attitudes toward subsidy reform in the rentier Gulf? I tested hypotheses 1, 2, and 3 using regression, with "share" as the main independent variable signifying a citizen's entitlement to subsidies, and the three "support for price increase" responses as dependent variables. I also inserted respondent demographics as predictor variables.

The regression results for the first two dependent variables displayed the expected signs and marshalled strong support for H1 and H2, finding that citizens who express entitlement to national resources are indeed more opposed to higher tariffs under the conditions described, as shown by the positive coefficients in table 9.2, at the top of columns 1 and 2. These findings bolster long-held rentier assumptions that portray reforms of energy subsidies as violations of citizen rights. As shown in the table, citizen "entitlement" to energy as a personal share of a national resource is strongly associated with higher levels of opposition to higher prices, when compared with the overall population, in models 1 and 2.

Table 9.2
Entitlement and subsidy reform results from ordinal logit regression

Model	1	2	3
Share (entitlement)	0.719***	0.663***	0.207
	(0.1711)	(0.1718)	(0.1681)
Age	0.046	-0.018	0.008
	(0.0668)	(0.0666)	(0.0669)
Income	-0.021	-0.040	-0.029
	(0.0625)	(0.0621)	(0.0619)
Education	0.172*	0.056	-0.149
	(0.0821)	(0.0812)	(0.0811)
Female	0.239	0.521**	0.217
	(0.1823)	(0.1825)	(0.1782)

Note: Dependent variables are willingness-to-pay variations in Dep1, Dep2, and Dep3.
* Significant at the 0.05 level; ** significant at the 0.01 level; *** significant at the 0.001 level; standard errors are in parentheses below coefficients.

Model 1 Results confirm that entitlement-minded citizens are less willing to pay the full cost for electricity in their homes when informed only that the government is paying for a portion of their consumption. This result provides strong support for H1. Also significant (at the 0.05 level) was level of education. However, contrary to what was surmised above, more educated respondents are actually *less* likely to support higher prices. Based on the other results of this model, there was no corroboration for assumptions that women or younger or wealthier people were also more likely to support higher prices.

Since the results of ordinal logit regression provide only log odds ratios, I also calculated the percentage change in odds for the statistically significant variables, to allow more intuitive interpretation of the results. In the case of model 1, the odds of being more opposed to higher prices are 105 percent higher for the "entitled" group, and 19 percent higher for each increase in a respondent's level of education.

Model 2 The results of the second model are given in table 9.2, column 2. Here again, citizens who expressed entitlement to natural resources were less supportive of higher electricity prices, in this case, when invoking the national interest. Again, this result is highly statistically significant and offers strong support for H2. Also significant (at the 0.01 level) was gender, but, again, contrary to what was surmised above, women were less likely than men to support higher prices, despite being informed it was in the national interest. Based on the results of this model, there was no support for assumptions that more educated, younger, or wealthier people were more likely to support higher prices. The odds of being more opposed to higher prices are 94 percent higher for the entitled group and 68 percent higher for women.

Model 3 The results of the third model are given in table 9.2, column 3. Entitlement has no statistically significant effect on whether a respondent would accept an alternate benefit in lieu of higher prices. Further none of the demographic variables were statistically significant at or above the .05 level. There is thus insufficient evidence to support H3, which declares that entitlement-minded citizens will demonstrate more support for higher prices if offered an alternate benefit.

9.5 Discussion

Analysis of the full range of citizen survey responses reveals a more nuanced view of the social contract than that implied in the literature. Citizens who express feelings of entitlement to subsidized energy accept the notion that they are entitled to that energy at a special price. Significant results from ordinal logit regressions were consistent with the subsidies-as-rights narrative in rentier theory. However, only a *minority* of respondents selected the entitlement option. That leaves a clear majority of citizens, nearly six in 10 respondents (312 of 541 total), who did *not* express entitlement to subsidized electricity.

How does citizen understanding of subsidy and potential reform contrast with that of experts? Broadly speaking, expert opinions reflect the portrayal of subsidies in the literature: citizens are entitled to subsidized energy and should be expected to oppose increased prices.

When asked a question related to that which informed H1, experts overestimated citizen opposition to proposals that would erode public "rights" to cheap domestic energy. Among the entire pool of citizen respondents (including the "entitled" and those who did not choose this option), 41 percent were either very or quite opposed and 41 percent were unopposed to higher prices.[42] By contrast, when experts were asked how citizens would respond, 92 percent of the expert respondents portrayed citizens as opposed, with just 5 percent portraying them as not opposed.

In the second survey question that informed H2, the percentage of total respondents "strongly opposed" to higher prices dropped from 26 percent to just 10 percent. Therefore a substantial portion of the public was actually willing to make a personal sacrifice to promote the national interest[43] in a more optimal allocation of exportable resources. (As shown above, those expressing entitlement happened to be much less likely to make this sacrifice.) The expert elicitation questionnaire did not contain this question, thus there is no comparison between cohorts.

What if citizens were offered an alternate benefit to replace subsidized prices for electricity, as occurred in Iran? Alaskans, who pay some of the highest electricity rates in the United States, also receive a yearly cash dividend as their portion of the state's oil revenues. Might a substitute benefit plan be accepted in lieu of higher prices in the Gulf monarchies? Responses to the survey question that informed H3 found that opposition was also assuaged by an alternate benefit. Opponents comprised 32 percent of respondents, with just 9 percent of those remaining in the "strongly oppose" category. Conversely, 51 percent of respondents did not oppose this hypothetical exchange of benefits. (As described above, there was no statistically significant difference in response between those who expressed entitlement to subsidies and those who did not.)

Table 9.3
Experts versus the public

	Public survey		Expert elicitation	
Variable/model	Public opposition to higher prices	Public support or indifference to higher prices	Experts who assume public opposition to higher prices:	Experts who assume public support or indifference to higher prices
Dep1: No explanation	41%	41%	92%	5%
Dep2: Nat'l interest explanation	32%	49%	n/a	n/a
Dep3: Alternate benefit	32%	51%	53%	47%
IV: Entitlement	% Public choosing "entitlement"		% Experts assuming public would choose "entitlement"	
Subsidies = "my share" of energy wealth	42%		75%	

Note: Figures do not add to 100 percent because "don't know" responses and missing values were deleted.

As table 9.3 shows, once again the expert respondents in the EE survey assumed a greater level of public opposition to a tariff increase, even when replaced by a *quid pro quo* benefit. Citizens were also less likely to claim entitlement to energy than elites anticipated. Whereas 75 percent of experts thought that a large majority of the public would have understood subsidies as an entitlement, in fact only 42 percent of public survey respondents made such a response.

The comparison of the two sets of results, one from the public survey, another from an expert elicitation, should be treated as broadly illustrative rather than statistically robust. The methodologies and questions used to gather opinions from both groups differed. While the public was asked for personal opinion, experts were asked to estimate how the public, in aggregate, would respond. Therefore the right-hand column in table 9.3 represents expectations of experts regarding results in the left-hand column. The differences between the two methods also extend to techniques of data gathering and selection of respondents. It was thus not feasible to use statistical methods to examine differences between the two groups, or to test hypotheses based on such a comparison. However, the varying percentages in table 9.3 provide a useful illustration that citizen perceptions of social contract benefits differ markedly from the assumptions of experts and portrayals within the literature.

9.5.1   Other Reasons to Support Higher Prices

The aggregate public survey results in figure 9.2 beg a further question: Why would anyone want to pay more for electricity? Overall, a surprisingly large fraction of the public did not oppose increased prices. This finding suggests that, while the subsidies-as-rights construct within the rentier literature holds among a subset of the public, alternate explanations for citizen perspectives toward energy may also be valid. One such explanation could be a citizen desire for more prudent stewardship of national resource patrimonies. Since the largest share of the rentier social benefit system rests on export revenues, citizens' best interests, at least in the long run, might be served more effectively by *reducing* domestic waste and the associated opportunity cost of foregone revenues, while ensuring long-term sales at the highest possible prices, both inside and outside the country. Rentierist constructs of subsidy "entitlements" appeal to some members of the public, but these constructs probably more closely represent regime needs for purchasing domestic loyalty.

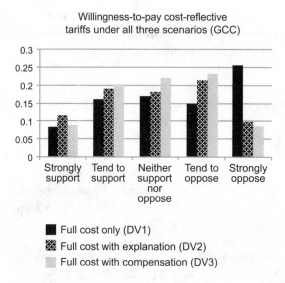

Figure 9.2
Public survey responses regarding higher electricity prices under three scenarios

Another explanation might also offer insight into this willingness to pay more. In the question informing Dependent variable 1, where respondents are given no rationale for higher prices, a surprising 24 percent of the public is nevertheless willing to pay more. This choice appears to run contrary to the public's immediate financial interest. One possible explanation flows from the implied terms of the authoritarian social contract. If a respondent disputed his or her role in exchanging political support for government subsidies and instead preferred more political participation, he or she might reject government subsidies.[44]

The survey did not ask respondents outright whether they would trade subsidies for a larger role in governance. However, if this rationale was driving some support for higher prices, it would provide an opposing message to governments considering subsidy reform. Whereas the "economic rationality" explanation by which citizens oppose waste in the name of long-term state distribution appears to *encourage* increased prices, the explanation of demands for increasing political participation does not. In fact, this explanation would validate regimes' cautious approaches to tinkering with subsidies, assuming ruling families do not wish to encourage participatory demands. In the past, regimes have demonstrated this stance by drip-feeding any political openings into their societies, ensuring that they pose no challenge to ruling family control. Recent repression of pro-democracy forces, including violent responses in Oman, Kuwait, and in Bahrain—where Saudi and Emirati forces joined in—provides another demonstration that regimes remain staunchly opposed to broader liberalization.

9.5.2 Policy Making and the Information Deficit

The gap in perceptions of the social contract—with citizen understandings diverging from those of experts and the literature—is consistent with the information deficit that is said to impair policy making in autocracies. Scholarship examining the institutional environment of authoritarian states has long argued that policy makers in autocracies suffer from much weaker awareness of public preferences than do their counterparts in democracies.[45] The democrat's advantage stems from institutions that offer avenues for criticism and amendment of unpopular measures. These range from freedoms of speech and press, independent judiciaries, and opportunity to vote for an organized political opposition. Since these constraining institutions are less common in autocracies, Wintrobe argues (in similar fashion to rentier scholars) that autocracies thus enjoy enhanced freedom of policy action. However, citizens in autocracies also tend to be reluctant to signal their displeasure with policy. Rulers are apt to fear the public since they lack information on public opinion. The phenomenon is known as the dictator's dilemma. Regime understanding of public preferences is thus negatively correlated with repression.[46]

The autocratic governance that typifies Gulf monarchies is consistent with the dictator's dilemma, but the information deficit stems not only from deficient institutions and signaling but also an absence of common consultative practices, such as use of survey and focus groups, that can illuminate public preferences. Social policy is fragmented, and regimes wield rent streams, business licensing and import restrictions to co-opt rivals with economic privileges that increase costs of defection.[47] Policy proposals are typically debated in traditional family–tribal networks and then launched.

A UAE government official's description of policy making reveals a process that pays little heed to public preferences:

Policy making isn't very mature in the government. People will just brainstorm around an idea, take it to the legal department and draft a law. From legal it goes to the *diwan* [ruler's court] and then to the sheikh. He will discuss whatever proposal they bring him. Most [policy makers] don't see the value in consultation.[48]

But while avenues of citizen protest are not institutionalized in the Gulf, they still exist. The freedom of policy action that the literature describes often disintegrates when a public backlash ensues. Complaints filter into the media and social networks. Prominent citizens go directly to the ruler or his agents. When the outcry is sharp enough, politics trumps economic expediency and the law is adjusted.

This is what happens when you announce the policy with no proper analysis or consultation. We don't have a mechanism for public complaints. We hear about it through the newspapers and our own social connections. We need channels of communication.[49]

Sensitivity to public opinion has inculcated in rentier governments a reflexive resistance to "extractive" proposals such as the subsidy reforms discussed here. Gray and other rentier scholars suggest that regimes grow increasingly responsive to society over time, while displaying little appetite for testing the boundaries of social contracts or encouraging vocal opposition to policy. Recent pan-Arab uprisings have only redoubled these sensibilities.[50]

Anonymous surveys offer the possibility of sidestepping the signaling problems and information deficits that obscure policymaking. Gathering survey responses allowed me to assess citizen responses to subsidies often described as a key component of the autocratic social contract. While the social contract is well understood as the *mechanism* governing the exchange of government benefits for public support, this research shows that citizen concepts of the *terms* of that bargain are not uniform or clear, nor are the boundaries for policymaking.

Elites, perhaps because of their lack of information on public opinion, believe that the public is overwhelmingly opposed to subsidy reform unless it receives an alternate benefit to compensate for those revoked. Public survey results challenge that perception. In model 1, where no replacement benefit was offered, the public was as supportive or indifferent to higher prices as it was opposed. The expert understanding was one of overwhelming public opposition. Public willingness increased substantially under model 2, when the national interest was invoked, and remained nearly identical to that in model 3, when a replacement benefit was offered. Given the urgency of reducing energy demand in these countries, the overestimation of public opposition to reform would seem a costly misperception.

9.6   Conclusion

The relationship between state and society in the rentier monarchies of the Gulf is more nuanced and complex than depicted in the rentier literature. A significant portion of the citizen public is indeed willing, under some circumstances, to relinquish a benefit portrayed as a "right." Those most willing are found among the large contingent of citizens who do not claim to feel "entitled" to cheap electricity. Willingness to pay is also pronounced among citizens who accept the notion that energy price reforms are a national economic priority. Further, many citizens appear prepared to trade one benefit for another, including many who consider themselves entitled to subsidized electricity.

These results lead to three subsidiary findings. First, citizens and elites in the Persian Gulf monarchies exhibit divergent views of the social contract's terms of exchange. Rigid theoretical understandings find more support among experts—elite policy makers, economists, and industry participants—and less acceptance among average citizens. This finding suggests a deficit in elite understanding of public preferences, which is consistent with the signaling problems described by Wintrobe.

Second, elites exhibit a conservative bias. The experts surveyed—whether in government or industry, expatriate or national—assume high levels of citizen entitlement and deep opposition to increased prices. Experts' views on subsidy rationale and reform reflect the inflexible tenets of the rentier literature. Individual citizen views often diverge.

Third, this disconnect between theory and public opinion points to a problem with the core assumptions of the literature. Those assumptions imply that autocracies govern with a fixed set of inputs and outputs: if there is a reduction in patronage, there must be a corresponding increase in repression or in political participation.[51] Public responses to my survey—and the public responses to subsidy reform in Dubai[52]—show that these assumptions are off base.

What do these findings mean for policy making? The survey results suggest that a segment of the populace would consent to price reforms.

Such reforms might extend the economic models of these states without compromising public support for regimes. Opposition would be concentrated among members of the public with a strong sense of entitlement to subsidies, based upon feelings of personal ownership of natural resources. Significantly, a third of the survey population remains opposed to higher energy prices, even when invoking the national interest or offering a substitute benefit. Even among those who claim to be willing to accept higher prices, one should keep in mind that a hypothetical survey is different from reality. Those who are indifferent or mildly supportive may be swayed by opponents once policies are proposed. And the presence of an anti-reform cohort appears to validate regime fears of antagonizing citizens in ways that could provide a conduit for protest and Arab Spring-style mobilization.

Even acknowledging the necessary caveats, these findings imply that governments in need of reducing energy consumption may have more scope for reform than they or regional elites believe. Although more work must be done to investigate public opinion in the Gulf, particularly at the country level, survey results suggest that reforms could be made more palatable via provision of alternate benefits and via a public campaign that highlights resource waste and intergenerational equity. Both of these efforts preceded Iran's subsidy reforms of 2010.[53]

However, Dubai's subsidy reform of 2011 was launched without either of these inducements. Dubai raised electricity prices by 15 percent, including on Emirati nationals, and did so without public discussion. Citizens complained, and the new prices became a temporary newspaper and talk-radio theme, but the increases were ultimately accepted without a *quid pro quo* benefit, such as that provided in Iran. Most important, the state utility registered a corresponding drop in average household consumption.[54] Either way, it seems that citizens may be willing to submit to higher prices.

Energy entitlement structures in the Persian Gulf monarchies appear frozen in time, with prices unchanged for decades in some cases.[55] The gains from these welfare benefits have long since been eclipsed by the harm caused by wasted resources and the political-economic threat embodied in the state's accumulating distributive burdens. With regional energy demand showing no sign of slowing, prospects for reforming subsidies appear more necessary, and more promising, than many would accept.

Appendix: Details of Public Survey, Coding of Survey Variables, and Demographics

Conducted by: YouGov; Fieldwork period: November 28 to December 4, 2011; Sample size: 730 respondents

Language: The survey was written in English and translated into Arabic. Display language was governed by the user's browser settings. The English text of the survey follows.

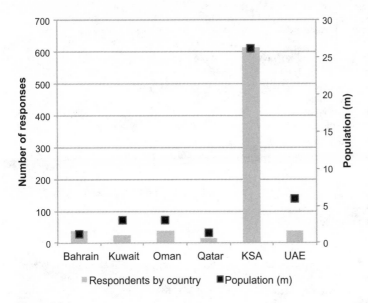

Figure 9A.1
Public survey responses by country, with population

Table 9A.1
Public survey text—English version

Introduction: In the GCC countries, there is increasing concern about energy issues. Some residents are concerned about rising prices, while governments worry about growing consumption. In this very short survey you are encouraged to have your say about energy issues.

Question JK1: In 2010, GCC governments paid, on average, more than 50% of the cost of electricity in nationals' homes. From what you know, why does the government contribute in paying for your electricity? (please select all that apply)

1 = Because it is my share of the country's energy wealth; 2 = Because it is the government's responsibility; 3 = Because the ruler is generous; 4 = Because energy is abundant in my country; 5 = Because I cannot afford to pay the full cost; 6 = Other; 7 = Don't know (*note: responses randomized in actual survey*)

Question JK2: How willing are you to pay the full cost of electricity consumed in your home? The true cost without government subsidies is more than the average price that nationals in your country pay now.

1 = Very willing; 2 = Quite willing; 3 = Neither willing nor opposed; 4 = Quite opposed; 5 = Very opposed; 6 = Don't know

Question JK3: Some people have said that because electricity is provided to nationals at an artificially low price some people waste it. This consumes oil and gas that could be exported. If the government sought to conserve energy by asking you to pay the full cost of electricity, would you:

1 = Strongly support; 2 = Tend to support; 3 = Neither support nor oppose; 4 =Tend to oppose; 5 = Strongly oppose; 6 = Don't know

Question JK4: If your government raised the prices of electricity to nationals and also compensated them with a benefit of equal value, would you:

1 = Strongly support; 2=Tend to support; 3 = Neither support nor oppose; 4 = Tend to oppose; 5 = Strongly oppose; 6 = Don't know

Question JK5: Which is the best way to distribute benefits from your country's oil and gas resources? (please choose one answer you think is the best)

1 = Spend it all now; 2 = Spend most now, save a little for future generations; 3 = Spend half, save half; 4 = Spend a little now, save most for future generations; 5 = Save it all for future generations; 6 = Don't know

The survey also included the following demographic question:

Are you a national of your country of residence or an expatriate?

1 = National of country of residence; 2 = Expatriate

Table 9A.1 (continued)

The survey cohort supplied the following demographic information:

Gender	1 = Male, 2 = Female
Age groups	1 = 18 to 24; 2 = 25 to 29; 3 = 30 to 34; 4 = 35 to 39; 5 = 40+
Income groups	1 = Less than $266; 2 = $266 to $532; 3 = $533 to $799; 4 = $800 to $1,065; 5 = $1,066 to $1,599; 6 = $1,600 to $2,132; 7 = $2,133 to $2,665; 8 = $2,666 to $3,999; 9 = $4,000 to $5,332; 10 = $5,333 to $6,665; 11 = $6,666 to $7,999; 12 = $8,000 to $10,665; 13 = $10,666 to $13,332; 14 = $13,333 or more; 15 = Prefer not to say; 99 = Don't know
What is the highest level of education you have completed?	1 = elementary school; 2 = secondary school; 3 = vocational college education; 4 = university first degree; 5 = university higher degree; 6 = professional higher education
To which of the following religions do you consider you belong?	1 = None—not religious; 2 = Islam; 3 = Christianity; 4 = Hinduism; 5 = Sikhism; 6 = Judaism; 7 = Buddhism; 8 = Jainism; 9 = Zoroastrianism; 10 = Other religion; 11 = Not specified
What is your current marital status?	1 = Single—never married; 2 = Married with Children; 3 = Married without Children; 4 = Divorced; 5 = Widowed; 6 = Not specified

Table 9A.2
Respondents by country and region

GCC	Bahrain	Kuwait	Oman	Qatar	KSA	UAE
730	36	18	36	4	611	25

Table 9A.3
Summary statistics

Variable	Obs.	Mean	Std. dev.	Min	Max
Dep1	465	3.41	1.37	1	5
Dep2	454	2.93	1.23	1	5
Dep3	468	3.01	1.17	1	5
Share	541	0.42	0.49	0	1
Age	541	2.44	1.28	1	5
Income	541	3.13	1.46	1	5
Edu	540	3.23	1.06	1	6
Female	541	0.39	0.49	0	1

Table 9A.4
Coding of the variables

Dependent variables

Dep1	Support for electricity price increase, no explanation	H1	1 = Very willing; 5 = Very opposed
Dep2	Support for electricity price increase, national interest explanation	H2	1 = Strongly support; 5 = Strongly oppose
Dep3	Support for price increase, with compensation by alternate benefit	H3	1 = Strongly support; 5 = Strongly oppose

Independent variables

Share	Entitlement		1 = Selected, 0 = Not selected
Female	Predictor-gender		0 = Male, 1 = Female
Edu	Predictor-education level		1–6
Income	Predictor-income level		1–15
Age	Predictor-age group	Age 18–24	1 = Selected, 0 = Not selected
Age	Predictor-age group	Age 25–29	1 = Selected, 0 = Not selected
Age	Predictor-age group	Age 30–34	1 = Selected, 0 = Not selected
Age	Predictor-age group	Age 35–39	1 = Selected, 0 = Not selected
Age	Predictor-age group	Age 40+	1 = Selected, 0 = Not selected

Note: Number coding of variables D1 to D3 were reversed from those in the survey to aid interpretation of results. Age group results were combined to form the variable age.

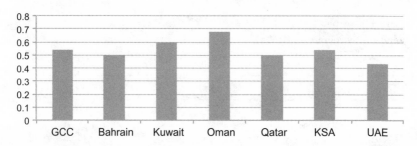

Figure 9A.2
Public survey respondents by gender (% male)

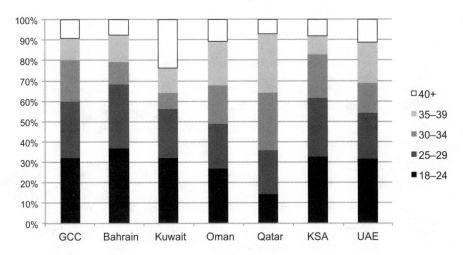

Figure 9A.3
Public survey respondents by age group

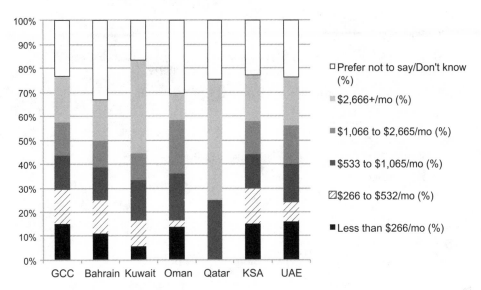

Figure 9A.4
Public survey respondents by income group

Notes

For their comments, the author wishes to thank the three anonymous peer reviewers, as well as Cees van Beers, Mary Ann Tétreault, and Sean Foley, along with Rice University colleagues Anna Mikulska, Richard Stoll, and especially Marwa Shalaby. This chapter would not have been possible without the generosity of YouGov Cambridge and Joel Faulkner Rogers who provided access to the YouGov Middle Eastern survey panel. GDF Suez provided crucial financial support, while travel and fieldwork expenses were covered by the Qatar National Research Fund, Peterhouse College, Cambridge, and the King Abdullah Petroleum Studies and Research Center in Riyadh.

1. Mahdavy (1970); Beblawi and Luciani (1987).

2. Mahdavy (1970); Beblawi (1987); Luciani (1987); Gause III (1994); Crystal (1990).

3. Such as Gray (2011) on the Gulf monarchies and Hertog (2010) on Saudi Arabia, Davidson (2005) on the UAE, Mitchell (2013) on Qatar. Earlier works touched on these themes, including Anderson (1986) on Libya and Tunisia, Chaudhry (1997) on Saudi Arabia and Yemen, and Vandewalle (1998) on Libya.

4. Wintrobe (2001); Tullock (1987); Desai, Olofsgard, and Yousef (2009).

5. Krane (2015).

6. Herb (2002).

7. Schlumberger (2006).

8. Beblawi and Luciani (1987: 16–17); Gause III (1994: 82, 61), specifically mentions state payment of citizen utility bills in this formulation; Gause III (1997: 80).

9. Schwarz (2008); Gause III (2011).

10. Yousef (2004: 6).

11. Farsoun (1988: 231).

12. Pierson (1996).

13. Heydemann (2003: 2).

14. Victor (2009); see also: Andresen (2008).

15. Crystal (1990: 191–92).

16. Gause III (1994: 147).

17. Davidson (2012: ix).

18. Hertog and Luciani (2009: 6–7).

19. Kazim (2007).

20. Gurr (1970: 338–40).

21. International Monetary Fund (2013a).

22. Uri and Boyd (1997).

23. Malaysia was not included in the IMF's case study report. See instead Chyi (2012) and International Monetary Fund (2013b).

24. International Monetary Fund (2013a).

25. First use of the term "rentier state" is generally credited to Mahdavy (1970) on Iran.

26. International Monetary Fund (2013a); Guillaume, Zytek, and Farzin (2011).

27. Tabatabai (2011).

28. Initial public support is documented in Guillaume, Zytek, and Farzin (2011).

29. FGE Gas Insights issue 216 (July 3, 2014). "What Happened to Iran's 'Most Radical Subsidy Reform Plan?'"

30. Middle East Economic Survey (April 30, 2012), "Second phase of subsidy reform plan to await budget approval," pp. 17–18. See also *Tehran Times* (December 31, 2011), "Petrol rationing saves Iran $38 billion: Official."

31. Guillaume, Zytek, and Farzin (2011).

32. International Monetary Fund (2013a).

33. Tabatabai (2011).

34. Note that 100 kWh is a fraction of Iran's average monthly consumption of 2,500 kWh (Guillaume, Zytek, and Farzin 2011).

35. Bozorgmehr (2012); International Monetary Fund (2013a).

36. International Monetary Fund (2013a).

37. International Monetary Fund (2013a: 6).

38. This author discussed its details with an adviser in the Saudi Ministry of Petroleum and Minerals, on October 17, 2012. The official displayed thorough understanding of the Iranian reforms and their relevance for the kingdom.

39. Sixty-one of 76 respondents (80 percent) said "yes" to the question "Several academics have stated that subsidies in the GCC are perceived by nationals as rights of citizenship. Do you agree?" 40. Numbers of responses are lower than 730 because I excluded "don't know" and incomplete responses from the dataset.

41. Robustness tests were also conducted for multicollinearity and parallel regression. Tests upon each of the three models revealed no multicollinearity and no violation of the parallel regression assumption.

42. The unopposed camp includes the 24 percent who were either "very" or "quite willing" and the 17 percent who were "neither willing nor opposed." I excluded the "don't know" responses.

43. All of the GCC countries have introduced campaigns asking the public to conserve energy.

44. I am indebted to Bill Nuttall at Cambridge for pointing this out. This hypothesis is undermined by the experience of Kuwait and Bahrain, however, where democratic openings have only intensified rent seeking. Also, if survey respondents support higher prices because they seek a corresponding increase in political participation, one would expect to see correlations between the "entitlement" explanation for subsidies and support for higher electricity prices. However, as shown in the retention of H1 and H2, this was not the case.

45. Bueno de Mesquita et al. (2002); Tullock (1987: 122–23); Kuran (1989); Wintrobe (2001).

46. Wintrobe (2001); Bueno de Mesquita et al. (2002); Bueno De Mesquita et al. (2003: 73–74); Kinne (2005).

47. Mares and Carnes (2009); Haber, Maurer, and Razo (2003).

48. UAE government official, interviewed by the author on condition of anonymity, April 8, 2012.

49. UAE government official, interviewed by the author on condition of anonymity, April 8, 2012.

50. Results from a separate expert elicitation the author conducted with UAE policy makers in March 2012 found that 15 of 25 respondents said the Arab Spring events made the government "less willing" to raise utility rates (one of three choices), while 21 of 26 respondents said the government was either "very sensitive" or "extremely sensitive" to citizen opinion on subsidies (of five choices). One respondent commented that the uprising had made the government "much, much, more sensitive and less willing to raise prices or antagonize anybody, anywhere, at any time."

51. Desai, Olofsgard, and Yousef (2009). I am indebted to Sean Foley for suggesting this input–output construct in his comments on an early draft of this chapter.

52. See Krane (2016) for a discussion of Dubai's electricity price reforms.

53. Guillaume, Zytek, and Farzin (2011).

54. The Media Office for HH Sheikh Mohammed bin Rashid al-Maktoum (2011); author interview with Dubai government official on condition of anonymity, Dubai (April 8, 2012).

55. Kuwait's current electricity tariff was set in 1966. Abu Dhabi's dates to 1989.

References

Anderson, Lisa. 1986. *The State and Social Transformation in Tunisia and Libya, 1830–1980.* Princeton: Princeton University Press.

Andresen, Nils August. 2008. Public choice theory, semi-authoritarian regimes and energy prices: A preliminary report. Working Paper 10. RUSSCASP Project. Fridtjof Nansen Institute, Norwegian Institute for International Affairs and Econ Pöyry.

Beblawi, Hazem. 1987. The rentier state in the Arab world. In Hazem Beblawi and Giacomo Luciani, eds., *The Rentier State*, 85–98. New York: Croon Helm.

Beblawi, Hazem, and Giacomo Luciani. 1987. Introduction. In Hazem Beblawi and Giacomo Luciani, eds., *The Rentier State*, 1–21. New York: Croon Helm.

Bozorgmehr, Najmeh. 2012. Subsidy dispute adds to Iran's woes. *Financial Times.* http://www.ft.com/intl/cms/s/0/a6ac4438-8ebe-11e1-ac13-00144feab49a.html.

Bueno de Mesquita, Bruce, James D. Morrow, Randolph M. Siverson, and Alastair Smith. 2002. Political institutions, policy choice and the survival of leaders. *British Journal of Political Science* 32: 559–90.

Bueno de Mesquita, Bruce, Alastair Smith, Randolph M. Siverson, and James D. Morrow. 2003. *The Logic of Political Survival.* Cambridge: MIT Press.

Chaudhry, Kiren Aziz. 1997. *The Price of Wealth: Economies and Institutions in the Middle East*. Ithaca: Cornell University Press.

Chyi, Lee. 2012. Kicking the subsidy habit. *Penang Monthly*. http://penangmonthly.com/ kicking – the – subsidy – habit.

Crystal, Jill. 1990. *Oil and Politics in the Gulf: Rulers and Merchants in Kuwait and Qatar*. Cambridge, UK: Cambridge University Press.

Davidson, Christopher M. 2005. *The United Arab Emirates: A Study in Survival*. Boulder: Lynne Rienner.

Davidson, Christopher M. 2012. *After the Sheikhs: The Coming Collapse of the Gulf Monarchies*. London: Hurst.

Desai, Raj M, Anders Olofsgard, and Tarik Yousef. 2009. The logic of authoritarian bargains. *Economics and Politics* 21 (1): 93–125.

Farsoun, Samih K. 1988. Oil, state, and social structure in the Middle East. *Arab Studies Quarterly* 10 (2): 155–75.

Gause III, F. Gregory. 1994. *Oil Monarchies: Domestic and Security Challenges in the Arab Gulf States*. New York: Council on Foreign Relations.

Gause III, F. Gregory. 1997. The political economy of national security in the GCC states. In Gary Sick and Lawrence Potter, eds., *The Persian Gulf at the Millennium*, 61–84. New York: St. Martin's.

Gause III, F. Gregory. 2011. Saudi Arabia in the new Middle East. Special Report 63. Council on Foreign Relations, New York.

Gray, Matthew. 2011. *A Theory of "Late Rentierism" in the Arab states of the Gulf*. *Scholarly Paper*. Doha: Georgetown University Center for International and Regional Studies.

Guillaume, Dominique, Roman Zytek, and Mohammed Reza Farzin. 2011. *Iran: The Chronicles of Subsidy Reform*. Washington, DC: IMF.

Gurr, Ted R. 1970. *Why Men Rebel*. Princeton: Princeton University Press.

Haber, Stephen, Noel Maurer, and Armando Razo. 2003. *The Politics of Property Rights: Political Instability, Credible Commitments, and Economic Growth in Mexico, 1876–1929*. Cambridge, UK: Cambridge University Press.

Herb, Michael. 2002. *Does rentierism prevent democracy?* Presented at Annual Meeting of the American Political Science Association, Boston, August 29.

Hertog, Steffen. 2010. *Princes, Brokers and Bureaucrats: Oil and the State in Saudi Arabia*. Ithaca: Cornell University Press.

Hertog, Steffen, and Giacomo Luciani. 2009. Energy and sustainability policies in the GCC. Academic Paper. Kuwait Programme on Development, Governance and Globalizsation in the Gulf States. London School of Economics.

Heydemann, Steven. 2003. *Toward a New Social Contract in the Middle East and North Africa*. Washington, DC: Carnegie Endowment for International Peace.

International Monetary Fund. 2013 a. *Energy Subsidy Reform: Lessons and Implications*. Washington, DC: IMF.

International Monetary Fund. 2013 b. *Case Studies on Energy Subsidy Reform: Lessons and Implications*. Washington, DC: IMF.

Kazim, Ayoub M. 2007. Assessments of primary energy consumption and its environmental consequences in the United Arab Emirates. *Renewable and Sustainable Energy Reviews* 11: 426–46.

Kinne, Brandon J. 2005. Decision making in autocratic regimes: A poliheuristic perspective. *International Studies Perspectives* 6: 114–28.

Krane, Jim. 2015. Stability versus sustainability: Energy policy in the Gulf monarchies. *Energy Journal* 36 (4). http://www.iaee.org/en/publications/ejarticle.aspx?id=2638.

Krane, Jim. 2016. Revolution and the rentier state: Theory of stability to theory of crisis? Working paper (forthcoming). Rice University's Baker Institute for Public Policy.

Kuran, Timur. 1989. Sparks and prairie fires: A theory of unanticipated political revolution. *Public Choice* 61: 41–74.

Luciani, Giacomo. 1987. Allocation vs. production states: A theoretical framework. In Hazem Beblawi and Giacomo Luciani, eds., *The Rentier State*, 63–82. New York: Croon Helm.

Mahdavy, Hossein. 1970. The patterns and problems of economic development in rentier states: The case of Iran. In M. A. Cook, ed., *Studies in the Economic History of the Middle East*, 428–67. London: Oxford University Press.

Mares, Isabela, and Matthew E. Carnes. 2009. Social policy in developing countries. *Annual Review of Political Science* 12: 93–113.

Media Office for HH Sheikh Mohammed bin Rashid al-Maktoum. 2011. Mohammed orders additional free water, electricity quotas. October 5. http://tinyurl.com/me46amz.

Mitchell, Jocelyn Sage. 2013. *Beyond Allocation: The Politics of Legitimacy in Qatar*. Washington, DC: Georgetown University.

Pierson, Paul. 1996. The new politics of the welfare state. *World Politics* 48: 143–79.

Schlumberger, Oliver. 2006. Rents, reform, and authoritarianism in the Middle East. In Michael Dauderstadt and Arne Schildberg, eds., *Dead Ends of Transition*, 100–13. Frankfurt: Campus Verlag.

Schwarz, Rolf. 2008. The political economy of state-formation in the Arab Middle East: Rentier states, economic reform, and democratization. *Review of International Political Economy* 15 (4): 599–621.

Tabatabai, Hamid. 2011. The basic income road to reforming Iran's price subsidies. *Basic Income Studies* 6 (1): 1–24.

Tullock, Gordon. 1987. *Autocracy*. Hingham, MA: Kluwer.

Uri, Noel D., and Roy Boyd. 1997. An evaluation of the economic effects of higher energy prices in Mexico. *Energy Policy* 25: 205–15.

Vandewalle, Dirk J. 1998. *Libya since Independence: Oil and State-Building*. London: IB Tauris.

Victor, David G. 2009. The politics of fossil-fuel subsidies. Working Paper. Global Subsidies Initiative IISD.

Wintrobe, Ronald. 2001. How to understand, and deal with dictatorship: An economist's view. *Economics of Governance* 18 (3): 35–58.

Yousef, Tarik M. 2004. *Employment, Development and the Social Contract in the Middle East and North Africa*. Washington, DC: World Bank.

10 Energy Benefits to Vulnerable Consumers: The Eligibility Criterion

Raffaele Miniaci, Carlo Scarpa, and Paola Valbonesi

10.1 Introduction

In this chapter we provide evidence on how the appropriateness of the eligibility criteria for household energy subsidies can be assessed using different definitions of energy affordability. In this regard we discuss the debate about the concepts of affordability and the statistical indexes that are typically adopted to assess the issue. Each approach can produce a somehow different picture of households' vulnerability in energy consumptions (see Hills 2012). The key point is that the ideal affordability indicator should accommodate—with appropriate weights—numerous elements. On the one hand, the indicator must be sensitive to changes in supply-side variables (i.e., energy prices, technology, quality of service), and on the other hand, it must take into consideration consumers' needs and preferences. This seems to be a particularly complex goal, given the heterogeneity of the households' living conditions (e.g., climate, type of housing), and composition (e.g., number of family members, presence of children, and/or elderly and disabled).

In our discussion on the *pros* and *cons* of the different affordability measures, we show how in the Italian retail energy markets alternative affordability indexes can affect the perception of the diffusion of energy poverty. More specifically, we use the 2012 European Union Surveys on Income and Living Conditions (SILC) to estimate indexes of affordability based on the incidence of the energy expenditure on the family budgets, as well as two ad hoc variations of the low income–high cost (LIHC) index proposed by Hills for fuel poverty in the United Kingdom. We also consider self-assessed indicators of energy vulnerability, such as the presence of leaking roofs or broken windows, the inability to keep the house adequately warm, and the presence of arrears for utility bills. As expected, the picture one gets on the extent of energy affordability problems substantially depends on how one defines and measures it.

Last, we evaluate the effectiveness of the energy benefit system introduced in Italy in 2008. In particular, we investigate to what extent the eligibility rules really benefit households with energy affordability problems. Our results highlight that the eligibility rules are affected by several limitations: overall, about 15 percent of the households in absolute poverty do not meet the criteria, only 43 percent of the households at risk of poverty and no more than 61 percent of those with energy affordability problems qualify for the benefits.

10.2 Energy Affordability Indicators and Their Measurement

In this section we first present the most common affordability measures, based on the incidence of energy spending on total household expenditure or income (subsection 10.2.1); we then illustrate indicators based on the LIHC approach suggested by Hills (2012), also proposing some modifications (subsection 10.2.2).

10.2.1 Affordability Indexes Based on Energy Budget Shares

Energy consumption is part of an essential basket of consumption goods that every household should be able to afford in order to have a "normal" standard of living, with the benefit of household heating and service appliances. A household is said to face an affordability issue if its energy budget share exceeds a critical threshold, determined—more or less arbitrarily—by policy makers. Such a household would then be considered as part of the target population of policy aimed at reducing energy poverty.

In this context, a headcount index (HI) is the percentage of consumers who spend on energy more than a given fraction of their income or total expenditure. In most studies this critical threshold has been fixed between 5 and 10 percent, depending on the good/service considered.[1] Such an index—as the underlying concept of affordability—does not, however, incorporate information on the desirable minimum amount of consumption of energy and other goods.

Formally, we define x_h as the total observed expenditure for household h, corresponding to the sum of the expenditure in energy, x_h^u, and the actual expenditure in all other consumption items, x_h^c. A household has problems of sustainability of its energy consumption if the ratio

$r_h = x_h^u / x_h$ is larger than a given threshold r^u. For a population, the extent of the sustainability problem is measured by the fraction of households for which $r_h \geq r^u$, namely by the headcount index:

$$HI \equiv \frac{\sum_h \mathbf{1}(r_h \geq r^u)}{N},$$ (10.1)

where N is the total number of households and $\mathbf{1}(r_h \geq r^u)$ is an indicator function, which equals one whenever the condition in parentheses holds, and zero otherwise. The HI in (10.1) tells us the fraction of households that spend more than a given "reasonable amount" (in proportion to available resources) for energy consumption. Notice that (10.1) does not incorporate any qualitative information on the amount of minimum/ desirable household energy, both for heating and other goods or services.

Also HI cannot provide useful indications on the extent of the affordability problem, or its depth. As for the affordability issue, the index does not include among the fuel poor those households in absolute poverty that decide—because of economic constraints—to spend very little on energy services. It may even label as "fuel poor" some relatively well-off households that consume high amounts of energy.[2]

10.2.2 Affordability Indexes Based on Low Income–High Cost (LIHC) Approach

As noted in Miniaci et al. (2008a, 2014b), indexes based completely on the budget share neglecting to account for spending in energy services can be problematic where a household has insufficient income to consume other goods or services because the household's "residual income" is too low. In other words, if the residual income is low after the energy bills are paid, the household does not have sufficient financial resources to fund the minimum level of consumption of other goods/services.[3] Similar circumstances may apply where the financial difficulties are induced by the consumption of public utilities (Stone 1993). For these reasons we need to disentangle at least three types of households with energy affordability problems of different origins:

1. No access to the minimum amount of both essential commodities and energy services In this case the problem of energy affordability can be alleviated by a mechanism of general income support, not conditional to the actual level of energy consumption;

2. Limited income but overconsumption of energy In this case, an appropriately targeted action should address why this is occurring (preferences, technological constraints, inefficient equipment, etc.);
3. Energy consumption below the minimum standard due to monetary or nonmonetary constraints (e.g., lack of access to gas or electricity networks) In this case, interventions should first be aimed at removing the constraints.

The low income–high cost (LIHC) approach due to Hills (2012), the residual income approach discussed above is combined with the budget share approach so that households are classified as energy poor if

• disposable income minus the *necessary spending* in energy results lower than the European Union relative poverty line,[4] and
• *necessary spending* in energy divided by disposable income results in the household having lower than the median national energy budget share.

Recall that the *necessary spending* in energy is the expenditure needed to keep the house adequately warm, regardless of actual energy consumption. By referring to *necessary* rather than to *actual* energy expenditure, this approach avoids "misclassifying" households that recklessly overconsume energy as well as those that underconsume energy but need to consume more to live in an adequately heated home. Although appealing, Hills' approach can hardly be applied to countries other than those of the United Kingdom, for at least two reasons:

• The data on households' energy needs must be accurate for the different types of accommodations, data that are often unavailable in continental Europe and in the United States.
• The data on national median energy budget shares may only be appropriate when applied to an area/country where climatic conditions are relatively homogeneous.

We thus consider a modified version of the LIHC approach, where we use *actual* energy expenditures (rather than *necessary* spending), and given the climatic differences within Italy, we adopt regional specific budget share thresholds.

Formally, consider an household h with an actual level of energy expenditure x_h^u; this household has a residual income defined as $RI_h = x_h - x_h^u$ that is the difference between its total disposable income and its energy expenditure x_h^u. Such an household is energy poor

according the LIHE approach if its residual income falls below the relative poverty line x^{rp} and its energy budget share $r_h = x_h^u / x_h$ is larger
than a given threshold r^u. The headcount index associated with the
modified LIHC approach, say LIHC1, is

$$HI^{LIHC1} \equiv \frac{1}{N} \sum_h \mathbf{1}(x_h - x_h^u \leq x^{rp}) \times \mathbf{1}(r_h \geq r^u). \tag{10.2}$$

In our opinion, both the original LIHC and its revised version LIHC1
are problematic: in order to assess the households' ability to pay, they
both refer to relative poverty rather than to absolute poverty in that the
residual income (i.e., net of energy costs) is compared to full income
(that includes resources for energy spending). By doing so, both criteria
do not treat as deprived those households with low income and low
(*necessary* or *actual*) energy expenditure. In other words, such criteria
are likely to exclude from the set of vulnerable consumers those households whose lack of income induces them to spend too little on energy
services.

In order to avoid misclassifying these households in need, we
suggest a further modification to the LIHC criterion, according to
which households we consider to be vulnerable:

• households whose disposable income is lower than the absolute
poverty line, or
• households whose ratio of actual spending in energy to disposable
income is larger than the regional specific median energy budget
share.

The headcount index associated with this modified LIHC approach,
say LIHC2, is

$$HI^{LIHC2} \equiv \frac{1}{N} \sum_h [\mathbf{1}(x_h \leq x^{ap}) + \mathbf{1}(r_h \geq r^u) - \mathbf{1}(x_h \leq x^{ap}) \times \mathbf{1}(r_h \geq r^u)],$$

where x^{ap} denotes the absolute poverty line.

By using the LIHC2 criterion, we would include all the households
that cannot afford the minimum quantity of energy without consuming
too little of the other goods (first criterion), plus the households that
consume "too" high a fraction of their income for energy. So, while
LIHC1 tends to excludes poor households not spending enough on
energy, LIHC2 tends to include some high-income household spending
too much on energy.

10.3 Electricity and Gas Benefits in Italy

The Italian policy on benefits for electricity and gas to vulnerable consumers was set by Law 205 on December 23, 2005, and then implemented through two Ministerial Decrees, respectively, in 2007 for electricity and in 2008 for gas. The declared aim of the policy is to provide support in energy consumption to (1) households living in poverty, or at its margins; (2) large households; in case of electricity, also to (3) households with a disabled or critically ill person (i.e., using medical device). The policy is funded through specific tariff components in transmission or distribution, paid by all consumers.

The income eligibility criteria for electricity and for gas benefits are the same; in both cases, the spending ability of the family is tested by using a synthetic indicator called ISEE (the acronym for "Indicatore di Situazione Economica Equivalente," i.e., Equivalent Economic Conditions Indicator). This indicator combines information about income, real and financial assets, family composition, and occupational status of household members. To be eligible, the household's equivalent income indicator must not exceed 7,500 euros, unless the family includes more than three dependent children; then the threshold is increased to 20,000 euros.

Because the benefits are paid in lump-sum discounts on the electricity and gas bills, a necessary eligibility condition is that the household be a domestic customer in its primary residence. In case of electricity, some limits to the installed power must be met (3 kW for up to 4 household members, 4.5 kW if more), unless the household includes a person who needs essential electro-medical appliances. In the case of gas, the benefit is given to the eligible households in the form of discount in bills for domestic customers having an individual contract, and with a postal order for customers having a condominium contract (i.e., usually because it has centralized heating).

All domestic customers that meet these criteria can apply for the benefits by filing a form with the municipality of residence. Given that the eligibility criteria are independent of consumption levels, the ubiquity of the power grid guarantees that (*de facto*) all households meeting the income requisites are potential beneficiaries of the electricity benefit. The coverage of the gas benefit is instead jeopardized by the non-universal diffusion of the natural gas. In particular, the gas distribution grid does not serve many mountainous areas and the entire Sardinia region. This, in practice, makes the pool of eligible households for the gas benefit a subset of the households eligible for the electricity benefit.

The amount of the electricity benefit depends on the number of households components, and it is independent of actual consumption (with the exception of the presence of electro-medical appliances, where it is calculated on the ground of the electricity usage intensity). In 2012, it ranged between 63 euros per year for a couple and 139 euros for a household with more than 4 members (plus 10 percent VAT). The amount of gas benefit is proportional to family size and depends on the classification of the municipality according to its typical winter temperature, and to the adoption of natural gas for heating. In this case, the value of the benefit ranged from 85 euros for a household with less than 5 members living in the warmest part of the county, to 318 euros for a household with at least 5 members living in the coldest areas (plus 21 percent VAT). However, it should be noted that the design of the gas benefit is such that households heating their homes with fuels other than natural gas are implicitly penalized by this system.

10.4   Energy Poverty and Energy Benefits in Italy

To describe the incidence of energy poverty in Italy using the alternative approaches introduced in section 10.2, and to assess to what extent the benefits policy described in section 10.3 is capable of channeling resources toward vulnerable consumers, we first need to define some parameters for the empirical analysis as follows.

10.4.1   Setting the Parameters for the Empirical Analysis

We developed our analysis of energy affordability in Italy by (1) defining the relative and absolute poverty lines (x^{rp} and x^{ap}, respectively) and (2) defining the threshold (r^u) above which the budget share indicates the presence of an affordability problem.

We used the Eurostat–Istat "Survey on Income and Living Conditions" (EU-SILC) criteria to estimate the crucial values. This Survey was particularly useful in that it provides information on demographic, housing, occupational, and income variables for a representative sample of about 20,000 Italian households.

Table 10.1 shows the preliminary descriptive statistics we used to frame the Italian context, namely based on 2012 average monthly disposable income[5] and the expenditure for energy, by household size and climatic classification of the area of residence in Italy. As already

stressed in Miniaci et al. (2008a, b, 2014a, b), the expenditure for gas
and other fuels shows significant variability across climatic areas: a
family composed of two persons in a cold region spends more than
double what a two-person family does in a warm region. For electricity,
however, it is the number of household members that mainly affects
the level of expenditure, while the area of residence plays a limited role.

Table 10.1
Average monthly disposable income and expenditure for energy, by household size and
climatic classification of the area of residence

Household size	Disposable income				
	Warm	Mild	Temperate	Cold	Total
1	1501.84	1893.44	1829.49	2026.90	1883.36
2	2219.11	2897.49	2816.17	3328.81	2984.20
3	2673.25	3363.66	3715.36	3980.92	3556.29
4	2966.35	3722.64	3911.38	4503.47	3863.51
5 +	3073.76	3907.92	4410.94	4459.07	3930.55
Total	2340.11	2895.95	2950.12	3238.69	2953.29

Household size	Electricity expenditure				
	Warm	Mild	Temperate	Cold	Total
1	36.38	31.30	29.08	30.32	31.37
2	50.29	42.07	39.65	41.74	42.87
3	59.73	52.44	47.04	50.19	52.09
4	61.64	53.09	54.46	58.35	57.34
5 +	67.38	59.50	64.59	61.69	63.20
Total	52.14	43.87	41.48	42.78	44.61

Household size	Gas and other fuels expenditure				
	Warm	Mild	Temperate	Cold	Total
1	34.71	56.74	60.50	91.06	70.17
2	47.92	71.21	82.81	119.40	92.33
3	53.01	78.55	87.56	118.44	92.80
4	57.52	75.99	90.07	125.22	92.20
5 +	59.15	78.94	105.90	126.45	93.70
Total	48.24	69.63	79.20	110.89	85.59

Source: Our estimates are based on ISTAT, "Survey on Income and Living Conditions"
(EU-SILC), 2012.

Table 10.2
Average monetary value of the minimum reference for total monthly expenditure and energy components, by household size and climatic classification of the area of residence

Household size	Relative poverty line	Absolute poverty line				
		Warm	Mild	Temperate	Cold	Total
1	740.71	603.19	707.96	709.10	797.64	733.91
2	1234.51	854.86	973.28	978.03	1102.34	1017.01
3	1641.90	1108.65	1231.26	1240.16	1399.71	1284.43
4	2012.26	1358.23	1489.40	1472.06	1698.63	1535.10
5 +	2434.20	1605.91	1752.95	1798.02	2010.59	1808.53
Total	1353.79	1002.09	1081.77	1067.36	1180.91	1109.51

Source: Our estimates are based on ISTAT, "Survey on Income and Living Conditions" (EU-SILC), 2012.

Table 10.2 shows the relative poverty line and the average monthly absolute poverty line categorized by household size and climatic classification of the area of residence. The computations used for the relative income poverty line are based on the definition of the expenditure poverty line for Italy adopted by the Italian Statistical Office (Istat). That is, the poverty line for a two-member household is equal to the average per capital household disposable income, and the value for other family sizes is adjusted using the Carbonaro equivalence scale. The disposable income is calculated as household income net of taxes and contribution to the social security system, and including imputed rents. The absolute poverty line for each family sampled by the survey is set following the definition of official Italian poverty line (Istat 2009), and it is, by construction, regional specific.

We chose to define the values of the threshold r^u based on the budget shares approach. In our analysis we therefore considered two criteria:

1. A "median budget share" that takes into consideration the balance sheets of households with low purchasing power and defines the maximum sustainable threshold (r^u) as the median value of the share of energy expenditure for the households in relative poverty. This threshold is conditional on household size and geographical area and varies over time due to changes in relative prices and household consumption decisions.
2. An European Commission (EC) criterion used in a European Commission Report (2010), that suggests a threshold that is twice the ratio of average energy expenditure to average total expenditure.

Table 10.3
Critical thresholds r^u for budget share approach

Household size	Median budget shares				EC criterion			
	Warm	Mild	Temperate	Cold	Warm	Mild	Temperate	Cold
1	10.10	13.97	15.83	17.51	9.47	9.30	9.79	11.98
2	9.46	10.51	10.23	13.13	8.85	7.82	8.70	9.68
3	9.43	8.56	8.69	10.82	8.43	7.79	7.25	8.47
4	6.64	7.79	7.92	9.22	8.03	6.94	7.39	8.15
5 +	6.61	7.29	6.11	6.92	8.23	7.09	7.73	8.44

Source: Our estimates are based on ISTAT, "Survey on Income and Living Conditions" (EU-SILC), 2012.
Note: Median budget shares: median budget shares of the relatively poor, by household size and climatic classification of the area of residence. EC criterion: 2 * Average expenditure / Average income, by household size and climatic classification of the area of residence.

We made two modifications to this criterion: we used disposable income instead of total expenditure, and we adopted averages of both expenditure and disposable income, conditional on household size and climatic area.[6]

Table 10.3 shows the difference between thresholds computed according to criteria 1 and 2 above. In particular, for households up to four members the threshold calculated according to the median budget shares approach is higher than that calculated with the EC criterion. Consequently we expect the incidence of energy poverty to appear to be lower when the threshold is set using the median budget share approach rather than the EC criterion.

10.4.2 Setting the Affordability of Energy Consumption and the Benefits Coverage

As already mentioned, we used EU-SILC data to empirically investigate the incidence of energy poverty in Italy; to assess to what extent policy is actually capable of channeling resources to vulnerable consumers, we used the Istat estimate of taxable labor income for each household in the survey. All this preliminary information was needed to compute the Equivalent Economic Conditions Indicator (ISEE), and therefore a household's eligibility status for the energy benefits.

However, the EU-SILC dataset did have some limitations. First, information on real and financial assets is not as detailed as information on income sources. So the amount of real and financial wealth can only be estimated from fiscal and financial income data (for details, see Miniaci et al. 2014a: app. C). Second, the data do not reliably identify the households that could use the electricity benefit for health reasons; therefore we had to focus exclusively on household eligibility due to economic hardship, which turned out to comprise the vast majority of candidate households. Third, an approximation had to be made for gas because the questionnaire does not distinguish between the use of natural gas and other kinds of gas (e.g., LPG), thereby leading to an overestimation of the pool of eligible customers.

Table 10.4 shows average income, percentage of income poor, eligible households, and households with affordability problems based on household size, area of residence, degree of urbanization, tenure status, and dwelling type. Here "poor" households are those with adult equivalent income below the absolute poverty line, and the households "at risk of poverty," according to Eurostat, are those with adult equivalent income lower than 60 percent of median adult equivalent income. We computed the percentage of households with affordability problems by three different methods: (1) the budget share approach (with thresholds set as the median budget share or according to the EC criterion); (2) the modified low income–high cost approach (i.e., LICH1 and LICH2 presented in section 10.2.2); and (3) self-assessed indicators of potential problems with housing conditions and energy costs. As for the third method, the EU-SILC questionnaire asks the households if: they have problems of leaking roofs, damp walls/floors, or rot in windows frames or floor; they can afford to keep their home adequately warm; they have been unable to pay on time due to financial difficulties for utility bills. The answers to these three questions are informative as to energy costs and energy efficiency of a household's accommodations.[7]

From the results in table 10.4 it should be clear that no matter which definition of energy affordability we adopt, low-income categories have the highest incidence of energy poverty. So, for instance, the "single parents" households are those with the lowest per capita disposable income (1,867.68 euros per month), and as a result are the households with the highest percentage in absolute poverty and at risk of poverty (23.7 and 38.3 percent, respectively) and thus affected by the highest incidence of energy poverty.

In general, changing the definition of energy poverty or a component of its indicator has two major effects on the assessment of energy affordability. On the one hand, it can change significantly the level of energy poverty measured: going from the "objective" criterion LIHC1

Table 10.4
Average income, percentage of income poor, eligible households, and households with affordability problems

| | Equivalent income (€) | Poor (%) | At risk of poverty (%) | Benefit eligible (%) | | With energy affordability problems (%) | | | | | | |
| | | | | | | Budget share approach | | Low income–high costs | | Self-assessed indicators | | |
				Electricity	Gas	Median budget shares	EC criterion	LIHC1	LIHC2	Leaking roof ...	Unable to keep home warm	Arrears on utility bills
Total	2,817.67	6.31	19.39	11.34	8.97	8.93	13.84	6.96	11.41	20.80	21.49	9.56
Household types												
Single	3,138.89	6.80	24.48	11.38	8.32	6.91	15.07	5.33	10.43	20.35	24.37	6.16
2 adults, less than 65 yrs	3,277.55	5.66	12.70	7.93	5.96	6.73	11.06	5.75	9.02	19.04	18.43	9.80
2 adults, at least one 65 yrs	2,892.89	1.06	12.43	9.03	7.43	5.75	12.28	3.22	6.16	20.46	20.26	3.86
Others, no children	3,021.59	2.06	11.04	5.97	5.01	6.48	8.68	4.18	6.98	23.41	22.36	10.64
Single parent	1,867.68	23.69	38.29	33.48	27.81	25.10	35.28	21.15	34.16	22.47	24.31	17.74
2 adults, 1 child	2,483.17	6.91	16.21	10.47	8.38	9.60	13.87	8.23	11.88	19.44	16.08	12.56
2 adults, 2 children	2,170.24	8.70	23.42	13.01	11.24	13.40	14.77	11.32	16.05	19.68	18.95	14.04
2 adults, 3 or more children	1,732.16	19.96	36.26	35.62	26.60	25.37	22.68	22.24	30.61	25.44	25.70	19.25
Others with children	2,294.41	7.52	21.81	12.27	10.54	13.19	10.36	9.95	15.36	23.69	24.15	18.56

Table 10.4 (continued)

| | Equivalent income (€) | Poor (%) | At risk of poverty (%) | Benefit eligible (%) | | With energy affordability problems (%) | | | | | | | |
| | | | | | | Budget share approach | | Low income–high costs | | Self-assessed indicators | | |
				Electricity	Gas	Median budget shares	EC criterion	LIHC1	LIHC2	Leaking roof …	Unable to keep home warm	Arrears on utility bills
Region												
North	3,152.95	4.58	11.83	6.47	5.51	6.45	12.92	4.45	8.58	18.80	12.66	7.36
Center	3,042.33	4.97	16.72	8.57	7.27	5.94	10.22	4.37	8.16	21.33	17.23	9.37
South and islands	2,166.71	9.80	32.57	20.50	15.30	14.58	17.50	12.39	17.75	23.51	37.60	13.01
Total	2,817.67	6.31	19.39	11.34	8.97	8.93	13.84	6.96	11.41	20.80	21.49	9.56
Degree of urbanization												
Densely populated area	3,058.29	6.63	17.53	11.10	9.36	7.65	11.85	5.99	10.51	18.88	18.35	10.07
Intermediate area	2,713.91	5.53	19.03	9.97	7.92	9.13	14.18	6.96	11.12	22.74	23.40	9.77
Thinly populated area	2,416.15	7.40	25.39	15.41	10.50	11.93	18.44	9.59	14.60	21.24	25.35	7.62
Tenure status												
Outright owner	3,064.90	3.18	17.41	6.24	4.71	7.13	11.69	4.91	8.13	18.90	19.87	5.48
Owner paying mortgage	3,018.82	3.02	9.23	3.76	3.13	7.32	9.78	4.90	8.35	18.58	13.85	12.92
Tenant at market rent	1,964.86	19.65	27.44	33.55	28.26	16.91	25.15	16.16	25.00	25.46	30.43	18.95

Table 10.4 (continued)

				Benefit eligible (%)		Budget share approach		Low income–high costs		Self-assessed indicators		
	Equivalent income (€)	Poor (%)	At risk of poverty (%)	Electricity	Gas	Median budget shares	EC criterion	LIHC1	LIHC2	Leaking roof …	Unable to keep home warm	Arrears on utility bills
Tenant at reduced rent	2,052.95	13.20	30.01	28.57	23.80	11.95	19.96	10.20	18.26	35.19	31.05	25.63
Free accommodation	2,547.16	8.55	30.47	14.34	9.23	9.81	14.04	8.18	13.91	22.15	25.35	8.96
Dwelling type												
Detached house	2,758.00	5.19	21.51	9.49	7.00	12.62	17.95	8.82	13.95	26.44	23.62	8.32
Semi-detached house	2,687.72	5.30	20.03	10.42	8.02	8.81	13.41	6.75	10.72	23.27	21.88	9.30
In building < 10 units	2,660.59	8.28	21.18	14.53	11.43	8.64	13.40	7.73	12.03	19.80	26.44	11.60
In building ≥ 10 units	3,141.28	6.05	15.26	10.39	8.94	6.58	11.64	5.03	9.40	15.09	14.86	8.83

Source: Our estimates are based on ISTAT, "Survey on Income and Living Conditions" (EU-SILC), 2012.

Note: Equivalent income (euros per month): household income net of taxes and contribution to the social security system, including imputed rents, divided by the equivalence scale used for the definition of the absolute poverty line. Poor: households whose adult equivalent income is below the absolute poverty line. At risk of poverty: households whose adult equivalent income is lower than 60 percent of median adult equivalent income. Median budget shares: median budget shares of the relatively poor, by household size and climatic classification of the area of residence. EC criterion: 2 * Average expenditure / Average income, by household size and climatic classification of the area of residence. LIHE1: (Income – Energy spending < EC relative poverty line) AND (Energy budget share > Median budget share). LIHE2: (Income < Absolute poverty line) OR (Energy budget share > Median budget share).

to the "subjective" criterion relying on the self-assessment of being able to keep the home warm shift the incidence of energy poverty in the entire population from 7 to 21.5 percent. On the other hand, it can remarkably change the identification of the group of household most/least in need. For instance, according to the budget share approach if one takes the EC criterion as a threshold, one-person households are more in need than the households classified as "others with children," but the conclusion is reversed if the critical threshold is the median budget share. The table provides illuminating evidence on how the choice of the instrument adopted to measure the phenomenon can have dramatic effects on the policy decisions, both in terms of assessment of its relevance and targeting of the intervention.

Although higher levels of energy poverty are typically associated with lower disposable income, the type of accommodation seems to play a major role in determining energy vulnerability. The second part of table 10.4 highlights that detached houses have the poorest maintenance conditions, and that their inhabitants are more likely to have energy affordability problems, despite the fact that they are relatively well off. The high incidence of energy poverty among tenants is also potentially due to the combination of their low income together with the low energy efficiency of their houses.

As the eligibility criterion is explicitly designed to target low-income households, we expect the percentage of eligible households to vary across groups together with the incidence of absolute poverty and the percentage of households at risk of poverty. The percentage of eligible households is always higher for the electricity benefit than for the gas benefit. This is particularly evident in the southern regions and islands because of the geographical limitation of the gas distribution grid and the differences in gas consumption in areas with different climatic conditions.

Table 10.5 shows the percentage of eligible households among poor households, households at risk of poverty and households with affordability problems according to the budget share or the low income–high costs approach. Among the absolute poor, we observe that about 15 percent are not eligible for the electricity benefits and 32 percent are not eligible for gas benefits. Among households at risk of poverty, only 43 percent are eligible for the electricity benefits and 34 percent for the gas benefits.

For the energy-poor households, we observe large changes in the eligibility rates as we change the definition of affordability. The eligibil-

Table 10.5
Percentage of eligible households among poor households, households at risk of poverty, and households with affordability problems

	Percentage of households eligible for electricity benefits						Percentage of households eligible for gas benefits					
			With energy affordability problems						With energy affordability problems			
			Budget share approach		Low income—high costs				Budget share approach		Low Income High Costs	
Household types	Poor	At risk of poverty	Median budget shares	EC criterion	LIHC1	LIHC2	Poor	At risk of poverty	Median budget shares	EC criterion	LIHC1	LIHC2
Single	75.47	34.19	45.30	31.83	57.35	55.18	55.31	25.07	38.01	26.70	48.10	40.91
2 adults, less than 65 yrs	81.95	48.32	49.39	39.20	57.75	57.30	61.34	35.42	37.34	31.07	43.66	42.74
2 adults, at least one 65 yrs	78.94	33.17	27.73	20.22	45.09	31.48	78.24	26.32	24.07	18.26	38.54	27.95
Others, no children	86.13	37.96	30.99	24.95	46.07	35.71	66.96	31.92	25.37	20.73	37.69	27.60
Single parent	93.52	70.51	70.57	61.75	83.76	76.36	75.53	58.54	63.89	54.50	75.83	63.88
2 adults, 1 child	89.40	51.60	50.15	43.96	58.38	58.67	79.05	42.71	44.68	39.69	52.00	51.26
2 adults, 2 children	88.54	48.55	52.97	50.57	62.70	58.70	75.84	41.18	49.01	48.91	58.02	51.57
2 adults, 3 or more children	98.12	76.80	73.29	75.12	83.11	77.66	78.13	60.31	58.77	59.42	66.54	61.27
Others with children	88.98	46.60	46.41	45.20	59.88	52.86	79.18	40.16	41.56	39.92	54.37	46.86

Table 10.5 (continued)

	Percentage of households eligible for electricity benefits						Percentage of households eligible for gas benefits					
	With energy affordability problems				Low income—high costs		With energy affordability problems				Low Income High Costs	
	Budget share approach						Budget share approach					
	At risk of poverty		Median budget shares	EC criterion				At risk of poverty	Median budget shares	EC criterion		
	Poor	poverty	budget shares	criterion	LIHC1	LIHC2	Poor	poverty	budget shares	criterion	LIHC1	LIHC2
Region												
North	75.62	36.80	35.57	26.67	50.44	45.02	66.87	32.00	32.68	24.80	46.48	40.05
Center	83.67	36.38	48.60	36.49	63.11	58.33	72.43	30.86	44.83	34.20	58.36	50.52
South and islands	91.26	49.24	57.07	51.82	66.73	63.44	67.46	36.76	47.18	42.38	55.13	48.02
Total	84.59	43.36	48.45	38.21	61.23	56.01	68.03	34.35	41.81	33.24	52.85	**45.48**

Source: Our estimates are based on ISTAT, "Survey on Income and Living Conditions" (EU-SILC), 2012.
Note: Poor: household whose adult equivalent income is below the absolute poverty line. At risk of poverty: households whose adult equivalent income is lower than 60 percent of median adult equivalent income. Median budget shares: median budget shares of the relatively poor, by household size and climatic classification of the area of residence. EC criterion: 2 * Average expenditure / Average income, by household size and climatic classification of the area of residence. LIHE1: (Income—energy spending < EC relative poverty line) AND (energy budget share > median budget share). LIHE2: (Income < absolute poverty line) OR (energy budget share > median budget share).

ity rates are the lowest among the households classified as energy poor according to the budget share approach with the EC criterion threshold (38 percent for electricity and 33 percent for gas benefits), and the highest with the LIHC1 approach (61 percent for electricity and 53 percent for gas).

Eligibility rates vary remarkably across household types and area: for example, among households in absolute poverty, the eligibility rate for the electricity benefit is 75.5 percent for the one-person households and 98.1 percent for households with two adults and at least three children. Similarly, for given income or energy poverty conditions, the eligibility rates in southern regions are higher than in the rest of the country.

The fact that the eligibility criteria exclude a significant portion of households in need from the benefits is due to a combination of different reasons, three of which refer to the adoption of the Equivalent Economic Conditions Indicator (ISEE):

1. The Equivalent Economic Conditions Indicator (ISEE), as used to assess the financial resources of the households, refers to a definition of income that differs from the one considered by standard poverty analyses. In fact the ISEE considers the gross household income together with an estimate of the income produced by real estate and financial wealth, while the poverty statistics refer to net household income including imputed rents due to primary residence ownership and social transfers. Accounting for homeownership and the value of real estate tends to decrease the eligibility rates of homeowners, in particular in the northern regions and large cities, where the values of the houses are considerably higher than in the rest of the country.

2. The Equivalent Economic Conditions Indicator (ISEE) is based on an equivalence scale that is slightly different from the one used for poverty definition. In particular, it attaches weight to the presence of disabled individuals, single parents with children, and occupational status, while the equivalence scale used for the poverty indicators considers only the size of the household and the ages of its members. This can explain some of the differences in eligibility rates across different household types.

3. The threshold value of the Equivalent Economic Conditions Indicator (ISEE) does not vary with the region of residence, while the components of the absolute poverty line are region-specific, as they include differences in prices, housing markets, and heating needs.

This generates different eligibility rates across the regions of the country.

4. The eligibility criteria do not depend on households' energy consumption; by design, the policy is not particularly well suited to support consumers who face affordability problems despite their spending ability is above the subsistence level.

5. To be eligible for the gas benefit, the households must be connected to the natural gas network, and this dramatically reduces eligibility among households living in areas not served by the gas distribution grid.

10.4.3 A Focus on the Eligibility for Benefits

So far, we have studied the eligibility and the energy poverty rates by relying on simple descriptive statistics. Although informative, these tables do not allow us to disentangle the effects of the determinants that are simultaneously at work. For instance, the difference across areas in the energy poverty rates may be simply due to the well-known differences in income across areas.

In order to further investigate the main drivers of energy poverty, and to evaluate to what extent the benefit policy adopted to support Italian vulnerable consumers in those market is able to target public resources to families in need, we resorted to a multiple regression approach. Our goal is to show the key determinant of the probability of being energy poor and eligible for electricity benefits. Recall that electricity and gas benefits have the same income eligibility criterion. Therefore a household that is eligible for the electricity benefit is eligible also for gas benefit if it uses natural gas. We analyze how the percentage of energy vulnerable households eligible for the energy benefits changes because of their ability to spend and also how it depends on other characteristics such as family composition, occupational and tenure status.

We modeled the joint probability of being energy poor and eligible for the energy benefits by applying a bivariate probit model (see Cameron et al. 2005). We consider a household to be energy poor according to the low income–high cost criterion, in which

• the "low-income" condition is assessed referring to the absolute poverty line, and
• the "high-cost" condition is satisfied if the incidence of energy spending on income is higher than the median energy budget shares

of the (relatively) poor households of similar size living in the same climatic area.

Here the probability of being energy poor is a function of income level and energy spending. For given level of income and spending, the energy poverty status is affected also by household composition, area of residence, housing conditions, and type of fuel used for heating.

Household's income is, in principle, the only determinant of the eligibility. In practice, this is not the case, since eligibility depends on an estimate of income from real estate and financial assets, which are not included in the standard definition of disposable income. The latter is instead routinely used in any household welfare analysis, both in Italy and in the European Union. This implies that the type and location of the accommodation and the tenure status affect the eligibility of the household due to the impact of real estate wealth.

Furthermore the way the eligibility criterion accounts for family composition and occupational status differs from the standard adjustment via the equivalent scale. We therefore consider household composition and occupational status as possible determinants of the eligibility status, also once controlled for household adult equivalent disposable income.

Overall, only the variables describing the type of fuels used and the incidence of energy spending on household disposable income affect exclusively the energy poverty status and not the eligibility status. We therefore specify the following multivariate model:

$$EnPov_h = \mathbf{1}(x_h'\beta_1 + z_h'\gamma > u_{h1}), \quad Eli_h = \mathbf{1}(x_h'\beta_2 > u_{h2}),$$

where $EnPov_h$ is a dummy variable equal 1 if household h is energy poor, zero otherwise; Eli_h is a dummy variable for the eligibility status; $\mathbf{1}(.)$ is an indicator function that equals one if the condition in parentheses hold true and zero otherwise; x_h is vector of household and accommodation characteristics, common to the two equations, z_h is a vector with information on the type of fuels used by the households and the incidence of energy expenditure on household income. The random components (u_{h1}, u_{h2}) are jointly normally distributed, independently and identically distributed with unitary variance and correlation ρ. The unknown parameters $(\beta_1, \beta_2, \gamma, \rho)$ are estimated via maximum likelihood.

As the bivariate probit model is highly nonlinear, it is easier to assess the effect of the covariates on the outcomes by looking at the marginal effects of x and z on the probability of being energy poor and eligible, rather than simply looking at the estimated parameters. We thus consider the marginal effect on the probability of being energy poor, that is $\partial \Pr(EnPov_h \mid x_h, z_h) / \partial x_h$ and $\partial \Pr(EnPov_h \mid x_h, z_h) / \partial z_h$, the probability of being eligible for the energy benefits $\partial \Pr(Eli_h \mid x_h) / \partial x_h$; and of the probability of being eligible, given that the household is energy poor, $\partial \Pr(Eli_h \mid EnPov_h = 1, x_h, z_h) / \partial x_h$ and $\partial \Pr(Eli_h \mid EnPov_h = 1, x_h, z_h) / \partial z_h$.

Table 10.6 shows estimated marginal effects computed at the average values of the covariates. As expected, an increase in income—Log(Adult equivalent disposable income)—reduces the probability of being energy poor and eligible for the benefits. Vice versa, keeping income and the other characteristics constant, an increase in the energy budget shares raises the probability of being energy poor. Family composition plays a role in both marginal probabilities, but usually with opposite signs: at the mean values, the single-person household is the one least likely to be energy poor according to the LICH2 criterion, but it is the type of household most likely to be eligible for benefits, together with single parents. The conditional probability $\Pr(Eli_h \mid EnPov_h = 1, x_h, z_h)$ confirms that—at the average values—the probability of a single-person household to be eligible is the highest.

There are significant territorial differences, also once controlled for compositional and income effects. The differences between homeowners and tenants are irrelevant for energy poverty, once income and other characteristics have been accounted for, though they persist as important determinants for eligibility: at the average values, the probability to be eligible for electricity benefits among the energy poor is about 13 percentage points higher for tenants with respect to outright homeowners.

As the estimated model is nonlinear, the differences between groups are not constant, and they depend on the value of all the variables at play. In particular, given the skewness of the income distribution, and the attention to the low-income households, it is worth considering how the differences between groups vary with income. In figures 10.1 and 10.2 we plot the three probabilities $\Pr(EnPov_h \mid x_h, z_h)$, $\Pr(Eli_h \mid x_h)$, and $\Pr(Eli_h \mid EnPov_h = 1, x_h, z_h)$ for different income levels and by different household subgroups. More specifically, we compute the probabilities at the 1st, 5th, 10th, 25th, 50th, 75th, 90th, and 95th percentiles of adult equivalent disposable income, keeping all other variables at their observed values. We expect the probabilities to be energy poor

Table 10.6
Marginal effects on the probability of being energy poor, eligible for energy benefits and eligible given that one is energy poor

	(1) Pr(Energy poor)	(2) Pr(Eligible)	(3) Pr(Eligible | Energy poor)	Sample averages
Household types				
Without children				
Single	-	-	-	0.3030
2 adults,	0.0007**	-0.0120***	-0.0495**	0.1037
both younger than 65 yrs	(0.0003)	(0.0030)	(0.0215)	
2 adults,	0.0004**	-0.0047	-0.0235	0.1490
at least one over 65 yrs	(0.0002)	(0.0031)	(0.0145)	
Others	0.0029***	-0.0133***	-0.0580**	0.1266
	(0.0010)	(0.0028)	(0.0254)	
With children				
Single parent	0.0030*	0.0144*	0.0135	0.0309
	(0.0017)	(0.0078)	(0.0186)	
2 adults, 1 child	0.0007**	-0.0134***	-0.0548**	0.1057
	(0.0003)	(0.0028)	(0.0229)	
2 adults, 2 children	0.0023***	-0.0120***	-0.0534**	0.1055
	(0.0008)	(0.0028)	(0.0235)	
2 adults, 3 or	0.0049**	0.0302**	0.0421	0.0213
more children	(0.0022)	(0.0124)	(0.0257)	
Others	0.0095***	-0.0083**	-0.0483**	0.0543
	(0.0031)	(0.0037)	(0.0239)	
Area of residence				
North	-	-	-	0.4828
Center	0.0015***	0.0037**	0.0051	0.1989
	(0.0005)	(0.0018)	(0.0057)	
South and islands	0.0008**	0.0131***	0.0342***	0.3183
	(0.0003)	(0.0027)	(0.0113)	
Degree of urbanization				
Densely populated area	-	-	-	0.4391
Intermediate area	-0.0003	0.0036**	0.0134*	0.3993
	(0.0002)	(0.0016)	(0.0070)	
Thinly populated area	-0.0005**	0.0118***	0.0403**	0.1615
	(0.0002)	(0.0030)	(0.0160)	
Tenure status				
Outright owner	-	-	-	0.6054
Owner paying mortgage	0.0001	-0.0021	-0.0080	0.1371
	(0.0003)	(0.0016)	(0.0062)	

Table 10.6 (continued)

	(1) Pr(Energy poor)	(2) Pr(Eligible)	(3) Pr(Eligible | Energy poor)	Sample averages
Tenant at market rent	0.0001	0.0579***	0.1454***	0.1335
	(0.0002)	(0.0079)	(0.0399)	
Tenant at reduced rent	-0.0003	0.0470***	0.1310***	0.0485
	(0.0002)	(0.0090)	(0.0415)	
Free accommodation	-0.0000	0.0092**	0.0293**	0.0755
	(0.0003)	(0.0036)	(0.0143)	
Dwelling type				
Detached house				0.2081
Semi-detached house	-0.0003	-0.0019	-0.0078	0.2565
	(0.0002)	(0.0023)	(0.0080)	
In building < 10 units	-0.0002	-0.0005	-0.0001	0.2575
	(0.0002)	(0.0021)	(0.0069)	
In building ≥ 10 units	0.0002	0.0003	-0.0002	0.2778
	(0.0003)	(0.0023)	(0.0072)	
Number of rooms	0.0003***	-0.0034***	-0.0127**	3.2733
	(0.0001)	(0.0009)	(0.0052)	
Occupational status				
Employee	-	-	-	0.3729
Self-employed	-0.0000	-0.0015	-0.0055	0.1251
	(0.0003)	(0.0010)	(0.0045)	
Unemployed	-0.0000	0.0070**	0.0233**	0.0457
	(0.0004)	(0.0028)	(0.0119)	
Retired	-0.0005*	0.0193***	0.0639***	0.3247
	(0.0003)	(0.0034)	(0.0234)	
Other out of labor force	-0.0000	0.0326***	0.0920***	0.1316
	(0.0003)	(0.0061)	(0.0303)	
Log(Adult equivalent	-0.0063***	-0.0699***	-0.1816***	10.2760
disposable income)	(0.0016)	(0.0060)	(0.0452)	
With gas	-0.0008**		0.0050	0.8742
	(0.0004)		(0.0036)	
Using gas for heating	-0.0004		0.0025	0.7231
	(0.0002)		(0.0021)	
Energy spending/	0.1003***		-0.6408	0.0584
Disposable income	(0.0257)		(0.4132)	

Note: Marginal effects computed at the mean values of the explanatory variables. Standard errors in parentheses, "-" denotes reference option for qualitative variables. Standard errors in parentheses; ***$p < 0.01$, **$p < 0.05$, *$p < 0.1$.

and eligible to be the highest for low values of income and drop to zero for affluent households. The speed at which this happens may differ among household groups.

Figure 10.1 shows the predicted probabilities for different level of income, by household type and occupational status. Looking at the probability of being energy poor, it is possible to observe how the predicted probability is different across different household types for low-income levels and how the difference vanishes as income increases, becoming negligible around the median value of income. For the eligibility rate, the picture is rather different: there are no differences between types for very low levels of income (1st percentile), where all households are predicted to be eligible, then the differences widens reaching their maximum around the fifth percentile, and subsequently decreases. Large differences in the eligibility probability are depicted also between different occupational status (second panel of figure 10.1) and housing tenure (first panel of figure 10.2), which instead do not affect energy poverty. The latter result is apparently in sharp contrast with the descriptive evidence provided in table 10.4, where a considerably higher incidence of energy poverty is reported for tenants. The use of a multiple regression strategy allows us to say that such difference is mainly due to income differences between tenants and homeowners, that is, when tenants and homeowners of similar income level are confronted, there is no relevant difference in their probability of being energy poor.

The regression analysis confirms the presence of a persistent difference in the regional eligibility rates: the second panel of figure 10.2 shows that among energy-poor households with adult equivalent income around the 5th percentile, the eligibility rate in the southern regions is about 65 percent, 10 percentage points higher than in the central and northern areas. As previously explained, this can be due to the heterogeneity in price levels, housing values, and different labor market participation rates.

Overall, the graphs make evident that, ceteris paribus, the eligibility criterion does not guarantee equal opportunity of access to the benefits, but it rather privileges the households with children, those households whose head is out of labor force, the tenants and the resident in the southern regions.

10.5   Conclusions

Alternative indexes of affordability in energy consumption focus on different aspects of the energy poverty; any sensible indicator should combine information on households income and the achievement of a minimum standard of quality of life, also considering underspending as a potential cause of deprivation. The actual implementation of these principles has to deal with the nature of the available data and it needs to be complemented by a precise analysis of the determinants of the affordability problem.

In this chapter we have briefly presented alternative indexes of affordability in energy consumption (i.e., using the budget share approach and low income–high cost approach), discussed their advantages and disadvantages, and suggested a way to assess households in need if a policy designed to support energy consumption of vulnerable consumers does include them.

We use the Italian energy markets to illustrate how the adoption of alternative indexes provides a strikingly different picture on the affordability of energy consumption. We then describe the Italian scheme of electricity and gas benefits that consists of a lump-sum contribution on the vulnerable consumers' bills. The amount of these benefits refers to the number of household components, is independent of the household's actual consumption; the gas benefit also depends on the climatic classification of the area of residence of the households. The policy provides a limited benefit to a potentially large number of beneficiaries. In 2012 the electricity benefit ranged between 63 euros a year for a couple and 139 euros for a household with more than 4 members (plus 10 percent VAT); the gas benefit ranged from 85 euros for a household with less than 5 members living in the warmest part of the county, to 318 euros for a household with at least 5 members living in the coldest areas (plus 21 percent VAT).

Our empirical results show that the judgment on the appropriateness of the eligibility criteria for energy benefits depends on the method used to identify households in fuel poverty. In Italy, regardless of the concept of energy affordability we refer to, the eligibility criterion prevents access to the energy benefits for more than 45 percent of the households with energy affordability problems. We discuss which characteristics of the eligibility criterion reduce the coverage rate: the lack of reference to the energy expenditure and prices actually faced

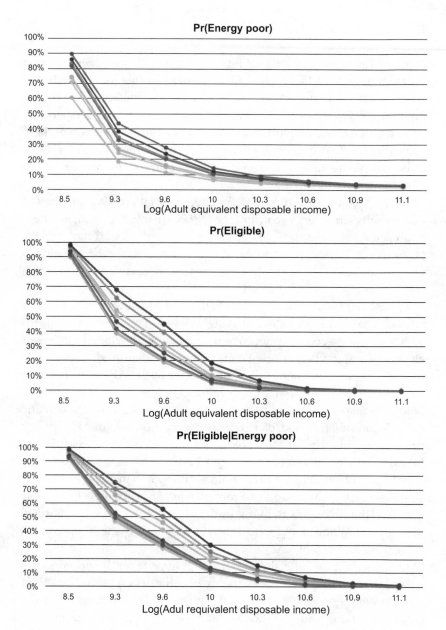

Figure 10.1
Predicted probability of being energy poor and eligible for energy benefits as function of adult equivalent disposable income, by household type and occupational status of the head of the households. Predicted values are computed at 1st, 5th, 10th, 25th, 50th, 75th, 90th, and 95th percentiles of adult equivalent disposable income, with all other variables at their observed values.

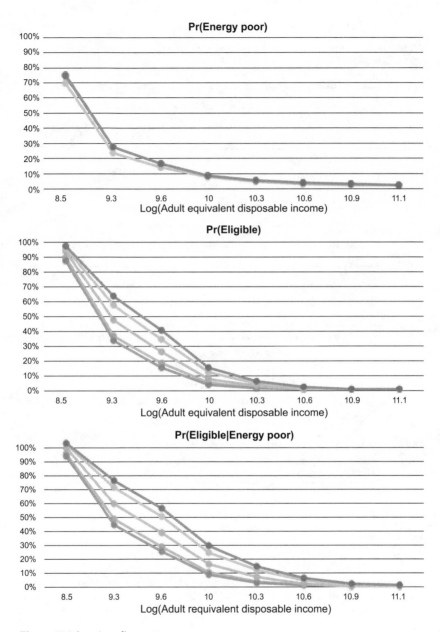

Figure 10.1 (continued)

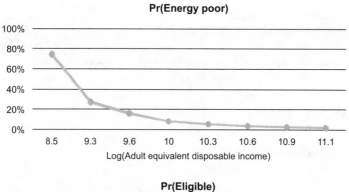

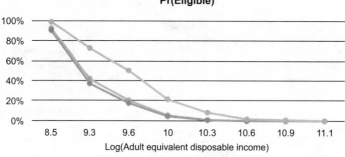

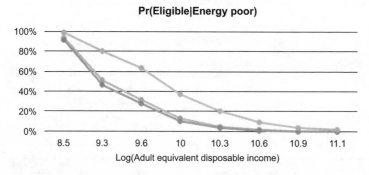

Figure 10.2
Predicted probability of being energy poor and eligible for energy benefits as function
of adult equivalent disposable income, by tenure status and area of residence. Predicted
values are computed at 1st, 5th, 10th, 25th, 50th, 75th, 90th, and 95th percentiles of adult
equivalent disposable income, with all other variables at their observed values.

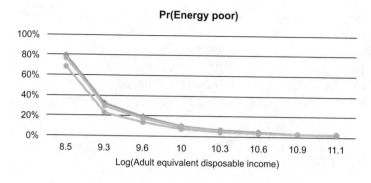

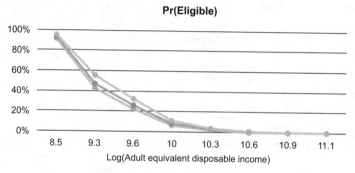

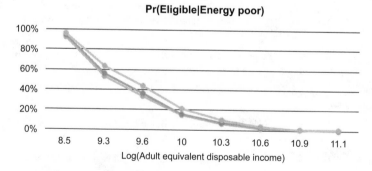

Figure 10.2 (continued)

by the households, and the exclusion from the benefits of consumers using fossil fuels other than natural gas.

Finally, we apply a multiple regression model to investigate the key determinants of the probability of being energy poor and eligible for energy benefits. As expected, an increase in income reduces the probability of being energy poor and eligible for energy benefits; keeping income and the other characteristics constants, an increase in the energy budget shares raises the probability of being energy poor. Family composition plays a role in both marginal probabilities, but usually with opposite signs: at the mean values, the single-person household is the one least likely to be energy poor, but it is the type of household most likely to be eligible for benefits, together with the single-parent household. There are significant territorial differences, also once controlled for compositional and income effects. Overall, our analysis shows that, ceteris paribus, the Italian eligibility criterion does not guarantee equal opportunity of access to the benefits, but rather, it privileges the households with children, those households whose head is unemployed, the tenants and the resident in the southern regions.

Notes

1. See, for example, Fankhauser and Tepic (2007), Chaplin and Freeman (1999), Hancock (1993), Healy (2001), Sefton, (2001), Sefton and Chesshire, (2005), Waddams Price et al. (2012).

2. The problem of affordability in energy consumption has been firstly investigated in United Kingdom where it has been labeled as "fuel poverty" (see Defra 2001, 2007).

3. The field where the notion of residual income was first introduced is housing economics (Thalmann 2003).

4. The EU relative poverty line may differ from the relative poverty lines computed by the national statistical offices because of the different equivalence scales adopted.

5. Disposable income is defined as the household income, net of taxes and contribution to the social security system, including imputed rents.

6. The first modification is dictated by the lack of a reliable measure of total expenditure in the EU-SILC dataset, and in any case, income is probably a more sensible denominator in such ratio. The second modification is suggested by the large differences in Italian energy spending across areas and family size, as shown in table 10.1.

7. The responses to these three questions in the EU-SILC questionnaire are included in the Eurostat multidimensional deprivation index.

References

Cameron, A. 2005. *Colin, and Pravin K. Trivedi. Microeconometrics: methods and applications.* Cambridge, UK: Cambridge University Press.

Chaplin, R., and A. Freeman. 1999. Towards an accurate description of affordability. *Urban Studies* 36 (11): 1949–57.

DEFRA. 2001. The UK fuel poverty strategy. First Annual Progress Report 2003. http:// www.dti.gov.uk/energy/consumers/fuel_poverty/index.shtml.

DEFRA. 2007. The UK fuel poverty strategy. First Annual Progress Report 2006. http:// webarchive.nationalarchives.gov.uk/+/http://www.berr.gov.uk/files/file29688.pdf.

Fankhauser, S., and S. Tepic. 2007. Can poor consumers pay for energy and water? An affordability analysis for transition countries. *Energy Policy* 32 (2): 1038–49.

Hancock, K. E. 1993. "Can pay? Won't pay?" or economic principles of "affordability." *Urban Studies* 30 (1): 127–45.

Healy, J. 2001. *Home sweet home? Assessing housing conditions and fuel poverty in Europe. Working Paper 01/13.* ERSR, University College Dublin.

Hills, J. 2012: Getting the measure of fuel poverty. Final Report of the Fuel Poverty Review. http://sticerd.lse.ac.uk/dps/case/cr/CASEreport72.pdf

ISTAT. 2004. *La povertà assoluta: informazioni sulla metodologia di stima, Approfondimenti— Famiglia e società.* Roma: ISTAT.

ISTAT. 2009. *La misura della povertà assoluta, Metodi e norme* no. 39.

Miniaci, R., C. Scarpa, and P. Valbonesi. 2008 a. Measuring the affordability of public utility services in Italy. *Giornale degli Economisti ed Annali di Economia* 121 (67/2): 185–230.

Miniaci, R., C. Scarpa, and P. Valbonesi. 2008 b. Distributional effects of the price reforms in the Italian utility markets. *Fiscal Studies* 29 (1): 135–63.

Miniaci, R., C. Scarpa, and P. Valbonesi. 2014 a. Fuel poverty and the energy system: The Italian case. Working Paper 66. IEFE.

Miniaci, R., C. Scarpa, and P. Valbonesi. 2014 b. Energy affordability and the benefits system in Italy. *Energy Policy* 75: 289–300.

Sen, A. 1976. Poverty: An ordinal approach to measurement. *Econometrica* 44: 219–31.

Sefton, T. 2002. Targeting fuel poverty in England: Is the government getting warm? *Fiscal Studies* 23 (3): 369–99.

Sefton, T., and J. Chesshire. 2005. Peer review of the methodology for calculating the number of households in fuel poverty in England. Final Report to DTI and DEFRA. http://www.berr.gov.uk/files/file16566.pdf

Stone, M. E. 1993. *Shelter Poverty: New Ideas on Housing Affordability.* Philadelphia: Temple University Press.

Thalmann, P. 2003. House poor or simply poor? *Journal of Housing Economics* 12: 219–317.

Waddams Price, C., K. Brazier, and W. Wang. 2012. Objective and subjective measures of fuel poverty. *Energy Policy* 49: 33–39.

11 Are Renewable Energy Subsidies in Need of Reform?

Carolyn Fischer, Mads Greaker, and
Knut Einar Rosendahl

11.1 Introduction

A great deal of attention is now being focused on fossil fuel subsidy reform, and rightly so. International organizations such as the International Energy Agency (IEA) and International Monetary Fund (IMF), as well as a variety of independent researchers, have engaged in large-scale efforts to quantify fossil fuel subsidies and the economic and environmental benefits from eliminating them (IEA, OECD, and World Bank 2010; Coady et al. 2015). The Group of Twenty (G20) has committed to phasing them out.

This chapter shines a light on renewable energy subsidies, particularly for electricity generation, and reviews some recent efforts by researchers to identify their costs and benefits, using both qualitative and quantitative methods. Renewable energy has important advantages over fossil fuels, in terms of both environmental and health impacts, as well as long-term sustainability. However, the use of subsidies for renewable energy is not without controversy.

11.2 Taxing Bads versus Subsidizing Goods

As highlighted in Coady et al. (2015), the economics of subsidies reveals some important disadvantages. First of all, they require revenue, and public funds do not come without their own costs; estimates of the marginal cost of public funds are typically above \$1 for every \$1 of revenue raised (e.g., Barrios, Pycroft, and Saveyn 2013). This revenue cost means that larger societal benefits (for example, a higher social cost of carbon) from a subsidy are needed to justify it from a welfare perspective. Second, subsidies tend to provide poor long-run signals, allowing less-productive firms to remain in the market.

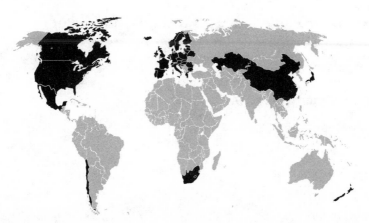

Figure 11.1
Countries implementing or considering carbon pricing in 2015

In general, if the primary problem is an environmental externality, such as greenhouse gas emissions, it is better to make the polluters pay for their emissions than to subsidize their substitutes. Charging fossil fuels for their carbon emissions would discourage their use, particularly the more emissions-intensive fuels, and make renewables more competitive. Simply subsidizing renewables, on the other hand, does not ensure that the most carbon-intensive fuels will be displaced.

Indeed, some progress is being made toward placing prices on carbon. The World Bank Group's *State and Trends Report* charts the global growth of carbon pricing (see figure 11.1). As of 2014, 39 nations, including 23 subnational jurisdictions, have implemented or are considering carbon pricing, covering nearly 15 percent of global emissions (World Bank 2015).

While promising, for the most part, these programs still have prices well below common estimates of the social cost of carbon (SCC) (World Bank 2015). For example, at the time of that report, the allowance prices in the EU Emissions Trading System (ETS) and the average prices for covered emissions globally were less than $8, compared with a central value of the SCC used by the US Environmental Protection Agency (EPA) of roughly $40. Figure 11.2 presents these prices as a share of the EPA-estimated SCC for the five largest jurisdictions in terms of emissions coverage.

Renewable energy subsidies, on the other hand, are far more popular, as documented in policy databases maintained by the International Energy Agency and International Renewable Energy Agency (IEA/

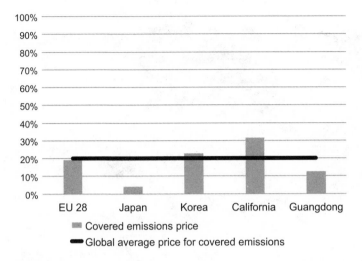

Figure 11.2
Carbon prices for covered emissions as a share of the social cost of carbon, for the five largest implementing jurisdictions and the global average, as of April 2015
Source: Own calculations with data from World Bank 2015

IRENA) and Renewable Energy Policy Network for the 21st Century (REN21).[1] Focusing on the electricity sector, 33 countries offer direct financial incentives for renewables (in the form of capital subsidies, grants, or rebates; tax incentives; or energy production payments), and 69 countries employ regulatory measures that use market instruments to subsidize renewable energy, such as feed-in tariffs (FITs) or tradable green certificates. Twenty-one countries also use public financing mechanisms (public investment, loans, or financing). Figure 11.3 shows the most recent map of countries deploying a more inclusive set of policies or targets for renewable energy, as documented by REN21 (2015: 7): "As of early 2015, at least 164 countries had renewable energy targets, and an estimated 145 countries had renewable energy support policies in place."

Thus the coverage of subsidy policies is much larger than that of carbon pricing policies. Furthermore, numerous opinion polls reveal greater voter preferences for renewable energy policies than for carbon pricing policies. In Germany, polls have found overwhelming support for an aggressive transition to renewable energy (Amelang 2015). A recent poll by Resources for the Future (RFF), the *New York Times*, and Stanford (2015) finds majority support for reducing greenhouse gas emissions and more for promoting renewable energy. Of the policy

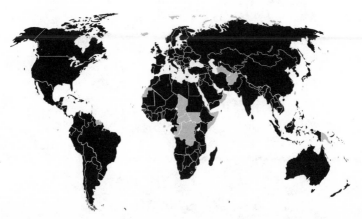

Figure 11.3
Countries with renewable energy policies and targets, early 2015

options given, tax breaks for renewables had the highest support, and taxes on electricity the lowest (see figure 11.4). Similarly a 2015 global survey by World Wide Views on Climate and Energy found the strongest support for subsidy policies for clean technologies (see figure 11.5).[2]

Not only do more jurisdictions subsidize renewable energy than price emissions, but nearly all of the countries and jurisdictions that do have carbon pricing also have renewable energy support mechanisms—and multiple mechanisms at that. This begs the question, given the policy context, how efficient are renewable energy subsidies?

11.3 Policy Interactions with Renewable Energy Subsidies

One must always take the policy context as a whole when evaluating the additive effects of a single policy such as a subsidy. Several studies underline the relevance of this analysis for renewable energy policies (e.g., Fischer and Preonas 2010 provide an overview of many of the issues). Toward this end, it is useful to distinguish between fixed-price policies, like most taxes and subsidies, and tradable credit programs, in which the market determines the price. Fixed-price incentives include direct subsidies such as production tax credits, investment subsidies, or feed-in tariffs (FITs), as well as taxes and fees on CO_2 emissions or on fossil fuels, which provide indirect support for renewables by making fossil sources less competitive. Tradable credit systems, on the other hand, have flexible prices that reflect the cost of compli-

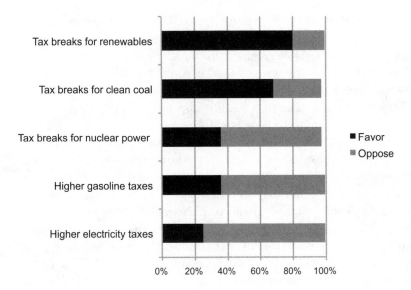

Figure 11.4
Percentage of respondents who favor or oppose each policy as a way for the federal government to try to reduce future global warming
Sources: Resources for the Future, *New York Times*, and Stanford University (2015)

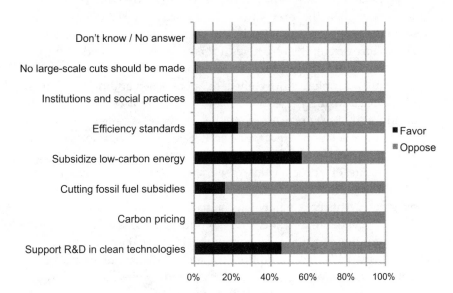

Figure 11.5
Responses to "Which of the following approaches do you prefer for making large-scale cuts in greenhouse gas emissions?"
Source: World Wide Views on Climate and Energy 2015

ance. Examples in the electricity sector include emissions trading schemes for CO_2 (aka, cap and trade) and renewable portfolio standards (RPSs, aka tradable green certificate schemes). Importantly, credit prices respond to changes in the market context—including changes in other policies.

Thus, in the presence of a binding cap on CO_2 emissions, supplementary policies offer no increase in environmental benefits. Instead, as subsidies make mitigation through renewable energy less expensive, the price of emissions allowances falls to allow other sources to expand and meet the cap. In fact Böhringer and Rosendahl (2010) show that the lower carbon price disproportionately benefits producers of the dirtiest fossil fuel, such as coal. Furthermore the allowance price no longer reflects the true marginal cost of abatement, as higher cost sources are being deployed by the subsidy. As a consequence these supplementary policies tend to increase the overall costs of reducing emissions. Indeed Marcantonini and Ellerman (2013) calculate the implicit marginal abatement costs of renewable energy policies (primarily feed-in tariffs) in Europe and find that reducing carbon through wind subsidies has cost 50 to 170 euros per ton CO_2 avoided, and solar subsidies cost 500 to nearly 1000 euros per ton—two orders of magnitude larger than the prevailing ETS allowance price. Some leading environmental economists have used such results to argue for the EU to scrap its overlapping objectives for renewable energy and let the ETS do the job of emissions reduction (Stavins 2014; Böhringer 2014).

A similar, counterintuitive effect happens when adding supplementary policies in the presence of a binding RPS: a renewable energy subsidy will either increase emissions or decrease renewable generation. The explanation is that while an RPS requires a certain percentage of electricity generation to come from renewables, it also requires a certain share of nonrenewable generation. A binding standard thus links the fate of renewable and fossil sources. Under a system of tradable green certificates, renewable sources receive subsidies in the form of credits, while fossil sources pay to purchase those credits, until the standard is met. Additional subsidies that increase the supply of renewable energy drive down credit prices, making fossil sources more competitive and allowing both sources—and emissions—to expand (Greaker, Hoel, and Rosendahl 2014).

Fixed-price policies, such as a carbon tax, allow renewable energy subsidies to have additive effects, as one might expect. Still, some rationales may exist for wanting to supplement carbon pricing—even a cap-and-trade system—with subsidies for renewable energy. That occurs when other market failures (besides the emissions externality) are present.

11.4   Market Failures Relevant for Renewable Energy Subsidies

11.4.1   Spillovers from Learning by Doing

Clean technologies are relatively new, compared with fossil energy sources, and continue to undergo more rapid rates of innovation, both through R&D and learning by doing. Learning by doing, in particular, implies that greater experience generating with renewables will drive down the costs of the technology. Several studies have shown these to be important in renewable energy technologies (e.g., Qiu and Anadon 2012; Nemet 2006, 2009; Swanson 2006; Schaeffer et al. 2004; Bruton 2002). Estimates of technological learning assumptions from EIA (2013) and IEA (2009, 2010) indicate that a doubling of cumulative production leads to a 7 percent cost reduction for conventional renewables like wind and a 19 percent cost reduction for solar. Many of these benefits prove to be industry-wide, meaning that individual producers may not be able to appropriate the full benefits arising from their innovations. As a result they lack sufficient incentive to develop and deploy new technologies (Jaffe, Newell, and Stavins 2005).

Fischer, Newell, and Preonas (2014) consider the rationale of knowledge spillovers, as well as other policy interactions, for optimal renewable energy subsidies. Since R&D spillovers and energy efficiency market failures can be addressed directly, the primary reason for generation subsidies is to internalize the undervalued gains from learning by doing. Using the US electricity sector as an example, they find that plausible optimal learning subsidies for wind are around 1 cent per kWh, while those for solar are in the range of 5 cents per kWh. These levels are significant but quite a bit more modest than subsidy payments in many countries. Hübler, Fischer, and Schenker (2015) perform a similar exercise for the European Union, also exploring second-best policy cases, and find similarly modest optimal subsidies. Like Fischer and Newell (2008), both of these studies find that emissions pricing is the single most cost-effective policy, and although supplementary renewable energy policies can lower costs somewhat, overly ambitious targets can increase costs much more.

11.4.2   Imperfect Competition

Several factors may limit the degree of competition in the supply of renewable energy equipment. Renewable energy technologies are relatively new in the market; they still involve the use of substantial intellectual property, restricted by patent protection, and they may have yet-to-be-realized scale economies. For example, the top five producers of wind turbines (firms located in the United States and Europe) supply roughly half the global market (REN21 2015). Typically, a consequence of imperfect competition is underprovision of the good, which may be corrected with a subsidy.[3]

Greaker and Rosendahl (2008) highlight the distinction between upstream suppliers of abatement technologies and the downstream markets in which they are deployed. They find that a strategic country may want to impose an excessively stringent environmental policy in order to reduce the markup of technology suppliers, and hence increase the diffusion of these technologies.

Fischer (2015) makes an attempt to quantify the potential magnitude of the distortion created by concentration in upstream renewable energy technology suppliers. Using a Cournot framework that allows for some of the observed large market shares, and representing a global market for renewable energy equipment based on demand by the major electricity markets, she finds an optimal subsidy on the order of 1 cent per kWh or less.

11.4.3   Emissions Leakage and Trade

Recognizing that renewable energy technology markets are increasingly global leads to another potential benefit of supporting clean technology: increasing diffusion in areas of the world where emissions are underregulated. In this case, however, the form of the subsidies may matter when the technologies are provided in a global market.

Downstream subsidies support domestic deployment of renewable energy. They shift out global demand, which tends to bid up global equipment prices, as long as the global supply curve is upward sloping. (Strong learning or scale effects may bend the supply curve downward in the longer run, but in the short run it is likely to be increasingly expensive to expand production.) Although total deployment increases, the rise in global equipment prices makes renewable energy more costly and decreases deployment in the rest of the world.

Upstream subsidies are offered to domestic manufacturers. They shift out total supply, which lowers global equipment prices, spurring

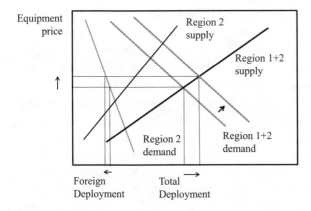

Figure 11.6
Effect of downstream subsidy in region 1

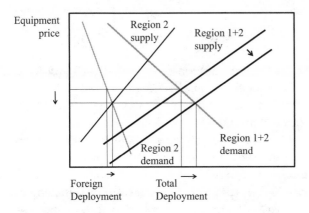

Figure 11.7
Effect of upstream subsidy in region 1

additional deployment at home and abroad. They also crowd out foreign producers, increasing producers' domestic market share.

Figures 11.6 and 11.7 illustrate these mechanisms. The figures are based on a stylized model with two regions that both supply and demand renewable technology. Thus each figure includes two supply and two demand schedules: region 2 for demand and supply of renewable technology, and total demand and supply of renewable technology (in both regions). Figure 11.6 shows the effect of a downstream subsidy in region 1. The downstream subsidy shifts out total demand but does not change demand in region 2. This increases the price on renewable technology in both regions, leading to less deployment in region 2 but higher deployment in region 1 and in total. Furthermore, since renewable energy technology is traded between the regions, both regions increase their supply, which causes a terms-of-trade effect that may not benefit the subsidizing region.

In figure 11.7 we illustrate the effect of an upstream subsidy. The upstream subsidy shifts out region 1 supply, leading to a higher total supply. Consequently the price on renewable technology decreases in both regions, and deployment is increased in both regions. Thus leakage is reduced. Moreover, because of the lower price, the supply of renewable technology from region 2 decreases, which through the terms-of-trade effect is likely to benefit region 1 (the subsidizing region). Therefore, with upward-sloping supply curves for renewable energy equipment, upstream and downstream subsidies have different implications for foreign deployment—and thus for emissions leakage.

11.5   Implications for Optimal Subsidies

Our recent work focuses on the question of subsidies for clean technologies and where to target them. Fischer, Greaker, and Rosendahl (2014) consider subsidies for an end-of-pipe abatement technology (e.g., carbon capture and sequestration) when emissions are regulated with a pollution tax. In a two-country model with Cournot competitors upstream and competitive trade-exposed industries downstream, we find stronger incentives for upstream subsidies than for downstream subsidies. Downstream subsidies tend to increase global abatement technology prices, reduce pollution abatement abroad, and increase emissions leakage. On the contrary, upstream subsidies reduce abatement technology prices and hence also emissions leakage. Moreover, as opposed to downstream subsidies, they provide domestic abatement technology firms with a strategic advantage.

Fischer, Greaker, and Rosendahl (2016) consider the setting of renewable energy technology when downstream markets are regulated with renewable portfolio standards (market share mandates). In reality, it is entirely plausible that renewable energy targets will have stronger market impacts than carbon targets, and that carbon targets may end up with little influence. In the European Union, ETS prices are low, in part because of the supplementary goals of renewable energy mandates and energy efficiency targets (OECD 2011; Böhringer and Rosendahl 2010). Most US states have renewable portfolio standards in place, and the emerging EPA climate regulation will take the form of a technology-based performance standard, rather than a cap-and-trade program. China's current Five Year Plan (2011–2015) also includes targets for the share of non–fossil fuels in primary energy consumption (Birol and Olerjarnik 2012).

Renewable energy targets can be achieved through market-based mechanisms such as blending mandates for biofuels and green certificates for renewable energy. In a setting with binding renewable energy targets, while subsidies can address the upstream market failure of imperfect competition, they also make the portfolio standard less binding. This effect allows dirty generation to expand; consequently, the leakage implications are reversed. Downstream subsidies raise all upstream profits and crowd out foreign emissions. Upstream subsidies have strategic advantages, increasing domestic upstream market share, but expand dirty output in both regions. This chapter thus highlights the critical importance of the policy context for evaluating the leakage performance

An interesting feature with these two-region models is that the strategic subsidies chosen noncooperatively by individual countries can be optimal from a global perspective, if each country values emissions at the global cost of carbon. Of course, if they undervalue carbon damages, the noncooperative equilibrium will be suboptimal, but this result indicates that the setting of both production and consumption subsidies simultaneously does not lead to trade distortions that are damaging to social welfare.

Fischer (2016a) generalizes the problem of upstream and downstream market failures and trade to deepen our understanding of these results. In a context of multiple market failures, she incorporates multiple asymmetric regions, including a nonproducing region that imports renewable energy technology, and multiple firms within the producing regions. The marginal benefits of deployment may differ across the downstream markets, as they may be driven by different levels of carbon taxation or by different fuel mixes that might be crowded out by expanded renewable generation. Using linear forms for supply and demand curves, closed-form solutions for optimal and strategic Nash subsidies can be derived as a function of the market failure parameters.

If no policy intervention is available in the third-party importing region, then the social planner would like the upstream subsidies to reflect the value of the emissions mitigation downstream in that region, as well as any upstream market failure due to imperfect competition. The producer regions should then use downstream deployment subsidies (taxes) to the extent that their marginal external benefits are greater (smaller) than those in the third-party region. Strategic countries, on the other hand, have different strategies. To the extent that they are net exporters to the rest of the world, they care about their terms of trade and do not care about foreign consumer surplus. As a result they prefer smaller upstream subsidies and larger downstream subsidies than the global planner. Thus, because of exports to the third-party market, even if they value global emissions at the global social cost of carbon, producer countries undercorrect the upstream market failure, and they also choose a subsidy mix that keeps global equipment prices higher. As a consequence foreign deployment is too low, and leakage and global emissions are too high, relative to the case of socially optimal subsidies.

Fischer (2016a) also presents a calibrated numerical exercise that estimates optimal and strategic equilibrium subsidies for renewable energy. Downstream markets are represented by the electricity sectors in the United States, European Union, China, and the rest of the world (ROW), calibrated using the models of Fischer, Newell, and Preonas (2014) and Hübler, Fischer, and Schenker (2015), as well as data from EIA's *International Energy Outlook*, taking 2020 as the target year. The upstream market is styled on the supply of wind turbines, where the largest firms have market shares of 14 to 15 percent; in a Cournot model this can be represented with seven or eight firms. Europe serves roughly half the market of the top producers, while the United States and China have similar market shares for the remainder. Europe's downstream market is also significantly cleaner, meaning that fewer emissions are displaced by deployment in the European Union than in other regions.

The results indicate that optimal upstream subsidies are on the order of $0.01 per kWh to correct the upstream market failure from imperfect competition and around $0.04 per kWh for the downstream market failure, assuming a social cost of carbon of $40 per ton CO_2. Furthermore the planner would like to tax EU deployment in order to shift more effort toward the rest of the world, where more emissions would be displaced. In the strategic equilibrium, by contrast, we observe the tension between avoided leakage and terms of trade: even assuming that producer countries value carbon at its global social cost, upstream subsidies are well less than half as large as is optimal, and all producer countries, including the European Union, want to subsidize deployment as well. While the net result of strategic subsidies is deployment levels in producer countries similar to those that would be achieved with the optimal subsidies, deployment is significantly lower—and emissions higher—in the rest of the world. As a result nearly one-fourth of the welfare improvements that might be achieved with optimal subsidies are forgone in the strategic equilibrium; furthermore, if one does not permit upstream subsidies, half of the potential welfare gains are lost.

Taking a global welfare perspective thus leads to starkly different conclusions from the early trade literature on subsidies. For example, Brander and Spencer (1985) showed that producer countries would be better off if they would restrict themselves (e.g., through a trade agreement) from subsidizing their producers. In essence, this collusion allows for higher prices for their exports. However, it ignores the fact that global welfare would be higher with larger subsidies than strategic producer countries provide, and this result is further strengthened when environmental externalities are taken into account.

Indeed leakage accounts for the vast majority of the welfare effects of climate and technology policies. Compared with a globally optimal policy—a global carbon tax to internalize the emissions externality plus an upstream subsidy to counteract underprovision due to market power—correcting the upstream market failure accounts for only 3 percent of the welfare gains. Not pricing carbon in "rest of world," on the other hand, means roughly 60 percent of the potential welfare gains are lost. While carbon pricing is important, it exacerbates the emissions leakage problem, while subsidies that lower global renewable energy costs mitigate leakage. In the Fischer (2016a) model, optimal subsidies among the main producer regions can capture similar magnitudes of welfare gains as a carbon price in the main producer regions, and significantly more than a carbon price that is applied only in the United States and the European Union.

11.6   Discussion

In summary, there are many reasons why we see an arguably greater reliance on clean technology policies, such as renewable energy subsidies, than on emissions pricing. Some of these rationales may be political, representing constraints on setting optimal policies. In that sense, expanding public awareness and designing emissions pricing policies that can meet these constraints—such as by using the revenues to meet distributional objectives—can improve environmental policy making, much in the same way as the effort to remove fossil fuel subsidies.

However, other reasons for relying on renewable energy subsidies may reflect legitimate rationales based on economic cost-effectiveness. Chief among these are innovation spillovers and emissions leakage. In these cases the market underprovides renewable energy, and subsidies are a standard tool for addressing underprovision. Combining results from some of our recent work, we find that plausible optimal subsidies for wind are in the range of $0.06 per kWh: $0.01 each for learning spillovers and imperfect competition, and $0.04 for addressing environmental externalities. This amount compares favorably with the levels provided by the US federal tax credit for wind and the implicit subsidies in European feed-in tariffs, which range from $0.01 to $0.09 per kWh for onshore wind energy and up to $0.13 for offshore wind (CEER 2015). However, since the largest benefits may be through encouraging deployment among countries without explicit climate policies, the most critical question is whether the subsidy policies succeed in making these technologies affordable in the rest of the world. Upstream support clearly contributes to this effect; whether downstream policies also do so through learning by doing or scale economies is a subject for further research. Fischer (2016a) considers the influence of scale economies at the global level and finds that they boost the effectiveness of both downstream and upstream subsidies, but upstream subsidies still maintain their relative advantage.[4]

While the analysis indicates that such "green industrial policy" may indeed be useful to combat emissions leakage, the use of these instruments is becoming contentious in trade policy. Under the Agreement on Subsidies and Countervailing Measures (Subsidies Code), World Trade Organization (WTO) members agreed to disallow many traditional forms of industrial policy, particularly subsidies to domestic manufacturing and exports, which discriminate against foreign suppliers. WTO law regarding tariffs also has at its core the principle of nondiscrimination, but Article XX of the GATT enunciates several exceptions to the disciplines, including reasons related to preserving human health and the environment. No such exceptions exist in the Subsidies Code, however. As renewable energy subsidies have become more pervasive, they have formed the basis of several recent and ongoing disputes in the WTO. Most of the complaints involve upstream subsidies and local content requirements. The European Union and United States have brought antidumping and antisubsidy complaints against China, charging that large Chinese subsidies in the form of cheap loans, land, and capital to photovoltaic producers constitute illegal aid.

WTO rules are not generally interpreted to hinder downstream subsidies toward the deployment and diffusion of green technologies (WTO 2011). Nonetheless, a recent ruling in the case of *Canada—Renewable Energy* raised some confusion, as explained in Charnovitz and Fischer (2015). The province of Ontario had instituted a feed-in tariff with local content requirements, a condition that renders the downstream deployment subsidy into support for upstream local manufacturing. When the European Union, Japan, and others complained, the WTO panel and appellate body decisively struck down the local content requirements. However, the complainants also asked the panel to rule that the feed-in tariff itself confers a benefit, a factor in determining whether a subsidy is actionable. The panel and Appellate Body both avoided doing so, with differing logic, raising fears among legal scholars that they had inadvertently opened a Pandora's box for infant industry protection, giving governments wide berth to create markets for products for which they design the demand (Cosbey and Mavroidis 2014).

Thus we have some clear tension between trade and environmental goals. The absence of an environmental exception for subsidies, with clear criteria for their justification, may be inadvertently undermining the application of the Subsidies Code, as dispute settlement panels seem loath to be seen declaring a popular environmental policy a subsidy. At the same time, pressures are building among competing producers of green technologies to protect industry at home and protest such protections abroad. In this setting, a broader discourse is needed about the role of environmental aims in trade policy, and more research is needed to understand when subsidies for green products are beneficial to society and when their costs may outweigh the benefits.[5]

Notes

The authors' research described in this chapter benefited from the support of the Norwegian Research Council's RENERGI program, the Mistra Foundation's ENTWINED and INDIGO programs, and US Environmental Protection Agency Grant 83413401. Fischer would also like to acknowledge the European Community's Marie Curie International Incoming Fellowship, "STRATECHPOL—Strategic Clean Technology Policies for Climate Change," financed under the EC Grant Agreement PIIF-GA-2013-623783, and the hospitality of the Fondazione Eni Enrico Mattei (FEEM). Greaker and Rosendahl are associated with CREE—Oslo Centre for Research on Environmentally Friendly Energy. The CREE centre acknowledges financial support from the Research Council of Norway.

1. Global Renewable Energy, accessed June 1, 2015, http://www.iea.org/ policiesandmeasures/renewableenergy/; and News from the REN21 Network, accessed June 1, 2015, http://www.map.ren21.net/.

2. World Wide Views on Climate and Energy, accessed June 1, 2015, http:// climateandenergy.wwviews.org/results/. Note that the total amount of all answers can be higher than 100 percent, since participants could choose among options to answer this question. The specific options were as follows: (a) Support for research and development of low-carbon technology, for example, research into effective car batteries. (b) Carbon pricing, for example, through taxes on carbon emissions, or emissions trading schemes. (c) Cutting fossil fuel subsidies. (d) Subsidization for low-carbon energy, such as wind, solar power, marine energies, geothermal energy. (e) Legislation of new standards, for example, to improve the energy efficiency of cars or buildings and appliances. (f) New socioeconomic institutions and practices, such as investment in public transportation systems or consumption of locally produced food. (g) No large-scale cuts should be made. (h) Don't know/Do not wish to answer.

3. This is the case with Cournot competition, which many of the subsequently cited studies use.

4. Fischer (2016a) considers an extension to scale economies.

5. Fischer (2016b) considers the value of restricting upstream subsidies when industry group lobbying distorts policy objectives, as compared to the value of reducing foreign emissions with upstream subsidies, and considers whether climate finance (i.e., subsidizing deployment abroad) can serve as an adequate substitute.

References

Amelang, S. 2015. Polls reveal citizens' support for Energiewende. Clean Energy Wire Factsheet. https://www.cleanenergywire.org/factsheets/polls-reveal-citizens-support-energiewende (last modified April 8, 2015).

Barrios, S., J. Pycroft, and B. Saveyn. 2013. The marginal cost of public funds in the EU: The case of labour versus green taxes. Working Paper 35–2013. Taxation Papers. Luxembourg: Publications Office of the European Union. doi:10.2778/15847.

Birol, F., and P. Olerjarnik. 2012. Will China lead the world into a clean-energy future? *Economics of Energy and Environmental Policy* 1 (1): 5–10.

Böhringer, C. 2014. Two decades of European climate policy: A critical appraisal. *Review of Environmental Economics and Policy* 8: 1–17.

Böhringer, C., and K. E. Rosendahl. 2010. Green serves the dirtiest: On the interaction between black and green quotas. *Journal of Regulatory Economics* 37: 316–25.

Brander, J., and B. Spencer. 1985. Export subsidies and international market share rivalry. *Journal of International Economics* 18: 83–100.

Bruton, T. M. 2002. General trends about photovoltaics based on crystalline silicon. *Solar Energy Materials and Solar Cells* 72: 3–10.

CEER (Council of European Energy Regulators). 2015. *Status Review of Renewable and Energy Efficiency Support Schemes in Europe in 2012 and 2013. C14-SDE-44–03.* Brussels: CEER.

Charnovitz, S., and C. Fischer. 2015. Canada—renewable energy: Implications for WTO law on green and not-so-green subsidies. *World Trade Review* 14 (2): 177–210.

Coady, D., I. Parry, L. Sears, and B. Shang. 2015. How large are global energy subsidies? Working Paper 15/105. IMF.

Cosbey, A., and P. C. Mavroidis. 2014. A turquoise mess: Green subsidies, blue industrial policy and renewable energy: The case for redrafting the subsidies agreement of the WTO. *Journal of International Economic Law* 17: 11–47.

Energy Information Administration. 2013. *Annual Energy Outlook 2013.* Washington, DC: DOE/EIA-0383.

Fischer, C. 2016a. Strategic subsidies for green goods. RFF DP 16-12, Resources for the Future, Washington, DC, and FEEM Nota di Lavoro 30.2016, Fondazione Eni Enrico Mattei, Venice.

Fischer, C. 2016b. Environmental protection for sale: Strategic green industrial policy and climate finance. RFF DP 16-13, Resources for the Future, Washington, DC, and FEEM Nota di Lavoro 31.2016, Fondazione Eni Enrico Mattei, Venice.

Fischer, C., M. Greaker, and K. E. Rosendahl. 2014. Robust policies against emission leakage: The case for upstream subsidies. Working Paper 4742. CESifo.

Fischer, C., M. Greaker, and K. E. Rosendahl. 2016. Strategic technology policy as supplement to renewable energy standards. Working Paper 1/2016. School of Economics and Business, Norwegian University of Life Sciences.

Fischer, C., and R. G. Newell. 2008. Environmental and technology policies for climate mitigation. *Journal of Environmental Economics and Management* 55: 142–62.

Fischer, C., R. Newell, and L. Preonas. 2014. Environmental and technology policy options in the electricity sector: Interactions and outcomes. Working Paper 4757. CESifo.

Fischer, C., and L. Preonas. 2010. Combining policies for renewable energy: Is the whole less than the sum of its parts? *International Review of Energy and Resource Economics* 4 (1): 51–92.

Greaker, M., M. Hoel, and K. E. Rosendahl. 2014. Does a renewable fuel standard for biofuel reduce climate costs? *Journal of the Association of Environmental and Resource Economists* 1: 337–63.

Greaker, M., and K. E. Rosendahl. 2008. Environmental policy with upstream pollution abatement technology firms. *Journal of Environmental Economics and Management* 56: 246–59.

Hübler, M., C. Fischer, and O. Schenker. 2015. Second-best analysis of European energy policy: Is one bird in hand worth two in the bush? ZEW Discussion Paper 15-079. Zentrum für Europäische Wirtschaftsforschung/Center for European Economic Research, Mannheim.

International Energy Agency. 2009. *Technology Roadmap: Wind Energy.* Paris: OECD/IEA 2009.

International Energy Agency. 2010. *Technology Roadmap: Solar Photovoltaic Energy.* Paris: OECD/IEA 2010.

IEA (International Energy Agency), OECD (Organisation for Economic Co-operation and Development), and World Bank. 2010. The scope of fossil-fuel subsidies in 2009 and a roadmap for phasing out fossil-fuel subsidies. Prepared for the G20 Summit, Seoul, November 11–12. http://www.oecd.org/env/cc/46575783.pdf.

Jaffe, A. B., R. G. Newell, and R. N. Stavins. 2005. A tale of two market failures: Technology and environmental policy. *Ecological Economics* 54 (2/3): 164–74.

Marcantonini, C., and D. Ellerman. 2013. *The cost of abating CO₂ emissions by renewable energy incentives in Germany. Working Paper 2013–005.* MIT Center for Energy and Environmental Policy Research.

Nemet, G. F. 2006. Beyond the learning curve: Factors influencing cost reductions in photo-voltaics. *Energy Policy* 34: 3218–32.

Nemet, G. F. 2009. Demand-pull, technology-push, and government-led incentives for non-incremental technical change. *Research Policy* 38: 700–709.

OECD (Organisation for Economic Co-operation and Development). 2011. *Interactions between Emissions Trading Systems and Other Overlapping Policy Instruments.* General Distribution Document, Environment Directorate. Paris: OECD.

Qiu, Y., and L. D. Anadon. 2012. The price of wind power in China during its expansion: Technology adoption, learning-by-doing, economies of scale, and manufacturing localization. *Energy Economics* 34 (3): 772–85.

REN21 (Renewable Energy Policy Network for the 21st Century). 2015. *Renewables 2015 Global Status Report: Key Findings.* Paris: REN21.

RFF (Resources for the Future), *New York Times*, and Stanford University. 2015. Global Warming National Poll. January, 2015. http://www.rff.org/research/collection/surveying-american-attitudes-toward-climate-change-and-clean-energy. Accessed June 1, 2015.

Schaeffer, G., A. Seebregts, L. Beurskens, H. H. Moor, E. Alsema, W. Sark, M. Durstewicz, M. Perrin, P. Boulanger, H. Laukamp, and C. Zuccaro. 2004. *Learning from the Sun: Analysis of the Use of Experience Curves for Energy Policy Purposes: The Case of Photovoltaic Power. Final report of the Photex Project. Report ECN DEGO: ECN-C–04–035.* Petten: Energy Research Centre of the Netherlands.

Stavins, R. 2014. Will Europe scrap its renewables target? That would be good news for the economy and for the environment. Posted on January 18, 2014. www.robertstavinsblog.org.

Swanson, R. M. 2006. A vision for crystalline solar cells. *Progress in Photovoltaics: Research and Applications* 14: 443–53.

World Bank. 2015. *Carbon Pricing Watch 2015: An Advance Brief from the State and Trends of Carbon Pricing 2015 Report, to Be Released Late 2015. State and Trends of Carbon Pricing.* Washington, DC: World Bank Group.

WTO (World Trade Organization). 2011. *Harnessing Trade for Sustainable Development and a Green Economy.* Geneva: WTO.

World Wide Views on Climate and Energy. 2015. http://climateandenergy.wwviews.org/results/. Accessed June 1, 2015.

Contributors

Carolyn Fischer, RFF
Mads Greaker, Statistics Norway
Mohammad Habibpour, Philipps-University of Marburg
Michelle Harding, OECD
Christina Kolerus, IMF
Christos Kotsogiannis, University of Exeter
Jim Krane, Rice University
Albert Touna-Mama, IMF
Raffaele Miniaci, University of Padova
Marco Pani, IMF
Ian Parry, IMF
Carlo Perroni, Warwick University
Leonzio Rizzo, University of Ferrara
Knut Einar Rosendahl, Norwegian School of Life Sciences (UMB) School of Economics and Business
Carlo Scarpa, Universtiy of Padova
Neda Seiban, Philipps-University of Marburg
Suphi Sen, IFO Institute
Jon Strand, World Bank
Paola Valbonesi, University of Padova
Herman Vollebergh, NEAA

Index